SUPERCHARGE

SUPERCHARGE

A NEW PLAYBOOK OF LEADERSHIP

DAVID T. NORMAN

PYP **Publish** Your Purpose

For permission requests, write to the publisher, addressed "Attention: Permissions Coordinator," at the address below.

Publish Your Purpose
141 Weston Street, #155
Hartford, CT, 06141

PYP **Publish**
Your Purpose

The opinions expressed by the Author are not necessarily those held by Publish Your Purpose.

Ordering Information: Quantity sales and special discounts are available on quantity purchases by corporations, associations, and others. For details, contact the author at info@davidtnorman.com

Edited by: Lily Capstick
Front cover design by: Calhoun Creative Solutions
Spine and back cover design: Rebecca Pollock
Cover photography: Calhoun Creative Solutions
Typeset by: Lydia Christine Hall
Graphics and Images created using Napkin.ai.

ISBN: 979-8-88797-166-7 (hardcover)
ISBN: 979-8-88797-167-4 (paperback)
ISBN: 979-8-88797-169-8 (ebook)

Library of Congress Control Number: 2025905154

First edition, June, 2025

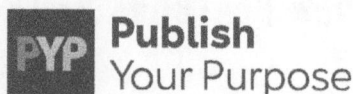

Publish Your Purpose is a hybrid publisher of non-fiction books. Our mission is to elevate the voices often excluded from traditional publishing. We intentionally seek out authors and storytellers with diverse backgrounds, life experiences, and unique perspectives to publish books that will make an impact in the world. Do you have a book idea you would like us to consider publishing? Please visit PublishYourPurpose.com for more information.

Contents

CONTENTS

Foreword

What David Norman presents here is a framework that combines very accessible operating models from the books *Traction* and *Scaling Up* with the essential relational means to bring them into being. It brings special insight to how we create change in our organizations and communities. The "playbook" he offers is an alternative to top-down authority and instead explores leadership as an act of collective engagement and shared purpose.

What resonates deeply in Norman's work is his understanding that true leadership power comes not from position or authority, but from our capacity to create spaces where authentic dialogue can flourish and where every voice contributes to both the larger narrative and the personal accountability needed to sustain what we, as leaders, know is needed.

In a world that often seems to be pulling apart and has a naïve and robotic version of what creates accountability for the whole, *Supercharge* affirms a vision of leadership that combines very grounded strategic tools with the conversational methodology that brings people together. This gives shape to authentic engagement and shared purpose. It's a vision that's both timely and timeless, practical and profound.

Peter Block
Cincinnati, Ohio

Preface

I began my management consulting career in 1973, and by 1995, I had started my own practice, joining the world of entrepreneurship as a solopreneur. Since 2007, I have been on concurrent paths, both associated with some form of management consulting. One path was my work as a business owner coach and one as a consultant to management. As a business owner coach, I started with Vistage International in 2007, and during that time (ca. 2012) I became familiar with the Entrepreneurial Operating System® (EOS®) model, based on the book *Traction* by Gino Wickman. I was trained in 2014 and quickly became a Certified EOS Implementer®. Coaches don't typically have access to a complete, yet simple, set of tools to use with owners of organizations wishing to improve. EOS augmented my work as a coach by providing clients with a proven set of tools to transform their organizations.

Through my change management consulting work, in 2016 as a member of the Institute of Management Consultants (IMC USA), I was introduced to Peter Block at our national conference. Block presented his book, *Community: The Structure of Belonging*,[1] and what he presented captured my interest, especially on how to create communities (or organizations, in my consulting world).

Most importantly, while it didn't happen in a flash or an epiphany, I came to deeply realize that Wickman's and Block's works can be connected to help transform organizations. Wickman's *Traction* contains a proven set of tools that can be used to improve the company, and Block's *Community* became the "how" to further build on those tools to create an even more vibrant and human-centric community.

---

1. Peter Block, *Community: The Structure of Belonging*, (Barrett-Koehler Publishers, 2008).

Combined, this business model and Block's work were transformative to my efforts on behalf of clients and led to this new playbook for leaders.

In sum, the genesis of this book was the understanding that by using an operating model concurrently with community, business owners can achieve more complete, lasting results than with an operating model alone. Thus, *Supercharge* was born.

Value of a Formalized Business Model

I was one of the early EOS Implementers® (somewhere around number 60) and worked with approximately 50 closely held companies implementing EOS. I loved the work. Clients loved the results. Those simple tools were valuable in getting everyone 100 percent on the same page with where the company is going and how it will get there and helped to build a more cohesive and healthy leadership team.

My consulting and coaching practices benefited from having a specific tool I could introduce to prospects and clients. Over seven years, I helped clients achieve much of what they hoped for.

Verne Harnish's *Scaling Up*, published in 2014 (revised 2022), includes similar tools but is focused on organizations beyond start-ups looking to scale up.

The tools in *Traction* and *Scaling Up* (both hereinafter referred to as "business models") are good and will work whether you do the implementation yourself or hire an outside consultant. Either will help you, through one simple and complete business model, create a better approach to running your organization and getting more out of it and will also do so virtually seamlessly, without angst.

The rub is that both business models are only business systems. Each is tried and proven. Each, perhaps in different stages of organizational growth, work. They provide a process, including forms, to help bring your people together, focused and potentially more accountable. In short, they help you build an organization of like-minded individuals with values consistent with yours and provide a framework for improving your leadership.

The problem is that, as with any business system, effective implementation requires, and in fact relies upon, people: Business models tend not to work without human intervention.

Clarity came to me after observing multiple implementations in which the outside "consultant/implementer" simply followed a canned approach for each client, irrespective of any particularities, needs, or differences associated with the client. The implementation approach was the same, while each client is different.

Something was missing. At some level, people must be involved, and neither of these two business systems will truly work without people.

VALUE OF COMMUNITY

Peter Block wrote *Community: A Structure of Belonging* to help build transforming communities [like your organization]. He says, "After all the thinking about policy, strategy, mission, and milestones, it gets down to this: *How are we going to be when we gather together?*"[2] [emphasis added]. "How are we going to be together?" for me sums up the behavioral component of building our organizations.

One of the more frustrating aspects of our current organizations is the fragmentation or gaps among functions. Even with implementation of a proven business model, each function is working hard on its own purpose, and those **parallel efforts added together do not make a community**. Organizations tend to be separated into silos; they are a collection of "programs operating near one another but not overlapping or touching."[3] This is important to understand because it is this dividedness that makes it so difficult to create a more positive or alternative organization. **The work is to overcome this fragmentation. The essential challenge is to transform isolation and self-interest (e.g., silos) within our organizations into connectedness and caring for the whole (e.g., accountability).** Neither business model alone is specifically designed to correct the lack of connectedness. It *may* happen, but it is not part of the design. Consciously building a better culture is totally based on introducing a new model of leadership and on your leadership skills and behaviors.

What if you, through the implementation of any business model, created a truly connected community—a community of possibilities, rather than a

---

2. Block, *Community*, 10.
3. Ibid.

community of continuing problems and separated silos—an organization that takes its identity from the generosity and accountability of all? As Block writes, "The essential challenge is to transform the isolation and self-interest within our [organizations] into connectedness and caring for the whole."[4] This transformation is your responsibility as a leader.

Additionally, Block wrote: "I especially like the word *structure* because it stands in relief to our concern about style. To offer structures with the promise of creating community gives leaders relief from the common story that leadership is a set of personal qualities we are born with, develop, or try on like a new suit to see if they fit . . . We can create structures of belonging even if we are introverted and do not like to make eye contact."[5]

Caring for the whole is at the root of positive change and accountability. You are the root of leadership.

Figure 1—Warp and Weft

COMBINED VALUE

Woven fabric is composed of two components, the warp and the weft. Together they transform thread and yarn into textile fabrics. The warp threads are the long, straight yarns on the loom, forming the strength/backbone of the fabric: These threads are generally stronger. The weft threads are woven (the "weave")

---

4. Block, *Community*, 2.
5. Block, *Community*, 1.

in and out between the warp. Together, the warp and the weft form the pattern, the design of the cloth, as diverse ways of weaving create different textures.

This works as an analogy for *Supercharge*, in that the tools presented in either business model act as the weft: They are composed of the individual threads/textures, as it were, of your organization; your people, your product or service, your operations, your values, and your present and future direction. Block's work, in *Community*, forms the warp, the strength of building your community/organization upon which we will weave the weft.

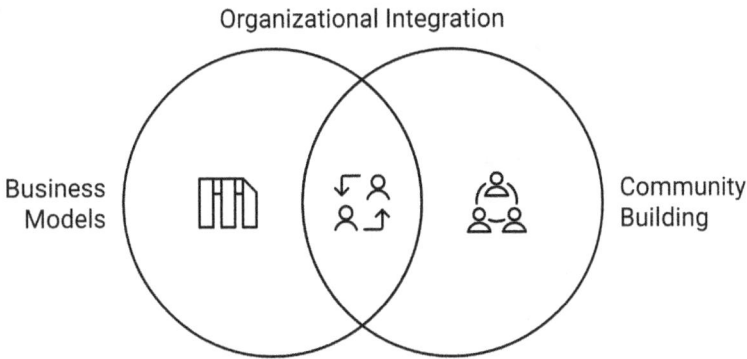

Figure 2—Should I adopt?

This book serves as a guide for truly building an organizational community using either of these models as the common design you integrate (weave) around the community/organization you are building in the process.

For Consultants/Outsiders Helping Organizations

As a lifelong consultant and executive coach, my desire is that you read this book with the warp and weft in mind and that it will work with more small- to mid-sized companies that need a simple, proven business model. There likely has been a time when a client of yours didn't get the most out of their experience. This diminished return primarily comes from the client who either tries to adapt the business model to suit their "culture" better (e.g., cutting meetings and agendas short, moving them to a different or even random schedule, missing meetings, and so forth) or uses the tools sporadically or haphazardly. We have all seen it. In short, they may have the highest expectations for success and become their own worst enemies.

Your current EOS or Scaling Up implementation likely delivers solid results for your clients. The tools work. The systems function. The metrics improve. But there's a gnawing sense that something more is possible. This isn't just intuition: It's recognition of a fundamental truth about organizations: Tools and systems, no matter how sophisticated, are just the beginning, not the end.

The journey from good to extraordinary begins with a profound shift in how we think about organizational life. Instead of seeing our business systems primarily as performance tools, we recognize them as frameworks for human connection and development. This isn't about choosing between structure and community. It's about weaving them together into something more powerful than either alone.

The tools your clients already have: The Vision/Traction Organizer® (V/TO®) or One-Page Strategic Plan (OPSP), their meeting rhythms, their metrics and rocks (priorities) become more powerful when viewed through the community lens:

- They become frameworks for discovery rather than just direction.
- They create spaces for dialogue rather than just discussion.
- They enable development rather than just deployment.
- They foster connection rather than just coordination.

The journey from good to extraordinary isn't about abandoning what works. It's about enhancing it through deeper understanding of the human community. Every tool, every process, every practice can either contribute to or detract from this integration.

I ask you to consider that perhaps something else is going on with your clients' and prospects' organizations and that some of this book will help you get a grip on how to truly Supercharge the organization. Read on with that in mind, as you are in a great position to continue to influence small- to mid-sized businesses and their leadership.

To the Reader

Here is a roadmap of what you'll experience in *Supercharge*:

The book progresses across three sections:

- Early chapters establish the foundational need and framework (Chapters 1–6).
- Middle chapters detail the specific mechanisms and approaches (Chapters 7–16).
- Final chapters focus on practical implementation and sustainable results (Chapters 17–20).
- Appendices 1 through 9 provide additional, in-depth resources.

At the beginning of each chapter, I have provided a short summary that highlights the content. Additionally, at the end of each chapter I also have Key Takeaways and a couple of "homework" assignments, in case you are interested.

Definition

Community-Enhanced Culture

/ kə'myo͞onədē ˌen'hanst 'kəlCHər / (n)

1. The essence of a community-enhanced culture is created through three shifts: viewing leadership as collective capacity rather than individual performance, asking questions instead of giving answers, and focusing on creating conditions for natural emergence rather than controlling outcomes.
2. A cultural social system or organization in which the practices, values, and knowledge are actively shaped and enriched through collective participation and shared contributions of members.
3. An organizational culture distinguished from traditional top-down cultural structure by emphasizing collaborative development, peer-to-peer learning, and distributed decision-making.

Related terms: Participatory culture, collaborative community, collective intelligence.

Nomenclature used in *Supercharge*:

1. When I refer to a book (physical or in electronic form), the name of the book will be Italicized, e.g., *Traction, Scaling Up,* or *Community: A Structure of Belonging.*
2. When I refer the operating system which the book is written about, it will not be italicized, such as the Traction® or Scaling Up system.
3. Entrepreneurial Operating System® is separate and additional from the Traction system in that it is more expansive and incorporates more tools than are in the book *Traction.* It is implemented by trained franchisees. Other than by general reference, I will not address the specific tools or implementation methodologies.

⚡⚡⚡⚡

CHAPTER I

Why Supercharge?

Summary: This chapter introduces two prominent business models, Traction and Scaling Up, that have transformed small- to mid-sized businesses, while introducing the book's core concept of "supercharging" these models through community-enhanced leadership. Using a medical prescription analogy, it explains that successful organizational transformation requires both the right business model (the medicine) and the right implementation approach through community-building (how to take it). The chapter emphasizes that while these models can create improvement on their own, lasting transformation requires a deliberate focus on building community alongside implementing systems, shifting from isolated efficiency to connected, interdependent growth.

Since the publication of *Traction* by Gino Wickman in 2011 and *Scaling Up* by Verne Harnish in 2014, each of these business models have gained traction (pun intended) as being incredibly transforming for small- to mid-sized businesses. Their popularity is buttressed not only by a simple business model of tools that helps the organization become healthier and achieve its goals, but also, typically, the implementation is supported by outside resources such as consultants. Additionally, there are likely a larger number of organizations self-implementing; that is, doing either business model (or both in sequence) without the aid of an outsider or consultant. In either case, congratulations are in order if you are using either business model.

The change can be truly remarkable, finally getting all out of your business that you wished for. Here's a small sample of some of the things my past clients have said:[6]

Traction integration, through David's leadership, equips the leadership of a company to make real change on a weekly basis while enabling the entire leadership team to promote the vision of the company. —CEO, manufacturing firm

Our EBITDA will improve by 200% this year by focusing on solving real problems. Enough said! —Managing Partner, Public Accounting and Advisory Firm

The business models work. Moreover, through my work with clients, I have discovered that the business model is a great foundation upon which to transform an organization; thus the title of this book, *Supercharge*.

First, what this book is not: **It is not a guide to implementing either business model.** It will present an overview of each business model only to point out how either may be used to build the organization you really, really want. I will also point out notable differences between the two. The choice of which fits you and your organization is yours. The analysis in this book will provide some guidance for your decision-making.

Second, you may self-implement either model. Improvements will happen in your organization. Contrariwise, you may implement either of the business models by using an outsider trained to assist. I will not opine on either approach. With either model, you will note improvements, and though progress will not be instantaneous or overnight, things will change by simply implementing either model. These improvements can be somewhat accidental,

---

6. For more client testimonies, please see *How Others Leveraged This Process*, near the end of this book.

as by simply using the tools, improvement happens.[7] But is it the enduring change you desire and want?

Third, this book does not address implementation, but rather presents a container, as it were, within which you may undertake the implementation. This container is designed specifically to help you build a stronger, more cohesive organization *beyond* that which the tools of either model will get you. In doing so, you change the very nature of both leadership and the conversations you participate in. **The compelling case made herein is that when attention is given to how, as leadership, you enlist your people in the implementation, you build a more enduring, collaborative culture focused on the future.** That change is not inconsequential or nuanced; you are actively shifting your culture to one focused on more than efficiency and effectiveness, but on people as a part of your community.

If your sole purpose is to implement one of the two business models, good for you, but don't be too hopeful about your results. They are, after all, simply business models, and business models require that people not only implement them but also keep them functioning. Few systems work in a vacuum.

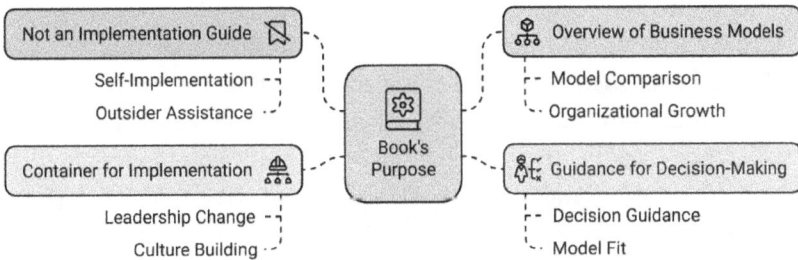

Figure 3—Book structure

This book, then, will serve as a guide to deciding which of the two business models is best for you and your organization and can help in your decision-making process. **This is a guide; it is not about how the chosen business model is implemented. Any implementation guidance provided herein**

---

7. Similar to the noted Hawthorne Effect. One account of this classic study: E. A. Spencer and K. Mahtani, "Hawthorne Effect," Sackett Catalogue of Bias Collaboration, 2017. Accessed December 12, 2024. https://catalogofbias.org/biases/hawthorne-effect/.

is *only* about how to use the business model, not its respective parts, to improve leadership and accountability.

Whether you are doing either of these with or without a consultant, you will sense there is possibly more available to you. By implementing the business model, you get a good start, but it is not the final goal. Perhaps after implementation you haven't gotten as much out of it as you had hoped for. Or, if you are not doing either business model, I would encourage you to do so, and there will be tips throughout this book that will help you along your journey and, by embracing the practices herein, improve leadership and accountability.

An Analogy

In medicine, a prescription, to have effective efficacy, has two parts: the medicine itself and the method of taking it (e.g., dosage, timing, constraints). Supercharge is like that prescription with two parts: The type of business system you chose is the medicine, and the how to "take it" is through a community-enhanced leadership effort. Both are necessary. Implementing either business model as medicine for your business is only part of the prescription and may leave you incomplete. You must have a way of creating and maintaining the new journey.

What I've learned from my clients is that each business model is a good tool (i.e., the right medicine) to help you consciously improve efficiency and accountability, and it is my intent to show you not only how to start to utilize these tools but, more importantly, how to become a better leader developing a better organization known for a culture of accountability and community.

Why a Management Business Model?

While startup advice overwhelmingly emphasizes hiring the best people, there's insufficient focus on the equally crucial element, business systems. Early employees undoubtedly shape company culture, but the management systems they build are equally vital to a company's future success.

Think of it like the relationship between musicians and a musical score, both the talent of your performers and the underlying structure of the composition are essential for creating exceptional music. Or think of it like a garden where both the quality of your seeds and the systems you put in place to nurture them determine how well your garden will thrive. While early employees establish behavioral norms, the early implementation of business models determines how the organization performs, from decision-making to goal setting and to accountability. These foundational systems are far easier to establish when a company is small, creating an environment where people can excel without constantly reinventing processes.

It is imperative to think about how to use a business model while creating an environment where people can do their best work (without having to reinvent everything every time) and create an organization with interdependence.

"Community is the container within which our longing to be is fulfilled."[8] *This is the warp, the strength of the fabric of your future organization.*

The key is to identify how this transformation occurs. We begin by shifting your attention from the problems of community to the possibility of community. . . . This begins the effort to create a future distinct from the past . . . change the narrative of what you want the future to be [emphasis added]."[9]

Would you be okay with getting 175 times return on your investment to transform your organization?

One client's experience was that for every $1 invested on [the business model's] implementation, the organization saw a return of $175 in increased, incremental shareholder value in only five years.

Chapter Summary

This chapter introduced the concept of enhancing two popular business models, *Traction* by Gino Wickman and *Scaling Up* by Verne Harnish, which have proven successful for small- to mid-sized businesses. While these models

---

8. Block, *Community*, xii.

9. Peter Block, Workshop on Leadership, Institute of Management Consultants annual conference, Toronto, Canada. November 2016.

provide valuable tools and frameworks for organizational improvement, the chapter emphasized that simply implementing them isn't enough for lasting transformation. The chapter proposed that these business models should serve as a foundation for deeper organizational change, comparing it to a medical prescription where both the medicine (the business system) and the method of taking it (community-enhanced leadership) are crucial for success. The chapter stressed the importance of creating strong management systems early while building a sense of community and interconnectedness, rather than just focusing on hiring talented individuals.

Key Chapter Takeaways

1. Business models (*Traction/Scaling Up*) provide foundational tools but may not create lasting transformation without proper implementation approach.
2. Early establishment of management systems is as crucial as hiring great people.
3. Successful implementation requires both the right tools ("medicine") and the right implementation method ("how to take it").
4. Community-enhanced leadership creates a container for lasting organizational change.
5. The focus should shift from solving problems to creating possibilities for community.

Suggested Homework

1. Evaluate your current situation: Are you implementing either business model? If so, assess whether you're getting the full potential from it. If not, research both models to understand their basic frameworks.
2. Consider your organization's current state of community and connection. Map out areas where isolation or self-interest might be preventing better outcomes.

⚡⚡⚡⚡

CHAPTER 2

Iceberg of Ignorance

Summary: The chapter explores the "iceberg of ignorance" concept in organizations, where leaders typically see only four percent of what's happening, the rest being beneath the surface. It introduces two key elements to combat this: a "source of truth" (centralized, reliable data for decision-making) and organizational rituals (regular review practices at annual, quarterly, and short-term intervals). Using a pilot's checklist analogy, the chapter emphasizes that success requires both systematic processes and consistent human engagement. The key message is that business models must combine reliable data with regular rituals to create accountability, build trust, and ultimately "flip the iceberg" by surfacing hidden issues and transforming organizational culture.

The sinking of the Titanic was not from what the crew could see of the iceberg, which was relatively small. It was what they could *not* see, the size of the problem beneath the cold waters.

Iceberg of ignorance: Business leaders, despite what they believe, really only know a very small portion, estimated at four percent, of what's going on in their organizations.[10]

---

10. Sidney Yoshida, "Iceberg of Ignorance," presented at International Quality Symposium, Mexico City, Mexico, 1989. Additional references addressing the Iceberg of Ignorance: Stephen R. Covey, *The Seven Habits of Highly Effective People*, Simon & Schuster, 1989; and Peter M. Senge, T*he Fifth Discipline: The Art and Practice of the Learning Organization*, Doubleday/Currency, 1990.

Despite our best intentions, our employees are in organizational silos, isolated and fragmented.

The predominant organizational behavior is that after annual goals are set, there's no ritual for reviewing them, so they quickly become out-of-date and there is no structure or effort to reduce fragmentation. It's hard to stay focused for 365 days, especially with organizational friction, silos, or inertia working against you.

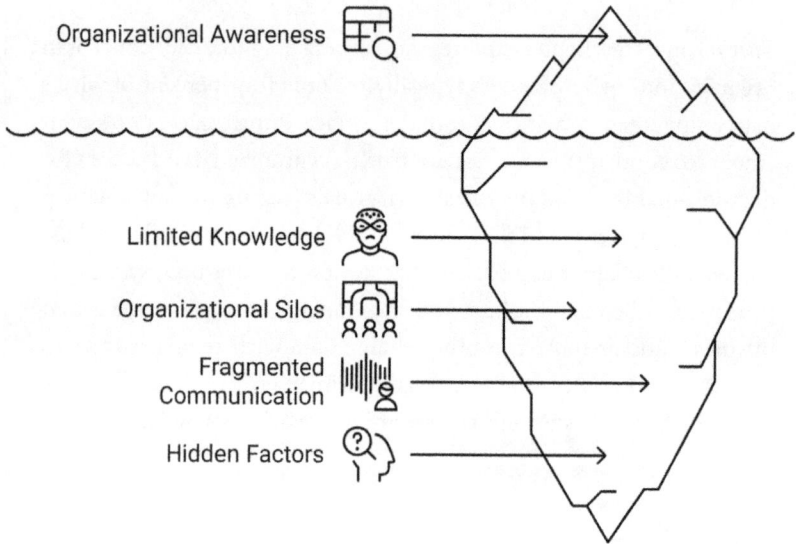

Organizational Awareness

Limited Knowledge

Organizational Silos

Fragmented Communication

Hidden Factors

Figure 4—Iceberg of Innocence

Without continual focus, employees start resenting the goals because the effort to create them now seems like a waste of time, and the interest in goals atrophies because no one looks at them anymore. The workplace becomes like an iceberg; most everything going on below the waterline is lost, purposefully buried, or accompanied by CYA[11] behaviors. As leaders, we need to surface and eliminate all those counterproductive behaviors, but how? The basic premise is to incrementally change and then institutionalize the way we behave.

---

11. Cover your a**

The effect of either business model implementation is to intentionally move away from the self-designed and self-protected collection of behaviors and spreadsheets and flip the iceberg, to move the organization toward higher efficiency and performance through consistency and repetition.

WHAT DOES SUCH A BUSINESS MODEL REALLY DO FOR LEADERSHIP?

While never overtly identified in either *Traction* or *Scaling Up*, the underlying strength of the tools is that each can be a very valuable leadership development tool that both defines and drives accountability through having a source of truth and creating rituals.[12] My takeaway is that **the tools are more than a business model.** They are about **leadership, accountability, source of truth, and ritual.** They are good tools but can be improved upon with a leadership playbook that focuses on building community.

The tools are intended to improve organizational performance, *through individual efforts* pushed or led by leadership. While a business model, or structure, is needed, true change requires more; it requires you to exert effort beyond "letting the business model do the heavy lifting" to institutionalizing that change through building a community.

"If we continue to invest in individuals as the primary targets of change, we will spend our primary energy on this and never fully invest in communities. In this way, *individual transformation comes at the cost of community* [emphasis added]."[13]

Essentially, you must have both an effective business model and a community-focused effort while implementing the tools.

Either business model requires repetition and consistency. There is a regular schedule of meetings/review inherent in each. These face-to-face meetings are not to be underappreciated or overlooked; they form the backbone of success.

---

12. I am indebted to Kevin Fishner's thoughts in First Round Review, February 29, 2024. https://review.firstround.com/focus-on-your-first-10-systems-not-just-your-first-10-hires-this-chief-of-staff-shares-his-playbook/.

13. Block, *Community*, 5.

Operating Rhythm

Operating rhythm tends to have three "speeds": Annual, quarterly, and short-term (either daily or weekly). Each rhythm consists of two fundamental foundations:

1. **Sources of Truth**, which defines success in a clear, ideally quantifiable way, and
2. **Ritual**, which is a consistent practice to review the sources of truth and build a community while improving accountability.

The tip here is *to set up your business models for regularly checking in on your strategic plan so you don't veer too far off course from initial goals.* These are not "set it and forget it" types of business models, as each requires human effort/intervention on a regular basis. Sometimes companies will focus on the sources of truth and not the ritual and that's one of the biggest mistakes that you can make. As a consultant, I often previously said, "Let the business model do the heavy lifting." This was short-sighted. The business model doesn't run itself; people are required. In 1973, my consulting mentor Nathaniel Hill said, "Regardless of what an organization's executives say is not working, it is always a people problem at its core." The purpose of an operating rhythm isn't to dogmatically stick to goals set at the beginning of the year; the rituals need to include a ritual of reflection and introspection.

I have a private pilot's license. As a pilot, your destination is obviously the goal or objective, but you don't just pronounce it, set it, and forget it. A completed flight is the outcome of many cadences, rituals, and adjustments. Before the engines are even started, the rituals begin: the flight plan, prestart check, after start check, before taxi check, before takeoff check, after takeoff check, climb check, cruise check, descent check, before landing check, after landing check, and the post-shutdown check.

The ritual and components of these checks support only the desired outcome, a safe flight. The actual outcomes always vary from your expectations (e.g., weather-related variables), and require adjustments to your plan. And so it goes; your success, and indeed your life, is intertwined with your learned ritual. It is not just the various procedures but the human-based cadence, or rhythm, and adjustments that are crucial to your safety. **The rhythm becomes learned rituals, which builds the framework so that the deviations from normal do not interfere with reaching your destination.**

WHAT'S YOUR ORGANIZATION'S TRUTH?

In the data world, the term "source of truth" refers to the authoritative and reliable source of information (data) within the company, a single, trusted data repository that contains accurate, up-to-date, and consistent data or knowledge that employees rely on for decision-making, problem-solving, and operational processes. It's centralized, not scattered haphazardly around in different silos. Does your organization have a leadership "source of truth?" Does it have a centralized, black-and-white set of information for decision-making? If not, I strongly suggest you do. Both business models lend themselves and their tools to becoming that source of truth.

While not addressed in these business models explicitly, each shows how leadership can create that source of truth through a couple of simple processes, including, but not limited to, a scorecard. The scorecard should be based on leading indicators (not lagging indicators like traditional accounting results), which are, in turn, tied to attainment of key results and goals. Using this source of truth, you cut straight through the CYA and excuses, which leads to increased accountability.[14] No more excuses; the data either supports it or not. Black and white. No alternative "facts." No equivocation and no more CYA.

By first setting the vision, goals, and expectations for behaviors and performance, you and your leadership team "own" this corporate source of truth around which your decisions are based and performance is judged. **Accountability is a predicate to trust. By performing against a source of truth, you foster a culture of trust, transparency, and continuous improvement, where everyone in your organization is accountable.** By prioritizing the use of the source of truth and, indeed, creating rituals around the analysis of this information, you establish a foundation for informed decision-making, improved communication, and overall organizational success.

Use your source of truth combined with organizational rituals to invert the iceberg of ignorance, uncovering all that is below the surface.

---

14. Throughout this book, please recognize that there are two types of accountabilities: compliance-based and natural. In some corporate cultures, accountability is based on compliance: a "you will do this" type of directive. In other cultures, such as the one developed in this book, natural accountability occurs, where employees hold themselves accountable out of, for example, a sense of purpose.

Chapter Summary

This chapter explored how business leaders typically only see about four percent of what's happening in their organizations, like the visible tip of an iceberg. It explained that without proper systems, organizational goals often get forgotten and employees become isolated in silos. The chapter introduced two key concepts for addressing this: "Sources of Truth" (clear, measurable definitions of success) and "Ritual" (consistent practices to review progress and build community). Using the analogy of a pilot's checklists, the chapter emphasized that success requires both reliable data and regular rhythms of reviewing that data. The goal is to "flip the iceberg" by bringing hidden issues to the surface through transparent, data-driven accountability systems and consistent team communication.

Key Chapter Takeaways

1. Leaders typically see only four percent of organizational reality; most issues remain hidden "below the waterline."
2. Operating rhythm requires both a source of truth (data) and consistent rituals (review practices).
3. Success demands both systematic processes and human engagement; business models alone aren't enough.
4. Regular review cycles (annual, quarterly, weekly) prevent goal atrophy and maintain focus.
5. Accountability emerges from clear metrics and consistent review, not from individual effort alone.

Suggested Homework

1. Audit your organization's "source of truth": Map out where key performance data lives and how it's accessed.
2. Document your current review rituals at each time scale (annual, quarterly, weekly) and identify gaps.

⚡⚡⚡⚡

CHAPTER 3

Small Business Realities

Summary: This chapter examines the challenges facing small businesses, supported by stark statistics: 20.4 percent fail in the first year, rising to 65.3 percent by year ten, with cash flow problems (82 percent) being the primary cause. It outlines common frustrations of business owners, categorized into five key areas: loss of control, financial instability, people problems (supported by employee engagement data showing 78 percent are not engaged), hitting growth ceilings, and initiative fatigue. The chapter addresses "small business imposter syndrome" affecting 84 percent of owners and introduces the concept that while business models like Traction or Scaling Up provide necessary tools, sustainable success requires combining these tools with community-enhanced leadership rather than relying solely on command-and-control implementation.

The U.S. Small Business Administration says small businesses accounted for 45.9 percent of U.S. employees[15] and 44 percent of U.S. economic activity.[16] There are approximately 34.8 million small businesses in the U.S. Over 1.3

15. U.S. Small Business Administration Office of Advocacy, "2024 Small Business Profile" (2024). https://advocacy.sba.gov/wp-content/uploads/2024/11/United_States.pdf.

16. Luisa Zhou, "Small Business Statistics: The Ultimate List in 2025," January 23, 2025. https://luisazhou.com/blog/small-business-statistics/#:~:text=20%25%20of%20small%20businesses%20fail%20within%20the%20first%20year&text=About%20 70%25%20of%20businesses%20with,their%2010th%20year%20of%20operating.

million new businesses opened between March 2022 and March 2023 (SBA) and, unfortunately, 1.1 million businesses closed in that same timeframe.

Surviving as a small business is difficult at best. U.S. Bureau of Labor Statistics reports that about 20.4 percent of small businesses fail the first year. The failure rate increases to 31.1 percent by the end of the second year, 49.4 percent by the fifth year, and 65.3 percent by the tenth year.

The reasons for failure are multiple, but the main causes are:[17]

1. Cash flow problems   82%
2. Lack of market need   42%
3. Ran out of cash   29%
4. Lack of right team   23%
5. Outcompeted   19%

Frustrations of Business Owners/CEOs

Given this data, get any group of business owners together in a safe space and they will freely share their frustrations at work. Here are some examples of what I've heard:

- Most small business owners work too hard and receive too little reward.
- Most businesses are in chaos. They lack a way of doing business that works.
- For most business owners, their businesses don't serve their lives; their businesses consume their lives.
- Most small business owners don't have a personal life plan that purposefully guides their daily actions.
- Most small business owners don't understand that they can and should create a business that works without them.
- Most small business owners perform too many functions (wear too many hats) and have no plan for freeing themselves from the technical work of their businesses.

---

17. Luisa Zhou, "Small Business Statistics: The Ultimate List in 2025."

- Most small businesses don't have a business model for recruiting, hiring, and training effective people.
- Most small businesses are organized around the existing people, rather than business processes. This leads to inconsistent performance and creates havoc when someone leaves.
- Most small business owners blame poor results on their people.
- Business owners do not feel they can depend on their employees, so they feel trapped in the business.
- There is usually confusion within organizations about who reports to whom.
- Accountabilities in small businesses often overlap and are unclear, adding to the confusion.
- Most small businesses don't produce consistent, predictable results.
- Most small business owners don't know who their preferred consumer is.
- They don't know how to identify and appeal to the emotional needs of their consumers.
- They don't examine the impact that their entire business process has on their customers.
- They market and sell "by the seat of their pants" rather than by applying proven marketing and selling strategies.
- Most business owners believe extraordinary people are the key to a successful business.
- Most small business owners don't realize that in the best businesses, business models run the business and ordinary people run the business models.
- Most people don't view business in a holistic way, as an integrated set of business models that interact with each other.
- Most small business owners don't use quantification to measure effectiveness and documentation to ensure predictability.

While you may see yourself in this list above (and likely in several places), don't despair; you are not alone. Let's try to bring some generalizations or grouping to these five frustrations:

Loss of Control: The business runs you instead of you running it. Chaos reigns, outcomes are unpredictable, and your time and resources feel constantly hijacked by urgent demands. Rather than steering the ship, you're being tossed by the waves.

Financial Instability: Sales fluctuate unpredictably while costs spiral. Poor accounting practices and cash flow management create constant financial pressure. Even during growth periods, working capital demands outpace available funds, and unexpected expenses erode margins.

People Problems: Without systematic hiring and training processes, the organization becomes dependent on individuals rather than systems. When key people leave, operations falter. Trust issues keep you chained to daily operations, while unclear reporting structures create confusion. Meanwhile, customer relationships suffer from inconsistent service and unclear profitability metrics. Employee engagement remains low.

Then you read the national research:

- 78 percent of employees are not engaged at work.[18]
- Only 39 percent see the value they create.[19]
- Only 34 percent thought they strongly contributed to their organization's success.[20]
- Only 28 percent feel connected to their company's purpose.[21]

No wonder business owners tend to be frustrated with people: their employees, their customers, their vendors, and their partners. They just don't get it, they don't listen, and/or they lack accountability.

Hitting the Growth Ceiling: Despite your efforts, you're stuck at a plateau. With no strategic roadmap, expansion feels impossible. Time and resources for meaningful growth or a profitable exit remain elusive. Something's blocking your path, whether it's the need for stability, better work-life balance,

18. Jim Harter, "Thriving Employees Create a Thriving Business," Gallup Workplace, June 26, 2020, updated April 14, 2021. https://www.gallup.com/workplace/313067/employees-aren-thriving-business-struggling.aspx.

19. Harter, "Thriving Employees Create a Thriving Business."

20. Harter, "Thriving Employees Create a Thriving Business."

21. Sally Blount and Paul Leinwand, "Why Are We Here?" *Harvard Business Review*, November-December 2019. https://hbr.org/2019/11/why-are-we-here.

or peace of mind. Larry Greiner wrote about these ceilings in *Harvard Business Review* in 1972.[22]

Initiative Fatigue: You've thrown everything at the wall from SEO, social media, to content marketing and nothing sticks. Your team has grown numb to the constant parade of new strategies and business books. Each month brings another flavor-of-the-month initiative, yet sustainable progress remains out of reach. They're reading all the books, the business books du jour, including *Traction* or *Scaling Up*.

In summary, you are working way too much without seeing the payoff; you're exhausted, physically and mentally.

SMALL BUSINESS IMPOSTER SYNDROME

Small business imposter syndrome for business owners/entrepreneurs happens, in part, because there is no handbook. We are all basically unqualified to run our own businesses. Critically, there is no book entitled, "How to Succeed as a Business Owner." Some say that earning an MBA is like that book; yet, it has been estimated that an "overwhelming 84 percent of business owners reported struggling with imposter syndrome at any given time."[23] There are many tips, videos, guides, and blogs online, and remember while reading those tips, the countervailing forces listed previously are hindering and pushing back against you. "If left unchecked, imposter syndrome can unintentionally become a self-imposed glass ceiling."[24]

No wonder we have difficulty and frustrations. Yet, from these very frustrations come growth.

A simple business model of proven tools is that business model for you and implementing these tools is only part of getting what you want out of your

---

22. Larry E. Greiner, "Evolution and Revolution as Organizations Grow," *Harvard Business Review*, July-August 1972/updated May-June 1998. https://hbr.org/1998/05/evolution-and-revolution-as-organizations-grow#:~:text=This%20article%20originally%20appeared%20in,%2C%E2%80%9D%20to%20update%20his%20observations.

23. Chantel Cohen, "The Entrepreneur's Roadmap to Overcoming Impostor Syndrome," Inc., March 11, 2024. https://www.inc.com/entrepreneurs-organization/the-entrepreneurs-roadmap-to-overcoming-imposter-syndrome.html.

24. Cohen, "The Entrepreneur's Roadmap to Overcoming Impostor Syndrome," Inc.

business. They are merely a set of particularly pertinent tools, but you must know how to use the respective tools to get the biggest benefits.

Consider that a hammer is also a tool and can be used to build or to deconstruct something. Most anyone can use a hammer similar to one a craftsman would use, yet results may differ greatly. What separates a novice from a craftsman? I submit it is the learned skills beyond merely banging away on a nail. The analogy stands. Both business models are very well-crafted and, just through their implementation, will produce improved results for organizations. Yet, their promise is so much more: improved leadership, accountability, an unambiguous source of truth, and, finally, rituals, all of which leverage the strengths of the business model. **Either business model has the tools; community is the structure**, the weft and the warp. As leadership, you weave them together to build the organization you want.

Yet, there are those of you who still are uncomfortable with the potential effects of changing your culture to a community-enhanced one. It is, of course, your right to resist this seemingly extra effort and go right to the implementation of the business model. In fact, you likely have been told this is the "preferred way." However, by implementing from the command and control/fiat approach, which may seem faster initially, you are likely to face several challenges:

- Without buy-in, employees may resist or only superficially adopt new practices.
- A top-down approach might miss crucial, context-specific adaptations that could make the business model more effective.
- The organization loses out on the insights and ideas that emerge from inclusive conversations.
- Employees may feel like subjects of change rather than agents of change, leading to lower motivation and engagement.
- Without deep understanding and commitment, the implementation may falter when leadership attention shifts or challenges arise.
- The business model may be implemented in a way that conflicts with existing cultural strengths, potentially damaging morale and effectiveness.

While initial implementation using a command-and-control approach might be faster, true integration and results may take longer due to these challenges. In contrast, the community-based approach may potentially take longer in the initial stages but is more likely to result in a deeper, more effective, and more sustainable implementation of your business model, with additional benefits to organizational culture and employee engagement.

Community-enhanced leadership isn't about diluting the rigor of your business system. Rather, it's about amplifying its effectiveness by creating the conditions where these tools can achieve their full potential. It's about understanding that while systems can direct behavior, only community can inspire commitment.

Chapter Summary

This chapter examined the challenging landscape of small businesses in America, highlighting that while they make up nearly half of U.S. economic activity, their survival rates are concerning, with over 65 percent failing within ten years. The chapter outlined common frustrations faced by business owners, including loss of control, financial instability, and people problems, noting that most entrepreneurs struggle with "imposter syndrome" due to lack of clear guidance. The chapter suggested that while business models and tools can help address these challenges, simply implementing them isn't enough. Instead, success requires combining these tools with a community-focused leadership approach, comparing it to how a craftsman's expertise with tools goes beyond just knowing how to use them.

Key Chapter Takeaways

1. Small business failure rates are significant (65.3 percent by year ten), with cash flow being the primary challenge (82 percent).
2. Most owners face five core frustrations; loss of control, financial instability, people problems, growth ceilings, and initiative fatigue.
3. Employee disengagement is widespread (78 percent not engaged), contributing to organizational challenges.
4. Business imposter syndrome affects 84 percent of owners, creating self-imposed limitations.
5. Command-and-control implementation of business models, while faster initially, often leads to superficial adoption and resistance.

Suggested Homework

1. Assess which of the five core frustrations most impact your business: Document specific examples.
2. Map your current implementation approach (command-and-control vs. community-based) and identify potential resistance points.

⚡⚡⚡⚡

CHAPTER 4

The Fundamentals of the Models

Summary: This chapter provides a detailed comparison of two business models, Traction and Scaling Up, examining their shared DNA (leadership focus, structural alignment, operational tools) and key differences. Traction emerges as more suitable for early-stage businesses (under $10 million revenue) seeking operational clarity through a streamlined approach, while Scaling Up targets larger or rapidly growing organizations needing more sophisticated tools for managing complexity. The chapter emphasizes that while both models improve leadership and accountability through structured processes, neither explicitly addresses "how" to enhance these aspects. It concludes that choosing between them should depend on organizational size, growth aspirations, leadership capabilities, and available resources, noting that successful implementation requires clear commitment to one system rather than attempting to cherry-pick from both.

WHAT ARE THESE BUSINESS MODELS?

Traction and *Scaling Up* are both sets of simple tools for organizations to improve operational performance and, ultimately, profitability. Let's briefly explore the two models (again, not from an implementation point of view).

Traction:
- Developed by Gino Wickman
- Focuses on six key elements: Vision, People, Data, Issues, Process, and Traction

o Aims to help businesses achieve better results through improved organization and accountability

Scaling Up:
  o Based on Verne Harnish's work
  o Emphasizes four major decision areas: People, Strategy, Execution, and Cash™
  o Designed to help companies scale effectively and manage growth

Both business models are indeed focused on business performance and growth, rather than explicitly on building a "better" organization in terms of community.

In short, both are designed to accomplish specific things:

- Streamline operations
- Clarify goals and vision
- Improve accountability
- Manage growth
- Optimize resource allocation

COMMON GROUND—
THE SHARED DNA OF TRACTION AND SCALING UP

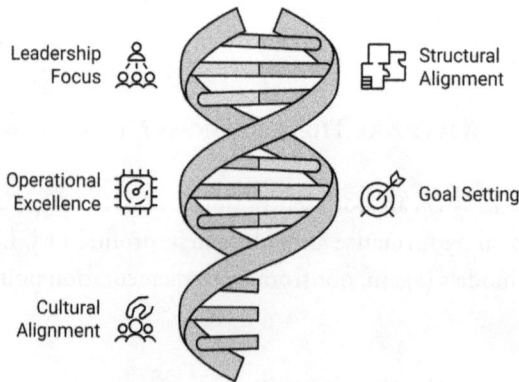

Leadership Focus

Structural Alignment

Operational Excellence

Goal Setting

Cultural Alignment

Figure 5—Shared DNA

At their core, both models emerged from a similar philosophy, successful businesses need structured models to achieve sustainable growth. These systems share remarkable similarities in their fundamental approach to business optimization, though they express these commonalities through different terminologies and specific tools.

Foundational Focus on Leadership

Both models recognize leadership as the cornerstone of organizational success. They share an unwavering commitment to developing strong leadership capabilities through systematic approaches. In both models, leaders are expected to clearly articulate vision, purpose, and core values. This isn't just about posting mission statements on walls, both systems require leaders to actively embed these elements into daily operations through specific tools and practices.

The data-driven decision-making emphasis appears prominently in both models. Whether it's Traction's Scorecard or Scaling Up's Critical Numbers, both systems insist on moving beyond gut feelings to measurable metrics. Leaders in both models are expected to regularly review key performance indicators and adjust, based on actual data, rather than assumptions.

Structural Alignment

The architectural similarity between these models is striking. Both employ a rhythm of regular meetings that cascade from annual planning sessions down to weekly team meetings. This isn't coincidental both systems recognize that regular, structured communication is essential for maintaining organizational alignment and momentum.

In terms of accountability, both models implement clear structural hierarchies and responsibility matrices. Traction uses its Accountability Chart, while Scaling Up employs the Function Accountability Chart, but the underlying principle remains the same that every key function needs clear ownership and measurable outcomes.

Operational Excellence Through Tools

Both systems provide comprehensive toolsets for executing their principles. Strategic planning documents serve as central reference points: Traction's Vision/Traction Organizer (V/TO) and Scaling Up's One-Page Strategic Plan (OPSP) both capture the organization's long-term vision and break it down into actionable components.

The commitment to performance metrics runs deep in both models. Regular measurement and review cycles are built into the core operations, ensuring that organizations maintain focus on their most critical numbers. Both systems emphasize the importance of leading indicators, rather than just lagging results, such as profits.

Meeting structures in both models follow similar patterns, though with different specific formats. The emphasis on regular, productive meetings from weekly team sessions to annual planning demonstrates their shared understanding that effective communication requires consistent, structured forums.

Shared Philosophy on Goal Setting

Both models emphasize the importance of setting and tracking goals at multiple time horizons. Whether it's Traction's Rocks or Scaling Up's Priorities, both systems recognize that organizations need to balance short-term objectives with long-term aspirations. They both advocate for breaking down larger goals into manageable quarterly objectives while maintaining alignment with the bigger picture.

Cultural Alignment

Perhaps most fundamentally, both models recognize that successful businesses need strong cultural foundations. They emphasize the importance of core values in hiring, firing, and daily decision-making. Both systems provide tools for ensuring that company culture remains strong and consistent as organizations grow and evolve.

Process Documentation

Both models stress the importance of documenting and standardizing core processes. This shared emphasis reflects their understanding that scalable growth requires consistent, repeatable operations. Both Traction's Process Documentation and Scaling Up's Process Accountability Chart provide ways to capture and optimize key business processes.

These shared elements reflect a collective understanding of what makes businesses successful. While the specific tools and terminology may differ, both models recognize that sustainable growth requires unclouded vision, strong leadership, consistent communication, measurable goals, and robust processes. This common foundation has proven effective across various industries and organization sizes, validating the fundamental principles both systems embrace.

DIVERGENT PATHS—
KEY DIFFERENCES BETWEEN TRACTION AND SCALING UP

While Traction and Scaling Up share common foundational principles, their approaches to implementing these principles differ significantly. These differences reflect their distinct target markets and the unique challenges faced by organizations at various stages of growth.

Complexity and Scope Variations

Traction deliberately employs a more streamlined approach, focusing on establishing and maintaining fundamental business practices. Its tools and processes are more standardized and generally easier to implement, making it particularly suitable for organizations that need to establish strong operational foundations. The model's simplicity is its strength, allowing organizations to focus on mastering basic but crucial business practices.

In contrast, Scaling Up embraces complexity, providing a more comprehensive framework designed for organizations dealing with the challenges of rapid growth. Its tools are more flexible and adaptable, acknowledging that growing organizations often need to customize their approaches based on specific circumstances. The model includes more sophisticated tools for managing both internal operations and external relationships.

Contrasting Leadership Philosophies

Traction's leadership model is built around the distinction between Visionary and Integrator roles. This clear delineation helps organizations separate strategic thinking from operational execution, often resolving common leadership conflicts in growing businesses. The focus is primarily on optimizing current leadership team dynamics and ensuring clear communication channels.

Scaling Up takes a different approach, emphasizing the development of leaders who can master what it calls the Four Decisions®: People, Strategy, Execution, and Cash.™ This model places more emphasis on developing future leaders and managing external stakeholders. It acknowledges that growing organizations need to build leadership capacity at multiple levels.

Financial Management Approaches

The treatment of fiscal management represents one of the starkest differences between the two models. Traction integrates financial considerations within its overall framework but doesn't emphasize them as a separate focus area. Financial metrics may be part of the scorecard, but the system doesn't provide specialized tools for financial management.

Scaling Up, by contrast, places significant emphasis on fiscal management, particularly cash flow. It provides specific tools and strategies for cash management, reflecting its focus on rapidly growing organizations where cash flow management is often critical for survival and continued growth. The Cash Acceleration Strategies (CASh) component is a distinctive feature of the Scaling Up framework.

Growth Management Philosophies

Traction's approach to growth management focuses on establishing and maintaining fundamental systems. Its quarterly priority-setting process provides a straightforward way to focus organizational energy on key objectives. The system emphasizes consistent execution over rapid scaling.

Scaling Up, true to its name, provides more sophisticated tools for managing rapid growth. It includes detailed models for scaling operations, managing increasing complexity, and maintaining organizational alignment during periods of rapid expansion. The system acknowledges that fast-growing organizations need more complex metrics and planning tools.

Customer and Market Orientation

Another significant difference lies in how these models approach market orientation. Traction maintains a primarily internal focus, emphasizing operational excellence and team alignment. While it doesn't ignore external factors, its tools and processes are primarily focused on internal optimization.

Scaling Up places more emphasis on external orientation, providing specific tools for managing customer relationships, market positioning, and competitive strategy. This reflects its focus on growing organizations that need to actively manage their market presence while scaling operations.

Meeting and Communication Structures

While both models emphasize regular meetings, their specific approaches differ. Traction's Level 10 Meeting® structure is more standardized, with a specific format and agenda that remains consistent across organizations. This standardization helps ensure consistency and efficiency in communication.

Scaling Up's meeting rhythm is more flexible, acknowledging that growing organizations may need to adapt their communication structures as they scale. It includes additional meeting types, such as daily huddles and monthly management reviews, reflecting the increased communication needs of larger organizations.

These differences highlight how each framework is optimized for different organizational contexts. Understanding these distinctions is crucial for choosing the right framework for your organization's specific needs and circumstances.

Choosing the Right System

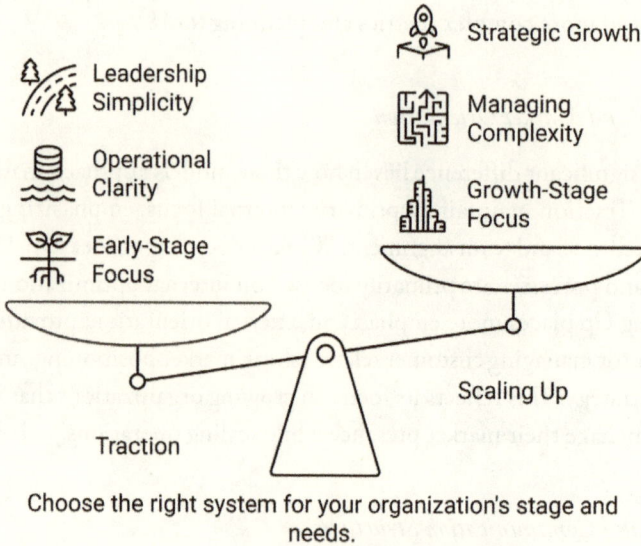

Choose the right system for your organization's stage and needs.

Figure 6—Choosing the Right System

The choice between Traction and Scaling Up represents a significant strategic decision that can profoundly impact your organization's future. Understanding when and why to choose one system over the other requires careful consideration of your organization's current state, future aspirations, and implementation capabilities.

When to Choose Traction

Traction proves most effective for organizations in specific situations:

Early-Stage and Small- to Medium-Sized Businesses: Organizations with revenue under $10 million typically find Traction's straightforward approach more manageable and immediately beneficial. The system's emphasis on establishing fundamental business practices makes it particularly suitable for companies still building their operational foundations. Its streamlined tools help create structure without overwhelming the organization with complexity.

Organizations Needing Operational Clarity: If your organization struggles with basic operational issues such as role clarity, meeting effectiveness, or consistent execution, Traction's structured approach can provide immediate benefits. Its clear models for accountability and communication can help resolve common operational challenges that plague many growing businesses.

Leadership Teams Seeking Simplicity: Organizations whose leadership teams prefer clear, straightforward tools and processes will find Traction's approach appealing. The system's standardized processes and well-defined roles can help resolve common leadership team dynamics issues while establishing consistent operational practices.

When to Choose Scaling Up

Scaling Up is typically more suitable for organizations with distinctive characteristics:

Growth-Stage Companies: Organizations with revenue over $10 million or experiencing rapid growth often find Scaling Up's comprehensive framework more appropriate. The system's more sophisticated tools for managing complexity and scale make it particularly valuable for organizations dealing with the challenges of rapid expansion.

Organizations Managing Complexity: If your organization is dealing with increasing operational complexity, multiple product lines, or diverse market segments, Scaling Up's more nuanced approach may be necessary. Its tools for managing complexity while maintaining organizational alignment become particularly valuable in these situations.

Strategic Growth Focus: Organizations with ambitious growth plans and the need for sophisticated strategic planning tools will find Scaling Up's comprehensive approach beneficial. Its emphasis on developing leadership capacity and managing external relationships supports aggressive growth strategies.

Consider your strategic planning process. Whether you're using Traction's V/TO or Scaling Up's OPSP, these tools become more powerful when treated as frameworks for collective wisdom rather than top-down directives. Create rituals that invite diverse perspectives into the planning process while maintaining clear accountability for decisions.

Considering a Hybrid Approach

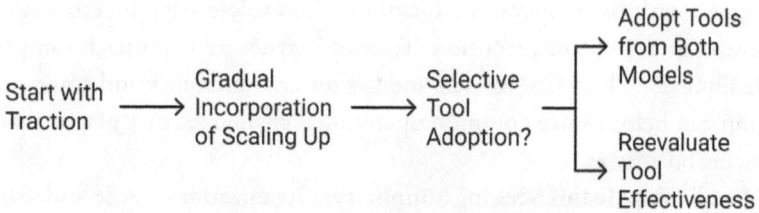

Start with Traction → Gradual Incorporation of Scaling Up → Selective Tool Adoption? → Adopt Tools from Both Models / Reevaluate Tool Effectiveness

Figure 7—Which Business Model?

Some organizations successfully adopt a hybrid approach, combining elements from both models:

Transitional Strategy: Organizations can start with Traction to establish fundamental practices and gradually incorporate elements of Scaling Up as they grow. This approach allows for a smooth transition as organizational needs evolve.

Selective Tool Adoption: Some organizations choose to adopt specific tools from each framework based on their particular needs. This approach requires careful consideration to ensure the selected tools work together effectively.

Implementation Considerations

Several factors should influence your final decision:

Resource Availability: Consider the time and financial resources available for implementation.

- Assess your team's capacity for learning and adopting new systems.
- Evaluate the availability of external support (consultants, coaches).

Organizational Readiness: Assess your team's appetite for change.[25] Consider your organization's current operational maturity.

---

25. See also Checklist in Appendix 9.

- Evaluate your leadership team's capabilities and development needs.

Long-term Alignment: Consider how each framework aligns with your long-term vision.

- Assess the scalability needs of your organization.
- Evaluate how each framework fits with your industry and market position.

Making the Final Decision

The ultimate choice between Traction and Scaling Up should be based on a careful assessment of:

1. your organization's current size and complexity,
2. your growth aspirations and timeline,
3. your leadership team's capabilities and preferences,
4. available resources for implementation, and
5. the desired level of system sophistication.

Remember that either framework, when properly implemented, can significantly improve organizational performance. The key is choosing the system that best aligns with your organization's current capabilities while supporting your future growth objectives.

The most successful implementations often occur when organizations make a clear, committed choice rather than trying to cherry-pick elements from both systems without a coherent strategy. Whichever system you choose, success will depend upon consistent, dedicated implementation and ongoing commitment to the chosen framework's principles and practices.

Further, there are interesting unstated comparisons between the two.

Since both business models imply that implementation will improve leadership and accountability, they appear similar in those respects. **Yet, neither specifically addresses the "how" of improved leadership and accountability, instead deferring to the implicit promise that improvement will happen.** It does, indeed, happen simply by adopting and embracing the respective processes; doing that alone will make leadership better and, as a result, accountability improves.[26] Some improvements will accrue to you simply by implementing the business model.

This is not an error of omission in the design, but it does represent in each case an unfulfilled promise. Experience has shown that it is indeed the leadership of the organization who determines the ultimate success and institutionalization of improvements. There is little explicit instruction for using the business model to fulfill deeper reasons for implementing either; that is, to improve leadership and accountability through sources of truth and rituals while building a community.

1. **Leadership**
    Traction: In this business model, leadership is viewed as a crucial element for creating a more efficient and effective organization that can execute the organization's vision. Relying on the roles of Visionary and Integrator, the model emphasizes clarity, accountability, and a systematic approach as the keys to running a business. The leadership principles implied in the book are designed to create a cohesive team that can effectively drive the organization towards its goals while maintaining a healthy and productive company culture, but it is still incumbent on ownership/leadership to determine how to change and lead others to a better culture.

    It's worth noting that this approach to leadership might be particularly effective in certain types of organizations or early stages of growth, especially where clarity and execution are key challenges. However, it might need to be balanced with other leadership approaches in situations that require more flexibility, innovation, or complex problem-solving, and the model itself provides no illumination on how to improve leadership.

    Scaling Up: This business model's view of leadership is more comprehensive and balanced, emphasizing both strategic thinking and operational excellence. It's designed for leaders who are driving significant growth and need to build organizations capable of scaling rapidly.

---

26. Due, in part, to the Hawthorne Effect.

This approach to leadership is more complex and multifaceted compared to some other business models, reflecting the challenges of managing rapidly growing organizations. It requires leaders to be adept at managing both internal operations and external relationships and to think simultaneously about current performance and future scalability. This definition of leadership might be particularly effective in high-growth environments or in organizations aiming to scale significantly.

2. **Accountability**[27]
    Traction: Accountability is not just about assigning blame or credit. It's part of a comprehensive business model that is designed to create clarity, drive performance, and ensure that every key area of the business has a responsible party.

    By implementing these tools and principles, organizations can potentially create a culture where everyone knows what they're accountable for and is empowered to deliver results.

    This approach to accountability is designed to be practical and actionable, providing clear structures and processes that can be implemented in any organization. The goal is to move from a culture of blame or ambiguity to one of clear ownership and problem-solving.

    Scaling Up: This approach to accountability is designed with growth in mind. It aims to create a business model where accountability is clear, aligned with strategy, and scalable as the organization expands. The focus on both functional and process accountability, along with regular rhythms for review and adjustment, sets it apart.

    This business model is particularly suited for companies experiencing or planning for rapid growth, as it provides structures to maintain clear accountability even as the organization becomes more complex.

3. **Source of Truth**
    Traction: It's worth noting that while Traction doesn't use the term "source of truth," the business model provides several key tools which

---

27. For more on accountability, see Chapter 9: How to Amplify and Augment Each Model with Community.

can become sources of truth, such as the Scorecard, To-do List, and Rocks, among others.

Scaling Up: It also does not explicitly use the term "source of truth," yet there are several tools which can serve this function, such as the One-Page Strategic Plan, Rockefeller Habits Checklist, and Critical Numbers, among others.

In each case, it is notable that the core foundational piece of institutionalized source of truth is specifically absent, although both models offer a variety of tools that can provide leadership with sources of truth.

4. **Ritual**

Traction: While not explicitly using the term "rituals," Traction does provide several key practices that serve to create an organizational ritual, e.g., annual, quarterly, and weekly meetings. These meetings:

- Create a rhythm for the organization, ensuring regular review, communication, and alignment
- Provide periodic forums for addressing issues and making decisions
- Embed the business model into the organization's culture and daily operations

Scaling Up: Similarly, while Scaling Up also doesn't explicitly use the term "rituals," it prescribes several regular practices and meetings that effectively function as organizational rituals, such as annual, quarterly, monthly, and daily meetings. These rituals are designed to create consistency, maintain alignment, and drive execution within rapidly growing organizations. Their tools:

- Create a structured rhythm for the organization, ensuring regular communication and alignment at all levels
- Provide consistent forums for addressing issues, making decisions, and adjusting strategies
- Reinforce the core components of the Scaling Up business model, particularly the Four Decisions (People, Strategy, Execution, Cash)
- Embed growth-oriented practices into the organization's culture and daily operations

○ Allow for regular recalibration and adjustment, which is crucial for rapid scaling companies

WRAP UP

Both business models can serve as the backbone to create a better organization through improved leadership, accountability, sources of truth, and rituals. Traction is oriented to early-stage organizations and Scaling Up to growth-oriented organizations. The models are good, proven systems. While there are implied promises about leadership and accountability, there is little guidance or discussion as to what to do, or how to use the tools, to improve existing leadership. The "how" is missing, and without other guidance, you must apply your own skills/experiences to purposefully improve leadership and accountability.

The choice is yours: one is likely better suited to you, your leadership style, and your near-term desires for your organization.

Critically, and the significance is that through their design and their core, each is still (1) a traditional approach to both strategic and operational planning and (2) a performance measurement and management business model, albeit streamlined and made easier for small- to mid-sized organizations.

Suggestion: Even if you already have or are in the process of implementing either of these two business models, you may want to go over the materials in Appendices 4 through 7 for reinforcement and/or suggestions for improvement.

Chapter Summary

This chapter provided a detailed comparison of two popular business models, Traction/EOS and Scaling Up, examining both their shared foundations and key differences. While both models focus on improving business performance through structured approaches to leadership, accountability, and regular meetings, they serve different organizational needs. Traction is presented as better suited for smaller businesses (under $10 million in revenue) seeking operational clarity through simpler, standardized tools. In contrast, Scaling Up is designed for larger or rapidly growing companies (over $10 million) that need more sophisticated tools to manage complexity. The chapter noted that while both models promise improved leadership and accountability, neither explicitly guides how to achieve these improvements; they simply provide the tools and frameworks, leaving the actual transformation up to the organization's leadership.

Key Chapter Takeaways

1. Both models share core DNA; leadership design, structured meetings, data-driven decisions, and process documentation.
2. Traction suits businesses under $10 million seeking operational clarity; Scaling Up fits larger organizations managing complexity.
3. Traction offers standardized, simpler tools; Scaling Up provides more sophisticated, flexible frameworks.
4. Neither model explicitly teaches "how" to improve leadership and accountability, though improvements occur simply through implementation.
5. Success requires committing to one system rather than mixing elements from both.

Suggested Homework

1. Evaluate your organization's current size, complexity, and growth goals against the models' characteristics to determine best fit.
2. Audit your current leadership practices and accountability systems to identify which model's tools would address your key gaps.

⚡ ⚡ ⚡ ⚡

CHAPTER 5

The Peril of a Formulaic Approach

Summary: This chapter critiques the "canned" or standardized implementation of business models, arguing that such approaches often lead to hidden costs and unintended consequences. It outlines specific risks across multiple areas: financial losses from resistance and workarounds, strategic vulnerabilities from over-standardization, reduced leadership effectiveness, damaged organizational culture, and decreased employee engagement. The chapter advocates for a shift from command-and-control to community-enhanced implementation, suggesting a transformation from controlling to enabling, telling to asking, and compliance to commitment. It concludes that combining proven business systems with community-building approaches leads to better outcomes in retention, engagement, innovation, and productivity.

THE FUNDAMENTAL SHIFT

Each of the two systems, when implemented, could be done by an outsider in a "canned" approach: "Here's the way to do it," without regard to your organization's culture. Sometimes it works and, in doing so, brings about a much improved, efficient organization, particularly when no such structure existed beforehand. However, implementation following "the rules" will likely not consider unique cultural elements, therefore leaving much unaccomplished, e.g., unfulfilled promises, as it were.

A "canned" implementation approach is fundamentally problematic. It is simply an extension of the command-and-control designed culture. Consider: Isn't it time to rethink and develop an alternate culture?

First and foremost a hierarchical (command-and-control) approach to implementation potentially has serious financial costs:

- Hidden costs of resistance and workarounds when people don't genuinely buy in. While the system might appear to work on paper, the reality of people creating elaborate workarounds often costs more than the inefficiencies the system was meant to solve.
- Lost opportunity costs when unique organizational strengths are suppressed by standardized approaches. The very capabilities that create competitive advantage often get damaged by rigid implementation.
- Implementation failure costs when the system doesn't stick because it wasn't adapted to organizational reality. The expense of multiple attempts at implementation often exceeds the cost of doing it right the first time.

Depending on your perspective or orientation, there are a few risks from a "by the book" implementation:

Market Orientation: If, as an owner/CEO, you are focused on market position, a "by the books" implementation might have risks for you by:

- reducing unique competitive advantages by forcing standardization where distinctive capabilities once created market differentiation,
- creating strategic vulnerability when competitors can easily copy your now-standardized approaches rather than having to decode your unique organizational magic, or
- limiting adaptive capacity precisely when market conditions demand increased agility and innovation.

Control Orientation: For many leaders concerned with control (e.g., "If I don't do it, it won't be done right" or any variation on that theme), a "canned" approach to implementation potentially causes:

- surface compliance, masking underground resistance, making it harder to know what's really happening in the organization,
- standardized metrics, often measuring the wrong things, creating blind spots about real organizational performance, or

- rigid systems, driving important conversations and decisions underground, reducing leadership's actual influence on key outcomes.

Task Orientation: If your focus is on tactics or measurable risk, a "by-the-book" implementation potentially:

- reduces, rather than improves, performance by damaging the informal systems that actually get work done,
- leads to compliance rather than commitment, resulting in mediocre rather than exceptional performance, or
- ignores organizational context, creating friction that wastes energy and resources.

Competitive Orientation: If you are concerned about competition, a structured implementation may:

- stifle the creative capacity that drives innovation,
- suppress the organizational characteristics that enable breakthrough thinking, or
- damage the cultural elements that support adaptation and evolution.

People Orientation: If you are concerned about your people, a "canned" implementation may:

- increase turnover caused by frustrations with rigid, standardized systems,
- damage the engagement that drives discretionary effort, or
- reduce the satisfaction that keeps good people.

Reputation Orientation: Finally, as you consider your legacy and reputation as an owner/CEO, such a "canned" implementation could:

- damage, rather than enhance, leadership credibility by focusing on problems, not possibilities,
- erode trust in leadership, or
- create cynicism about leadership wisdom.

All implementations cost money in both direct and indirect costs. Remember the iceberg image from Chapter 2. Imagine for a moment that the visible part of the iceberg, above the waterline, are costs you can see (and perhaps are concerned about) like implementation expenses, training time, and system costs. The insidious or hidden costs, under the waterline, are lost organizational wisdom, reduced engagement, damaged information networks, suppressed innovation, and increased turnover; some of the very hidden costs you were hoping the system could alleviate.

But it does not have to be that way. No organizational system needs to be implemented the same way in each company; after all, every company is different, unique from the others, especially yours. One size doesn't fit all. **The goal isn't to reject the systems but to implement them in a way that creates sustainable value rather than superficial compliance.**

BEYOND FORMULAIC IMPLEMENTATION— CREATING SUSTAINABLE CULTURAL CHANGE

Communities thrive on authenticity, where relationships drive results, local wisdom matters, and engagement requires personal ownership.

Wrap the implementation of your model in the container of community. In doing so, the key shifts will be:

From		To
Controlling	→	Enabling
Telling	→	Asking
Compliance	→	Commitment
Standardization	→	Adaptation

Figure 8—From Formulaic to Sustainable

What becomes possible when you implement with wisdom rather than just compliance? Would you be pleased with these results?

- Employee retention: a significant reduction in turnover
- Engagement scores: improvement in engagement
- Innovation metrics: increase in new ideas
- Productivity: improvement in team output over that brought solely by the business system's implementation

Consider that by creating a community-enhanced culture supported by a proven business model, engagement drives performance, relationships enable innovation, trust creates efficiency, and community builds resilience. **People and purpose power performance and profits.**

Chapter Summary

This chapter warned against implementing business models in a standardized, "one-size-fits-all" manner without considering an organization's unique culture. It outlined the risks of "canned" implementations from different leadership perspectives: market, control, people, and reputation. While standardized implementations might seem cost-effective initially, they often carry hidden costs like reduced engagement, lost innovation, and damaged organizational wisdom. The chapter suggested that sustainable change requires building community and adapting the business model to fit each organization's unique characteristics.

Key Chapter Takeaways

1. "Canned" implementations risk damaging unique organizational strengths and culture.
2. Hidden costs of standardized implementation often exceed visible costs.
3. Command-and-control implementation leads to compliance rather than commitment.
4. Success requires shifting from standardization to adaptation.
5. Community-enhanced implementation improves retention, engagement, and innovation.

Suggested Homework

1. Audit potential hidden costs in your current implementation approach.
2. Map specific areas where standardization might be suppressing your organization's unique strengths.

⚡⚡⚡⚡

CHAPTER 6

So How Does Reality Work vs. the Models?

Summary: This chapter critiques traditional annual planning processes and their cascading control mechanisms (quarterly, monthly, weekly, daily), highlighting how this approach damages organizations. It outlines key costs: The deficit trap of focusing on problems rather than possibilities, the limitations of top-down hierarchy, overreliance on metrics, and loss of narrative. The chapter particularly emphasizes the human toll: how traditional planning erodes engagement, relationships, creativity, and purpose, ultimately undermining the organization's capacity for innovation and sustainable success. It concludes that organizations need planning systems that enhance rather than diminish human capability while still meeting coordination needs.

THE LIMITS OF TRADITIONAL STRATEGY

The Tyranny of Traditional Planning: The Annual Ritual

Picture the scene: A hotel conference room in late November. Leadership teams gather around tables covered with laptops and spreadsheets. The air is thick with the pressure of next year's numbers. PowerPoint slides flash by with market analyses, competitor comparisons, growth projections. The conversation revolves almost entirely around metrics: How much? By when? At what cost?

This annual planning ritual has become so normalized that we rarely question its underlying assumptions or count its hidden costs. **Yet this approach to planning shapes not just our strategies but our organizational cultures, our relationships, and our capacity for genuine innovation.** There are significant problems caused by the traditional approach to planning: control, hierarchy, meaning, and innovation, among others.

The Cascade of Control

From this annual event, a cascade of control mechanisms flows through the organization:

Quarterly Checkpoints: Quarterly, teams gather to assess progress against the annual plan. The questions are predictable: Are we on track? Where are we falling behind? How do we close the gaps? The focus narrows further to numerical targets and variance analyses.

Monthly Reviews: As pressure builds, monthly reviews become exercises in gap identification and problem-solving. The conversation centers on deficits: what's missing, what's behind, what's not working. Success becomes defined as the absence of problems rather than the presence of possibility.

Weekly Updates: Drilling down further, we reach weekly meetings, the focus narrowed entirely to task completion and deliverable tracking. The broader purpose that might inspire innovation or energize teams has disappeared beneath the weight of immediate demands.

Daily Huddles: At the daily level, work becomes reduced to its smallest measurable units. Daily huddles track immediate deliverables with an almost mechanical precision. The human elements of work, e.g., creativity, relationship, and meaning, fade into the background.

The Cost of Control: This cascade of control exacts several profound costs. When organizations focus primarily on gaps and problems, several things happen:

Energy is depleted as people increasingly focus on what's wrong.

- Innovation suffocates under the pressure to fix problems rather than create opportunities.
- Risk-taking declines as psychological safety becomes the default choice.
- Creativity loses out to finding solutions to predefined problems.
- Possibility thinking gets replaced by problem-solving.

The organization becomes better at avoiding failure than pursuing excellence; more focused on fixing weaknesses than leveraging strengths.

The Hierarchy Hangover

Traditional planning's top-down approach creates multiple limitations:

First, it wastes the **collective intelligence** of the organization. When goals cascade down from the top, they carry implicit messages about who can think and who should merely execute. Valuable perspectives from those closest to customers, products, and processes get lost.

Second, it reduces **ownership and engagement**. When people are merely implementing others' decisions, their commitment naturally decreases. The energy that comes from genuine participation gets replaced by compliance.

Third, it limits **adaptability**. When decisions flow primarily downward, the organization's ability to sense and respond to change becomes constrained by the bandwidth of its hierarchy.

Loss of Meaning

The Metrics Mirage: Perhaps the most subtle but significant cost comes from over-reliance on metrics, derived from the very system we implemented to improve the organization.

The Narrative Loss: When numbers dominate planning, the richer narrative of organizational life gets lost. Customer stories, employee experiences, cultural patterns, all the qualitative data that might inform genuine innovation gets filtered out.

The Time Trap: Short-term metrics create pressure for quick wins over sustainable value creation. Quarterly targets can drive decisions that optimize immediate results at the cost of long-term health.

The Meaning Gap: When planning focuses primarily on numbers, it loses connection to purpose and meaning. The questions that might energize and align people: "What difference are we making?" "What's possible?" "What matters most?" All get replaced by "How much?" and "By when?"

The Innovation Impact

This traditional approach particularly impacts innovation in several ways:

Scope Limitation: Innovation gets confined to safe, incremental improvements rather than transformative possibilities.

Risk Reduction: The pressure to meet predictable targets discourages the experiments and failures that genuine innovation requires.

Perspective Narrowing: The focus on predetermined metrics blinds organizations to unexpected opportunities and emerging possibilities.

THE HUMAN COST

Understanding the Deep Impact of Traditional Planning

Beyond the organizational metrics and visible inefficiencies, traditional planning extracts a profound human toll that often goes unrecognized until the damage is deeply institutionalized. This cost manifests in the gradual erosion of what makes work meaningful and organizations truly effective.

When people begin to feel like interchangeable resources rather than unique contributors, their engagement withers at the root. This isn't just about job satisfaction; it's about the fundamental human need to matter, to make a difference, to bring one's whole self to work. As people feel increasingly commoditized, their discretionary energy, that extra effort that often makes the difference between adequate and exceptional performance, quietly dissipates.

The relationship landscape transforms in equally troubling ways. What might have been rich, developmental connections become mere transactional exchanges.

Conversations that once explored possibilities and built shared understanding reduce to status updates and task assignments. The human fabric of the organization, which provides its resilience and adaptability, gradually thins and tears. People who might have been partners in creation become merely roles interfacing with other roles.

Learning, which in healthy organizations flows naturally from curiosity and shared exploration, becomes confined to prescribed processes and procedures. Instead of following the organic emergence of knowledge through experience and collaboration, development gets reduced to checkboxes on spreadsheets and steps in a procedure. The rich territory of unexpected discovery and collective wisdom remains unexplored as people stick to safe and sanctioned approved learning paths.

Creativity suffers a particular kind of diminishment. Rather than serving as a force for imagining new possibilities and expanding what's possible, it gets narrowly channeled into problem-solving mode. While solving problems matters, limiting creativity to this function misses its deeper potential to envision and create new futures. The organization loses its capacity to dream bigger dreams and imagine breakthrough possibilities when focused on fixing problems.

Perhaps most fundamentally, purpose (the deeper meaning that energizes and directs human effort) gets buried under an avalanche of performance metrics. The question "What difference are we trying to make?" gets replaced by "Are we hitting our numbers?" This shift might seem subtle, but it fundamentally changes how people relate to their work and each other. **The soul of work and its capacity to contribute to something larger than ourselves gets lost in the relentless focus on measurable outputs.**

These human costs, while harder to measure than traditional metrics, often have the most significant long-term impact on organizational success. They show up in the gradual decline of innovation, the slow erosion of customer relationships, the subtle decrease in quality, and the quiet departure of your best people, not dramatically, but in a steady trickle that depletes organizational capability.

The tragedy lies not just in the immediate human impact but in how these losses undermine the very things most organizations say they want when they decide to implement a proven business model: engaged employees, strong cultures, continuous innovation, and sustainable success. **In our attempt to control and optimize through traditional planning, we often destroy the human foundations that make exceptional performance possible.**

This human toll requires us to fundamentally rethink how we approach planning and organizational design. We need approaches that enhance, rather than diminish, human capability; that strengthen, rather than weaken, relationships; that expand, rather than contract, possibilities; and that connect, rather than separate, people from deeper purpose.

The challenge lies in creating systems that serve human flourishing while meeting legitimate organizational needs for coordination and focus. This isn't about choosing between structure and humanity but about finding ways to have both, understanding that the highest performance comes when human spirits are free to soar within enabling structures, rather than be confined by controlling ones.

Chapter Summary

This chapter critiqued traditional annual business planning approaches, highlighting how they often prioritize control and metrics at the expense of human elements. It described how the typical planning cascade, from annual meetings to daily huddles, creates a rigid hierarchy that stifles innovation and creativity. The chapter argued that when organizations focus primarily on numbers and problem-solving, they pay hidden human costs: reduced engagement, weakened relationships, limited creativity, and loss of deeper purpose. While these metrics-driven systems aim to improve performance, they often undermine the very elements that make organizations successful: engaged employees, strong culture, and sustainable innovation. The chapter suggested that businesses need to find a balance between necessary structure and human flourishing.

Key Chapter Takeaways

1. Traditional planning's cascade of control undermines innovation and engagement.
2. Over-focus on metrics and problem-solving creates a deficit mindset.
3. Top-down planning wastes collective intelligence and reduces ownership.
4. Numerical focus overshadows important qualitative data and narrative.
5. Human costs include eroded relationships, diminished creativity, and lost purpose.

Suggested Homework

1. Audit your planning meetings; document time spent on problems versus possibilities.
2. Map how current metrics might be constraining innovation and employee engagement.

⚡⚡⚡⚡

CHAPTER 7

Community: The Missing Dimension

Summary: This chapter addresses the transition from merely installing business models to achieving true organizational transformation. It emphasizes that while both Traction and Scaling Up are effective tools, their full potential is only realized through community-enhanced leadership, an approach that combines operational excellence with authentic human connection. The chapter argues that perfect implementation of systems alone won't create lasting change: instead, organizations need to focus on how people think, work, and relate to each other using these tools. It concludes by emphasizing that while consultants can help install systems, true implementation must be owned by the organization's leadership and embraced by its people.

If you have already decided which business model works best for you and your organization, congratulations. I hope it works for you and achieves all that was promised.[28] If you haven't yet made the decision between the two business models, let's wrap up the previous chapters in a context that will not only ensure you get the expected benefits you desire, but also greatly improve your organizational culture.

Whether you self-implement or use an outsider/consultant, the rest of this book shows how you can go even further by creating a truly stronger, more vibrant organization. Remember that both business models are simply that, business models with a set of tools; no more, no less. They are well thought out and accepted in the marketplace of small- to mid-sized organizations. They

---

28. For a summary of the benefits of each business model, see Appendix 1.

are well designed as business systems. Each will help you make gains in your organization, perhaps even significant gains.

Yet neither was designed specifically to help you overtly build a stronger organization; this is not a design fault in either. Paying purposeful attention to the benefits described in the previous chapters, moreover, allows you to attain the results you potentially will achieve. Some benefits accrue simply by implementing your respective model. However, the efficacy of any business model requires people. Your people make the difference in the implementation, and they are often overlooked if an outsider installs the model for you with a canned methodology.

Here's an uncomfortable truth that many leaders discover after implementing Traction/EOS or Scaling Up: You can execute the system perfectly and still miss its full potential. You can have every tool in place, follow every prescribed practice, and still feel that deeper transformation remains elusive. If this resonates with your experience, you're touching the edge of an important insight into organizational change.

The distinction between installation and transformation is subtle but profound. Installation is about putting tools and practices in place. Transformation is about fundamentally shifting how people think, work, and relate to each other using these same tools. While proper installation is necessary, it's not sufficient for genuine transformation.

Consider a common scenario: Your organization has implemented Traction/EOS or Scaling Up. The tools are in place. People are using them. You're seeing improvements. But something still feels mechanical. Your weekly meetings run efficiently but lack energy. Your short-term goals/key results get completed but don't seem to drive real change. Your scorecards track metrics but don't inspire improvement. You've installed the system and it is working, but you haven't achieved transformation.

THE MISSING DIMENSION

In today's rapidly evolving business landscape, organizations are continually seeking ways to optimize their operations, enhance performance, and create sustainable growth. There is a growing recognition that these models alone may not be sufficient to navigate the complexities of the modern business world. Enter community-enhanced leadership: An innovative approach that combines the best of these operating models with the transformative power of community-building principles.

At its core, this leadership model is about creating organizations that not only deliver exceptional business results but also nurture the human spirit and create a deep sense of belonging. **It recognizes that the true source of organizational vitality lies not just in efficient processes and smart strategies, but in the collective wisdom, creativity, and engagement of the people who bring those processes and strategies to life.** Systems *and* people.

The community-enhanced leadership approach begins with a choice between two proven operating models. But community-enhanced leadership takes these models a step further by infusing them with the community-building principles articulated by thought leader Peter Block. Block's work emphasizes the power of belonging, ownership, and collective possibility in creating thriving organizations. He invites us to shift our focus from problem-solving to possibility-seeking, from top-down control to shared ownership, and from individual achievement to collective well-being.

By integrating these principles into the implementation of Traction or Scaling Up, the new leadership playbook creates potent alchemy. **It transforms the process of organizational change from a mechanical exercise in tool adoption to a deeply human journey of growth and connection. It invites every member of the organization to bring their whole selves to the table, to share their gifts and their challenges, and to co-create a future that works for all.**

The benefits of this community-enhanced approach are manifold. Engaging the hearts and minds of every employee unleashes a level of creativity, commitment, and resourcefulness that traditional top-down systematic approaches can rarely match. It builds trust and resilience, enabling organizations to weather the storms of change with grace and agility. It creates a culture of continuous learning and adaptation, where everyone is encouraged to grow and contribute their unique talents.

Perhaps most importantly, community-enhanced leadership helps organizations tap into a deeper sense of purpose and meaning. When people feel truly seen, heard, and valued; they know that their work matters not just for the bottom line but for the greater good and they bring a level of passion and dedication that can transform entire industries. They become not just employees, but ambassadors and changemakers, inspired to make a positive impact in the world.

Of course, this journey is not always easy. **It requires a willingness to challenge long-held assumptions, to change your language, to embrace vulnerability and discomfort, and to let go of the illusion of control.** It demands a level of courage and commitment from leaders at all levels to model a new way of being and doing. But for those who are ready to embark on this path, the rewards are immeasurable.

Making the Right Choice

To make an informed decision, it's essential to grasp the fundamental tenets and methodologies of each operating model. Armed with a deep understanding of each model and your organizational context, you're equipped to make an informed decision. This process can be aided by a decision framework that weighs the key factors: size and growth stage, leadership and culture fit, resource availability, and specific operational pain points or aspirations. By systematically evaluating your organization against these criteria, you can determine which model, Traction, Scaling Up, or another approach is best positioned to drive your new leadership journey.

However, it's essential to understand that implementing any operating model requires sustained commitment and effort; this is a transformational journey, not a quick fix. Success comes from clearly communicating expectations, embracing it as a collective learning opportunity, and recognizing that while the choice of model is important, it's just the beginning of creating an organization that achieves both operational excellence and true community.[29]

Getting the most out of either business model depends fundamentally on the steps *before* you implement your chosen business model.

But please note there's a difference between installation and implementation. You may use an outsider/consultant to help you install your chosen system. The outsider/consultant cannot implement it; that is your responsibil-

---

29. See Chapter 14 for suggested scripts.

ity. Those outside resources are not there every day, within your organization, working alongside your people. To be clear, the system can be installed (including training in the tools, for example) through a standardized approach. Implementation, however, considers you, your leadership, your people, your customers, your culture, etc., and you cannot abdicate implementation to an outside resource. You have to "own" it.

Follow the process outlined and your employees will embrace your efforts and assist with organizational transformation.

Chapter Summary

This chapter emphasized that while choosing and installing the right business model (Traction or Scaling Up) is important, true organizational transformation requires going beyond mere installation of tools and systems. The chapter argued that many leaders discover they can perfectly execute these systems yet still miss their full potential because they focus only on the mechanical aspects while overlooking the human element. The chapter introduced the concept of "community-enhanced leadership" as the missing dimension: An approach that combines proven business models with community-building principles to create organizations that deliver both exceptional results and nurture human connection. It concluded by noting that while consultants can help install a system, the actual implementation and transformation must be owned and driven by the organization's leadership.

Key Chapter Takeaways

1. Perfect system implementation doesn't guarantee transformation.
2. Installation and implementation are distinct—consultants can install, but organizations must own implementation.
3. Community-enhanced leadership bridges the gap between systems and transformation.
4. Both business models are tools that require human engagement to reach full potential.
5. Successful transformation requires shifting how people think and relate, not just following processes.

Suggested Homework

1. Evaluate current state: Map where your organization shows signs of installation versus transformation.
2. Assess leadership ownership: Document specific ways your leadership team could take greater ownership of implementation versus delegating to consultants.

⚡⚡⚡⚡

CHAPTER 8

One More Time, Why Community?

Summary: This chapter examines how organizations often reduce human interactions to transactional exchanges, manifesting in three key areas: mechanically efficient meetings, reductive performance reviews, and artificial team-building events. It contrasts this current reality with the potential of community-enhanced leadership, where meetings become meaning-making spaces, performance conversations explore genuine growth, and team connections emerge naturally. The chapter argues that while business tools and structures are necessary, their implementation often reinforces the very silos and disconnections they aim to eliminate, suggesting that true organizational effectiveness requires balancing operational efficiency with authentic human connection.

THE HUMAN COST AND POTENTIAL LOSS
OF ORGANIZATIONAL INTERDEPENDENCE

The Current Reality: The Transaction Trap

In most organizations today, human interaction has been distilled into a series of carefully choreographed exchanges, each designed to maximize efficiency and minimize the messiness of genuine human connection. This reality manifests in three key areas that shape organizational life.

The Meeting Mirage

Picture a typical organizational meeting: Team members file into a conference room, laptops open like shields. The agenda, a rigid taskmaster, dictates every minute. Numbers flash across screens as people report their KPIs with mechanical precision. Questions are brief, answers briefer. Efficiency reigns supreme.

In these spaces, human beings simply become data points. The rich texture of their experiences, insights, and intuitions is flattened into metrics and status updates. "On track" or "behind schedule" becomes the primary vocabulary of interaction. Connection, if it happens at all, is accidental, a moment of shared humanity sneaking through the cracks of the agenda.

Time is treated as the enemy, structure and efficiency count in each incremental topical block of time. Every minute must be "productive." The unspoken message is clear: We're here to exchange information, not to understand each other. The human cost? Disengagement, missed insights, and the slow death of creativity that only emerges through genuine interaction.

The Performance Review Paradox

Once or twice a year, managers and employees engage in an elaborate ritual called the performance review. Armed with standardized forms and behavioral competency matrices, they enact a carefully scripted dialogue that reduces a year of human effort and growth to a series of numerical ratings.

The conversation follows predictable channels: Goals met or missed, competencies demonstrated or lacking, development needs identified through the narrow lens of organizational requirements. The rich context of challenges faced, lessons learned, and wisdom gained is lost in the pursuit of "objective" assessment.

This approach creates a peculiar paradox. In trying to measure human performance with mechanical precision, we miss the very human elements that drive exceptional performance: passion, purpose, personal growth, and the deep satisfaction of meaningful contribution.

The Team Building Illusion

Organizations recognizing the need for connection attempt to manufacture it through structured, so-called "team building" events. The annual retreat, the mandatory fun day, the networking mixer are all designed with good intentions but often achieving the opposite effect.

Picture the forced laughter at team building exercises, the awkward small talk at networking events, the superficial sharing in "getting to know you" activities. These efforts, despite their intentions, often highlight the very disconnection they aim to address.

The underlying assumption seems to be that connection can be scheduled, that relationships can be built through prescribed activities in designated time slots. The result? Surface-level interactions that leave people longing for genuine connection while becoming increasingly cynical about the possibility of finding it at work.

We Have Created the Very Things We Don't Want

These traps, paradoxes, and illusions create invisible walls. You know the ones, the subtle resistance to cross-functional collaboration, the "not my department" mentality, the unspoken territories that divide your organization into isolated silos. Even with the right tools and structures in place, these silos remain some of the most stubborn challenges in organizational life.

What's particularly frustrating is that our business systems can inadvertently reinforce these divisions. When each department has its own Rocks/key results, metrics, and accountabilities, we may be strengthening the very walls we're trying to break down. The tools themselves aren't the problem; it's how we use them.

THE POTENTIAL: FROM TRANSACTIONS TO TRANSFORMATIONS

This is where community-enhanced leadership offers a fundamentally different perspective. Instead of seeing your organization as a collection of separate functions, imagine it as a living fabric where every thread is interconnected. This isn't just a nice metaphor, it's a practical approach to organizational design that transforms how we use our business systems.

Now imagine that different possibility. Envision organizations where:

Meetings Become Meaning-Making Spaces. Meetings transform from information exchanges to spaces where real thinking happens together. They begin with genuine check-ins that honor the full humanity of participants. Agendas serve as guides rather than masters, flexible enough to follow the energy of genuine engagement and discovery.

In these spaces, metrics and KPIs become starting points for deeper exploration rather than ends in themselves. Questions like "What are we learning?" and "What possibilities do we see?" create space for insights that numbers alone could never reveal.

Time is still respected, but not at the expense of connection. The efficiency paradox is resolved: When people feel truly seen and heard, they engage more fully and think together more effectively.

Performance Review Conversations Deepen. Performance discussions evolve from evaluation exercises to explorations of contribution and growth. They begin with questions that invite the whole person: "What gives you energy in your work?" "What have you learned?" and "What impact do you hope to make?"

These conversations honor the complexity of human performance and development. They create space for both celebration and challenge, for both accountability and aspiration. They recognize that the greatest contributions often emerge from the intersection of personal passion and organizational needs.

Team Connection Emerges Naturally. Rather than trying to manufacture connection through artificial events, organizations create conditions where authentic relationships can emerge naturally. This happens through:

- Small group projects where people can work closely together on meaningful challenges
- Regular spaces for story sharing and collective sensemaking
- Celebration of both professional and personal milestones
- Recognition of the informal moments where real connection happens

The Transformation Path

Moving from transactional to transformative interactions requires:

- **courage** to challenge the efficiency-at-all-costs mindset,
- **patience** to allow real relationships to develop at their own pace,

- **trust** in people's natural capacity for meaningful connection,
- **wisdom** to create structures that enable, rather than force, interaction, and
- **commitment** to the human element in organizational life.

The goal isn't to eliminate structure or metrics but to create a container where both task and relationship can flourish together. When we honor the full humanity of organizational life, we create spaces where both people and performance can reach their highest potential.

The choice between transaction and transformation begins with a simple question: **Are we here merely to exchange information and labor, or are we here to create something meaningful together?** The answer shapes everything that follows.

Chapter Summary

This chapter examined how modern organizations often reduce human interactions to purely transactional exchanges in the pursuit of efficiency. It highlighted three key areas where this occurs: Meetings that prioritize data over human connection, performance reviews that reduce complex human contributions to numerical ratings, and artificial team-building activities that fail to create genuine relationships. The chapter argued that these practices, while intended to maximize efficiency, create organizational silos and barriers to true collaboration. The chapter then presented an alternative approach through community-enhanced leadership, where meetings become spaces for meaningful discussion, performance reviews explore deeper contributions, and team connections develop naturally. The goal is to transform organizations from purely transactional environments to spaces where both human connection and performance can thrive together.

Key Chapter Takeaways

1. Current organizational practices often reduce human interactions to transactions.
2. Traditional meetings, reviews, and team building often create artificial connections.

3. Business tools can inadvertently reinforce silos they aim to eliminate.
4. Effective organizations need both operational efficiency and authentic connection.
5. Community-enhanced leadership transforms transactions into meaningful interactions.

Suggested Homework

1. Audit your meeting structures; document where genuine dialogue happens versus pure information exchange.
2. Map how performance conversations could shift from evaluation to exploration of growth and contribution.

⚡⚡⚡⚡

CHAPTER 9

How to Amplify and Augment Each Model with Community

Summary: This chapter examines how business models (Traction and Scaling Up) can be transformed through a community-building lens, shifting from pure operational tools to frameworks for creating authentic organizational connections. It contrasts how each model can support community development: Traction through intimate, closely-knit structures, and Scaling Up through networks of interconnected communities. The chapter details how traditional tools like Traction's V/TO or Scaling Up's OPSP can be reimagined to foster possibility thinking, collective wisdom, and genuine participation, rather than just tracking metrics and goals. It emphasizes that success comes not from perfect implementation but from using these frameworks to create environments where both operational excellence and human flourishing can coexist.

THE POWER OF COMMUNITY IN BUSINESS MODELS

This vision of community building fundamentally transforms how we view organizational models. By overlaying community-enhanced leadership principles onto your implementation of Traction and Scaling Up, we discover new possibilities for creating belonging within business structures. This combination examines how these business models can create an authentic community, rather than just improve operational performance.

SHARED FOUNDATIONS:
COMMUNITY-BUILDING ELEMENTS IN BOTH MODELS

Traditional business models inadvertently reinforce problem-focused thinking. However, when viewed through this community-building lens, these same tools can become powerful catalysts for possibility thinking and collective aspiration. For example, consider the following points each model to reimage the benefits of community.

Transforming Traction's Vision/Traction Organizer®

The V/TO®, traditionally used as a planning document, can be reimagined as a container for possibility conversations. Rather than simply documenting goals and metrics, it becomes a living tool for exploring collective potential:

Creating Space for Possibility: instead of starting with current problems or gaps, begin V/TO sessions with questions like:

- What difference could we make in the world?
- What gifts might we offer?
- What future is trying to emerge through us?
- How might we serve in unexpected ways?

The Core Values component transforms from a list of behavioral standards to an exploration of collective gifts. Core Focus™ shifts from defining business boundaries to articulating unique contribution potential, away from the past to what's possible.

Enabling Collective Visioning: The 10-Year Target becomes more than a quantifiable goal; it becomes an invitation to imagine transformed possibilities:

- What impact might be possible?
- How could our gifts evolve?
- What future might we create together?
- What legacy might we build?

Marketing strategy shifts from competitive positioning to exploration of unique value creation potential. The Three-Year Picture becomes a canvas for collective dreaming rather than just milestone setting.

Reimagining Scaling Up's One-Page Strategic Plan

The OPSP framework, when approached through a possibility lens, becomes a powerful tool for collective meaning-making and future creation:

Shared Vision Creation: Rather than top-down vision setting, the process becomes collaborative exploration:

- Core Values emerge from gift recognition.
- Purpose connects to collective calling.
- Big, Hairy, Audacious Goal (BHAG)[30] grows from shared aspiration.
- Targets reflect meaningful impact.

The different time horizons, e.g., three to five years, one year, and quarterly, become platforms for exploring possibilities at different scales. Each horizon invites different questions and perspectives about what might be possible.

Model for Collective Aspirations: The plan's structure helps organize possibility thinking across dimensions:

- People: How might individual and collective gifts develop?
- Strategy: What new value might we create?
- Execution: How might we work together?
- Cash: What resources enable possibilities?

Principles with Either Model

Each of the business models support similar guiding principles; start with possibility, enable collective wisdom, maintain future focus, and support the learning journey.

---

30. Jim Collins and Jerry Porras, *Built to Last: Successful Habits of Visionary Companies*, 1994.

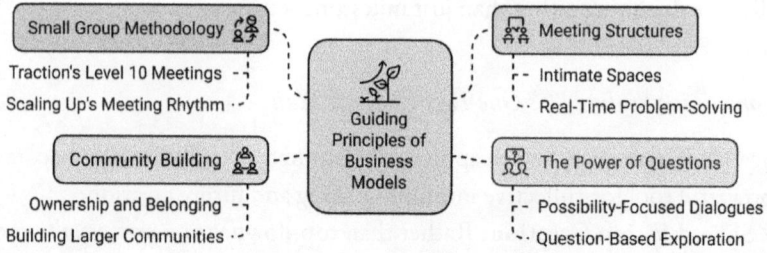

Figure 9—Guiding Principles

Small Group Methodology: Both models inadvertently align with community-enhanced emphasis on small group transformation:

Meeting Structures

Traction's Level 10 Meetings®
- Create intimate spaces for authentic dialogue.
- Enable real-time problem-solving in small groups.
- Foster accountability through relationship.

Scaling Up's Meeting Rhythm
- Build community through regular connection.
- Create multiple contexts for small group interaction.
- Enable cross-functional relationship building.

The Power of Questions: Both models can be enhanced by emphasis on powerful questions, not just answers:

Strategic Planning Processes

Traction
- Quarterly conversations can become possibility-focused dialogues.
- Issues lists can transform into question-based exploration.
- Rocks can emerge from collective inquiry, not simply from task identification.

Scaling Up
- ○ Strategy sessions can incorporate more possibility-focused questions.
- ○ Growth challenges can become opportunities for collective exploration.
- ○ Priorities can emerge from shared discovery of possibilities.

Distinctive Approaches to Community Building

Traction's simpler structure offers unique opportunities for reimagining as seen through the community lens:

Ownership and Belonging
- ○ Simple tools enable broader participation.
- ○ Clear accountability supports employee ownership.
- ○ Standardized processes can create safe spaces for engagement.

The Six Conversations through Traction
1. Invitation: through meeting structures and core values
2. Possibility: through Vision/Traction Organizer
3. Ownership: via clear accountability structures
4. Dissent: through Issues List and Identify, Discuss and Solve (IDS®) process
5. Commitment: via Rocks and quarterly planning
6. Gifts: through Right Person, Right Seat

Scaling Up's complexity can support sophisticated community building:

Building Larger Communities
- ○ Tools for managing complexity while maintaining connection
- ○ Models for scaling relationship networks
- ○ Structures for maintaining intimacy despite size

The Six Conversations through Scaling Up
1. Invitation: through culture and relationship management
2. Possibility: through BHAG and long-term planning

3.   Ownership: via Function Accountability Chart
4.   Dissent: through meeting rhythm and feedback loops
5.   Commitment: via priorities and metrics
6.   Gifts: through talent development and coaching

Key Differences in community approach (interdependence, not independence)

- Traction: builds intimate, closely-knit community
- Scaling Up: creates networks of interconnected and interdependent communities

Aligning Your Community-Building Path

Let me expand on how to align organizational frameworks with these core principles of community building while maintaining operational effectiveness: **Align Organizational Systems with Community Principles:** The choice between Traction and Scaling Up isn't just about operational fit; it's about how each model can support or hinder the development of authentic community. Understanding how each model aligns with these principles helps organizations make choices that serve both practical needs and community aspirations.

Create Containers for Connection: Traction's simpler structure naturally supports intimate group dynamics. The framework's emphasis on regular, focused meetings with consistent teams creates stable containers for relationship building. Level 10 Meetings, when properly facilitated, can become powerful spaces for:

- deep connection development,
- authentic dialogue emergence,
- collective wisdom sharing,
- natural gift expression, and
- mutual support building.

The quarterly and annual rituals provide regular opportunities for deeper community building without overwhelming the organization's capacity for meaningful connection.

While more complex, Scaling Up offers sophisticated structures for creating interconnected communities. Its framework enables:

- multiple layers of small group interaction,
- cross-functional team collaboration,
- network-based learning systems,
- distributed leadership development, and
- interconnected and interdependent support structures.

The challenge lies in maintaining intimacy while scaling, requiring intentional design of connection points and communication flows.

Foster Genuine Participation: Traction provides clear structures for individual ownership through:

- direct accountability assignments,
- clear role definition,
- simple decision rights,
- straightforward metrics, and
- regular feedback loops.

These elements, when approached through a community lens, can become platforms for authentic contribution rather than mere task assignment and reporting on completion.

The more sophisticated framework of Scaling Up enables:

- multiple levels of participation;
- complex contribution patterns;
- layered decision processes;
- interconnected responsibilities; and
- distributed leadership opportunities.

While offering more possibilities for diverse forms of employee ownership, this complexity requires more intentional management to prevent confusion or disconnection.

QUESTION-DRIVEN CULTURE: ENABLING GENUINE INQUIRY

The nature of Traction, with its straightforward approach, creates natural openings for deeper inquiry and community building. Its simple meeting structures provide clear moments in which questioning can naturally emerge without feeling forced or artificial. The regular rhythm of check-ins opens space for reflection and connection, allowing people to pause and consider deeper meanings in their work.

Questions often prove more powerful than answers. Leaders who master the art of inquiry unlock potential that command-and-control leadership never reaches.

The model's clear intent creates natural invitations to explore purpose; not just what we're trying to achieve, but why it matters. Even its straightforward metrics, rather than being merely numbers to track, can spark meaningful conversations about what we truly value and how we measure what matters most. The direct communication patterns inherent in the system support authentic, open dialogue, making it easier for people to speak truthfully and listen deeply.

This simplicity becomes a strength when building community, as it allows organizations to maintain consistent practices without getting stuck in procedural rigidity. People can focus on deepening their connections and understanding, rather than mastering, complicated processes.

In contrast, Scaling Up presents a more sophisticated landscape for community building; its complexity offers multiple layers where inquiry can take root and flourish. The model's various components create rich opportunities for pattern recognition, allowing communities to develop deeper understanding of how their systems work and interact.

The sophistication of Scaling Up enables development of more nuanced strategic questioning capabilities, supporting communities in exploring complex challenges and opportunities. Its interconnected elements create possibilities for rich learning cycles that can strengthen community wisdom over time.

Yet successful implementation of either model requires careful attention to community readiness and capacity.[31] Organizations must honestly assess their current community strength; not just formal structures, but the quality of relationships and trust. They need to consider their capacity for growth, not merely in size but in complexity of interaction and depth of connection.

Your leadership capability becomes crucial as not just technical skill but the ability to hold space for community emergence. The organization's systems need to be ready to support deeper community engagement, and there must be a clear path for progressive development of both structures and relationships.

Supporting infrastructure proves essential for success with either model. You need to create physical and virtual spaces that enable real connection, establishing communication patterns that support authentic dialogue rather than merely the exchange of information.

Feedback loops need careful design to support community development, more than mere performance reviews. Celebration practices must be established that honor not just achievement but growth, learning, and deepening relationships.

Perhaps most critically, you must maintain several crucial balances in their implementation approach. You need to find the sweet spot between providing helpful structure and maintaining flexibility for emergence. You must balance the appeal of simplicity with the need for sufficient sophistication to address complex challenges.

The tension between individual and collective needs requires constant attention, as does the balance between task accomplishment and relationship building. Organizations must learn to coexist with efficiency (i.e., improving the "known") and emergence (i.e., examining the "unknown") creating space for both predictable progress and unexpected possibilities.

Success with either model ultimately depends not on perfect implementation but on thoughtful adaptation that serves both organizational needs and community development. The key lies not in choosing between simplicity and complexity but in finding the right combination that enables your specific community to flourish.

---

31. See Appendix 9: Transformational Capabilities Development Checklist.

Consider your weekly meetings. In a typical implementation, these meetings follow the prescribed format, tick all the boxes, and get the job done. But in organizations that have embraced community-enhanced leadership, these same meetings become something more. They transform into spaces where real dialogue happens, where team members don't just report status but engage in meaningful conversation about what matters most. Look at your standard agenda and find spaces to improve them with openness and exploration though questions.

The same principle applies to your quarterly planning sessions. Traditional implementations focus on setting quarterly goals and reviewing metrics. But when infused with community-enhanced leadership, these sessions become a crucible of opportunities for collective wisdom to emerge. They create space for diverse perspectives, encourage genuine dialogue about challenges and opportunities, and foster the kind of deep engagement that turns plans into committed action.

This transformation extends to how we think about accountability. **In standard implementations, accountability often becomes about tracking numbers and following up on commitments, but in community-enhanced organizations, accountability shifts from an external force to an internal motivation.** People step up not because they have to, but because they feel genuinely invested in the organization's success.

The question isn't whether your current implementation is working; if you're following the system, it probably is. The question is whether it's delivering everything it can. Are your tools creating compliance or commitment? Are they fostering coordination or genuine collaboration? Are they driving performance or inspiring excellence?

The most powerful insight I've gained from working with dozens of organizations is this: **The tools themselves are just the beginning. They provide the structure, the framework, the necessary foundation, but it's the quality of human connection within that framework that determines whether an implementation merely succeeds or truly transforms.**

This isn't about adding more complexity to your implementation. In fact, it's quite the opposite. Community-enhanced leadership simplifies by aligning your tools with basic human needs for connection, meaning, and purpose. When these needs are met, many of the challenges that plague traditional implementations such as resistance, lack of buy-in, and inconsistent execution naturally dissolve.

The goal isn't to implement either model perfectly but to use them as frameworks for building an authentic community that can support both operational excellence and human flourishing. The art lies in maintaining focus on community development while using these models to create enabling structure rather than constraining control.

Implementation Through Community Lens

For either framework:

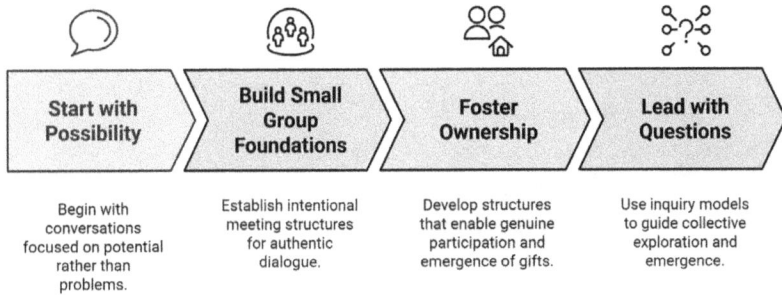

Start with Possibility	**Build Small Group Foundations**	**Foster Ownership**	**Lead with Questions**
Begin with conversations focused on potential rather than problems.	Establish intentional meeting structures for authentic dialogue.	Develop structures that enable genuine participation and emergence of gifts.	Use inquiry models to guide collective exploration and emergence.

Figure 10—Cultural Change

1. Start with Possibility.
   - Begin with possibility conversations.
   - Focus on "what could be" rather than problems.
   - Create space for collective visioning.
2. Build Small Group Foundations.
   - Use meeting structures intentionally.
   - Create intimate spaces for dialogue.
   - Enable authentic relationships.
3. Foster Ownership.
   - Develop ownership structures.
   - Enable authentic participation.
   - Create space for gifts to emerge.
4. Lead with Questions.
   - Transform tools into inquiry models.
   - Enable collective exploration.
   - Create space for emergence.

Beyond Business Models

The true power of either model emerges when viewed through this community-building lens. By intentionally incorporating the principles, the business models become vehicles for creating authentic community and belonging, not just tools for operational efficiency. It's about bringing greater consciousness and intention to how you use the tools you already have. It's about creating the conditions where the full potential of your business system can emerge through the engagement and growth of your people.

Success lies not in perfect implementation of tools, but in how they enable:

- authentic relationships,
- collective possibility,
- employee ownership,
- transformative questions,
- small group magic, and
- the gift of each person's contribution.

True transformation happens when you mindfully and purposefully leverage your existing tools and systems. Rather than simply implementing new processes, it's about cultivating an environment where your organization can reach its full potential by empowering and developing your team members.

When leadership is strengthened through community, it creates workplaces where people flourish while achieving outstanding results. In these environments, tools and methods enhance human growth instead of limiting it. What begins as implementation evolves into real transformation, powered by authentic connections among people.

Choose the model that best supports your community-building aspirations, then intentionally infuse it with community-enhanced principles and practices to create true belonging alongside operational excellence.

Chapter Summary

This chapter explored how to transform two broadly accepted traditional business models (Traction and Scaling Up) from purely operational tools into frameworks that build authentic community and connection within organizations. It demonstrated how each model's existing components, like Traction's V/TO or Scaling Up's One-Page Strategic Plan, can be reimagined to foster genuine engagement and collective possibility rather than just tracking metrics and goals. The chapter emphasized that while both models can improve business performance, their true potential is realized when they're implemented through a "community-enhanced leadership" lens that prioritizes meaningful relationships, authentic dialogue, and shared purpose. Instead of focusing solely on perfect implementation of tools, organizations should use these frameworks to create environments where both operational excellence and human connection can flourish together.

Key Chapter Takeaways

1. Business models can be reimagined as community-building tools rather than just operational frameworks.
2. Traction suits intimate community-building while Scaling Up enables networked communities.
3. Traditional planning tools can be transformed to foster possibility thinking over problem-solving.
4. Success requires balancing operational excellence with human connection.
5. Implementation should prioritize authentic participation over mere compliance.

Suggested Homework

1. Audit current meetings and tools; document how each could be redesigned to foster more meaningful dialogue and collective wisdom.
2. Map your organization's current "community structures," identify where genuine connection happens versus where it's blocked by purely operational focus.

⚡⚡⚡⚡

CHAPTER 10

Embracing Transformation

Consider that it is *not* the absence of leadership potential that inhibits the development of more leaders; it is the persistence of the myth that leadership can't be learned. —Peter Block

Summary: This chapter explores leadership myths and the transformation from traditional leadership to community-enhanced leadership. It debunks common misconceptions about leadership being innate, emphasizing that leadership skills can be learned and developed. The chapter identifies four key benefits of business models (Leadership, Accountability, Source of Truth, and Ritual) while arguing that successful implementation requires moving beyond command-and-control to build genuine community. It introduces a reimagined approach to planning that focuses on possibilities rather than problems, emphasizing collective wisdom and authentic participation. The chapter concludes by advocating for establishing a strong community foundation before implementing business tools, using the metaphor of warp (community) and weft (tools) to create a resilient organizational fabric.

LEADERSHIP

The Dalai Lama once said that if you think you are too small to make a difference, try sleeping with a mosquito in the room. One person can make or break an organization. The skills lie in figuring out how to be on the side that makes the organization. Further, consider that every leadership team is one decision away from oblivion. Simply look at the leadership at Enron, Kodak, Motorola, Blackberry, and, more importantly, just about every local business that is no longer in existence. (See the statistics in Chapter 3: Small Business Realities.)

Leadership can be a heavily ladened word in the business vernacular. On the one hand, leadership can remove most frustrations and on the other hand, leadership is responsible for failures.

COMMON LEADERSHIP MYTHS[32]

The Seven Leadership Myths

- Empowerment myth: leaving employees alone, hands-off management is perceived as empowerment
- Fairness myth: the way to be "fair" is to treat everyone the same irrespective of who they are or their skills
- Nice Guy myth: being domineering, directive, a "jerk"
- Difficult myth: avoiding conflicts by being "hands-off"
- Red Tape myth: managers are precluded from leading because of bureaucracy, procedures, and rules
- Time myth: too much to do to even manage people
- Natural leader myth: you are either born a natural leader or not

---

32. Bruce Tulgan, "Seven Leadership Myths That Are Holding Managers Back," Forbes.com, January 26, 2024. https://www.forbes.com/sites/brucetulgan/2024/01/24/seven-leadership-myths-that-are-holding-managers-back/.

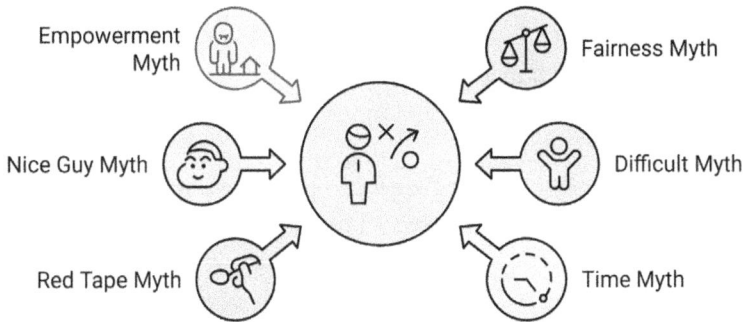

Figure 11—Common Leadership Myths

Leadership is a skill that can be learned and developed. It is not a trait limited to a select few individuals.

However, there is a persistent myth in many organizations that leadership is innate, and individuals are either born with it or not. This haunting myth that leadership is something you innately have is a far more powerful deterrent to leadership development than is the nature of leadership itself.

This misconception inhibits the development of more leaders within an organization. When organizations believe that leadership cannot be learned, they often fail to invest in leadership development programs and initiatives. As a result, potential leaders are left to figure things out on their own, limiting their growth and potential impact.

You don't have to have that "something special" to fulfill the leadership role. You don't have to be tall, well-spoken, and good looking. You don't have to be male. You don't have to have charisma. **What you do have to have are clearly defined values and convictions and, more importantly, the courage of your convictions to see them manifest into reality.** Only when you understand your role as a guide and steward based on your own deeply held values can you move from manager to leader.

Your people are looking for someone in whom they can place their trust. Someone they know is working for the greater good for them and for the organization. They are looking for someone not only who they can trust but also follow.

Leadership can be learned and practiced. Let's put all of the leadership myths to bed here and now.

Four Key Hidden Benefits of These Tools

By debunking the myth that leadership cannot be learned, organizations can create a culture that encourages and supports the development of leaders at all levels.

Effective leadership in setting expectations, addressing performance gaps, and fostering accountability is essential for organizational success. By using the business models' tools, leaders can create a culture where employees take ownership of their responsibilities, strive for excellence, and contribute to the overall growth of the organization. It is through purposeful, not command-and-control, leadership that organizations can achieve their goals, adapt to change, and thrive in today's competitive business landscape.

The very nature (and popularity) of each business model supports four critical elements of a successful organization: Leadership, Accountability, Source of Truth, and Ritual, although referenced more implicitly with the last two.

Leadership is about influencing, not directing, others by influencing their thinking, their values, and their desire to do the right things. Management, in contrast, focuses on details, instructions, structures, or results. You lead people and manage things.

Rather than seeing themselves as the sole visionaries and decision-makers, community-centric leaders become architects of spaces where collective wisdom can emerge. They focus less on having all the answers and more on asking the right questions. They measure their success not by compliance, but by engagement and contribution.

The journey from installation to transformation isn't about adding more tools or practices to your implementation. It's about you, as a leader, bringing greater consciousness and intention to how your people use the tools you already have. You create the conditions where the full potential of your business system can emerge through the engagement and growth of your people.

The promise of community-enhanced leadership isn't just better business results, though those certainly come. It's the creation of organizations where people can thrive while delivering exceptional performance, where tools and practices serve human development rather than constraining, and where installation becomes transformation through the power of genuine community.

Simon Banks wrote, "You are not a leader until you have produced a leader who can produce another leader."[33]

BUILDING A STRONGER ORGANIZATION— THE IMPORTANCE OF COMMUNITY

After more than 50 company implementations, I have seen those organizations that used a business model grow, thrive, and transform. Similarly, I have seen more than a few that have not received the "promised" benefits. **What differentiates the two groups simply comes down to leadership:** While the tools of each model are universal and proven, the critical fault comes down to the use of the tools.

Do not pretend that by simply installing the chosen system in your organization, your responsibility as a leader is over; it is only the beginning. Successful implementation is your responsibility and, well, accountability.

The biggest influences on ultimate success are you and your ability to adapt yourself, the model, and your culture to the new reality, thus making the future different from the past. Implementation by fiat, e.g., command-and-control, will work only partially and may disrupt your attempts.

By itself, installation will not substantively change your organization. Assuming that, by installing the tools, change will happen automatically results in the waste of both time and resources (e.g., money). Perhaps worse yet is that the organization's people can become disillusioned; "one more program" was introduced and ... well ... failed to get traction thus creating organizational whiplash.

Success in implementing the tools depends primarily on the behavior of your leadership, both as individuals and collectively. Miss a meeting? You demonstrate it's not important. Come in late? It's not important to you and, therefore, to everyone else. Shorten an agenda? Remove topics? It's all the same negative message that you don't believe in the very business model you are attempting to implement. You are sabotaging your own efforts.

---

33. Simon Banks, "You are not a leader until you have produced a leader who can produce another leader," LinkedIn, August 16, 2017, https://www.linkedin.com/pulse/you-leader-until-have-produced-who-can-produce-another-simon-banks/.

The Problem Is Disentangling[34]

Using the tools to build for the future involves disentangling from the past. Problem-solving is fixing the past and making incremental changes. It doesn't create a new future; it only prolongs the past.

This is where you come in. You start to create a new future by changing the context of your meetings and your discussions from problems to possibility. A new model does not shift the context, it simply adds an effort to the current context. Your current organization, whatever its size, is separated into silos. We have "trained and rewarded" our employees to be too interested in individuality and independence, rather than interdependence.

To get the true promise from implementation, start by building the right culture. What follows will be real accountability and, in all likelihood, a much better performing organization.

Accountability is the willingness to care for the whole. This communal conversation stems from the question "What can we create together that we cannot create alone?"[35]

REIMAGING HOW WE PLAN

Understanding the limitations of traditional planning doesn't require us to abandon planning altogether. On the contrary, it invites us to fundamentally reimagine what planning could be. This reimagining opens doors to approaches that might better serve both organizational needs and human flourishing.

Imagine planning that begins not with current constraints but with possibility. Before diving into budgets and timelines, we might create space to dream bigger dreams, to envision futures that excite and energize. This isn't about ignoring practical realities but about allowing vision to lead while bringing practicality alongside as a creative partner rather than a primary constraint.

In this reimagined approach, planning taps into the collective intelligence of the entire organization. Instead of relying on a small group of leaders or experts, it engages the wisdom distributed throughout the organization. The frontline

---

34. See also Appendix 8: Strategies to Disentangle Oneself.
35. Block, *Community*, 127.

worker's intimate knowledge of customer needs, the technical expert's understanding of emerging possibilities, and the support staff's grasp of operational realities, all these perspectives weave together to create richer, more nuanced plans.

Such planning finds ways to balance the necessary metrics of business with the deeper meaning that drives human engagement. Numbers remain important but become contextualized within larger narratives of purpose and possibility. Performance indicators serve as feedback for learning rather than tools for judgment, helping guide the organization's journey rather than constraining its imagination.

This innovative approach creates deliberate space for emergence alongside execution. While clear goals and milestones matter, the plan remains flexible enough to accommodate unexpected opportunities and unforeseen challenges. It builds in regular pause points (e.g., at quarterly meetings) for sensing what's emerging and adjusting course accordingly, recognizing that the best opportunities often arise unexpectedly during the year.

The reimagined planning process connects numbers to narrative, understanding that metrics tell only part of the story. It creates space for the qualitative alongside the quantitative, recognizing that some of the most important aspects of organizational life, e.g., trust, innovation, and commitment, can't be reduced to numbers alone. **The plan becomes a story of possibility that people can see themselves in, rather than just a set of targets to hit.**

Perhaps most importantly, this approach fosters genuine ownership through authentic participation. Instead of plans being handed down from above, they emerge through collective engagement with possibility and purpose. People own the plan because they've helped create it, seeing their fingerprints and hearing their voices in its formation.

This isn't just idealistic thinking: organizations that plan this way often discover they execute more effectively because people bring their full energy and creativity to the journey. The plan becomes a living document that guides collective action rather than a static target that demands compliance.

The Practice of Possibilities

Instead of starting with problems to solve, the conversation opens with possibilities to explore. When challenges arise, they're reframed as questions of possibility:

- **Traditional:** "How do we fix our customer service issues?"
- **Transformed:** "What would remarkable customer care look like?"

Or:

- **Traditional:** "How do we reduce costs?"
- **Transformed:** "How might we create more value for everyone involved?"

Or:

- **Traditional:** "How do we beat the competition?"
- **Transformed:** "What unique gift could we offer the world?"

Enabling Collective Visioning: The power of possibility thinking multiplies when it becomes collective. Instead of one leader sharing their vision, the whole group engages in creating a shared view of what could be. This happens through several practices:

> **Story Sharing:** People share stories of times when the organization was at its best, when work felt meaningful, when impact was greatest. These stories reveal patterns of possibility and potential.
> **Pattern Finding:** The group looks for themes in these stories: What conditions enable excellence? What values underlie success? What possibilities keep emerging?
> **Future Casting:** Together, they imagine not just what's probable but what's possible. "If everything went extraordinarily well, what could we create together?"

Space for Gifts and Possibility

We begin by looking inward, asking ourselves what gifts already exist within our community. These aren't just skills on resumes or completion of responsibilities on job descriptions, but deeper capacities that emerge when people are truly engaged. "What unique perspectives have we developed through our journey?" "What work makes our hearts sing?" "What contribution might we be uniquely positioned to make in the world?"

From this foundation of gifts, we expand our vision outward. "Who might we serve in ways that matter deeply?" "What transformations could we enable?" "What legacy might we create together?" "What future are we drawn toward?" These questions aren't just about dreaming, they're about connecting our unique capabilities to real possibilities for impact.

As possibilities emerge, practical questions naturally arise. "What would make these dreams possible?" "Who else might join this journey?" "What first steps await?" "What support would enable progress?" "How might we begin?" **These aren't limitations on dreaming but bridges between vision and action.**

The space where these conversations happen matters. Physical spaces need to encourage movement and interaction, offer tools for visual thinking, and welcome natural light and fresh air. They should provide comfortable settings for sustained dialogue while including quieter spaces for reflection. The environment itself should invite creativity and connection.

Time needs equal attention. Groups need adequate space for exploration, regular moments for reflection, and time to integrate new insights. Action planning needs to emerge naturally rather than being rushed or forced, and celebration needs to be built into the rituals of work rather than treated as an afterthought.

Perhaps most crucial is the psychological space creating conditions where people feel genuine permission to dream, where wild ideas are welcomed rather than immediately judged, where risk-taking receives support rather than criticism. Differences need to be appreciated as sources of creativity rather than obstacles to overcome.

When groups engage in this kind of possibility thinking, something magical tends to emerge. Purpose becomes clearer and more compelling. Energy rises naturally. Collaboration flows without forcing. Creative solutions appear from unexpected directions. Commitment deepens, not through pressure but through genuine connection to possibility.

The movement to action requires particular artfulness. The key lies in maintaining connection to larger possibility, even while taking practical steps forward. This means keeping purpose alive in planning discussions, finding concrete first steps while holding space for larger dreams, creating structures that support innovation rather than just efficiency, and celebrating progress while staying open to emerging possibilities.

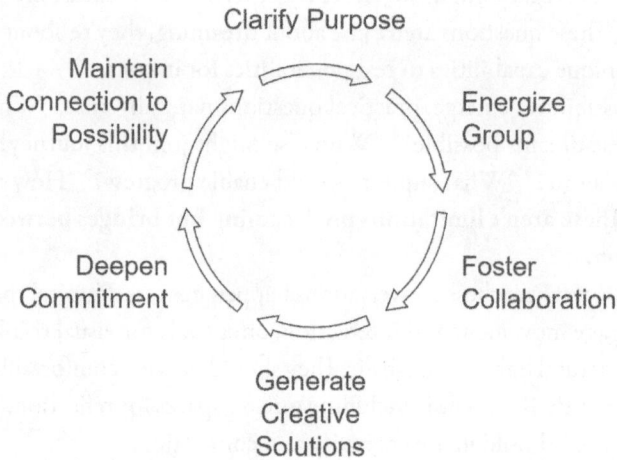

Clarify Purpose

Maintain
Connection to
Possibility

Energize
Group

Deepen
Commitment

Foster
Collaboration

Generate
Creative
Solutions

Figure 12—Cycle of Possibility to Action

This journey from gifts to action isn't linear but cyclical each step forward reveals new possibilities; each new possibility suggests new actions. The art lies in maintaining movement while staying connected to both purpose and possibility.

The goal isn't to abandon practical planning but to infuse it with larger possibility. When we start with "What could be?" before narrowing to "What's realistic?" we often find that more is possible than we initially imagined. **The future becomes not just a projection of the past but a creative act of collective imagination and commitment.**

The art lies in creating planning processes that maintain rigor while opening space for possibility, provide direction while enabling emergence, and establish accountability while fostering creativity. This requires new skills from leaders such as the ability to hold space for collective thinking, to balance structure with flexibility, to trust in collective wisdom while maintaining clear focus.

The reward for mastering this art is plans that people genuinely commit to because they connect to deeper purpose and possibility. Such plans

don't just direct action; they inspire it, creating momentum that carries organizations through challenges toward compelling futures.

The goal isn't perfect prediction (virtually impossible) but rather, creating conditions where people can think, create, and contribute their best. This requires a fundamental shift from planning as control to planning as creating space for possibility.

WHERE TO START?

The power of change can be started by changing the context by which it is approached.

In the Preface, I wrote: "Together, the warp and the weft form the pattern, the design of the cloth. . . . This works as an analogy for *Supercharge*, in that the tools presented in either business model act as the weft; they are composed of the individual threads/textures . . . of your organization: Your people, your product or service, your operations, your values, and your present and future direction. Block's work, in *Community*, forms the warp, the strength of building your community/organization upon which we will weave the weft." Without the warp's strength, the weft simply doesn't work to create a lasting fabric.

The business models' success lies in the tools and their effective use. **At their core, though, each is still a traditional approach to planning and a performance management business model, albeit streamlined and simplified for small- to mid-sized organizations.** As to the planning aspect of each, it follows the tradition of taking the past, analyzing it, adding another action plan to it for the upcoming planning timeframe. **This process works, but you are simply extrapolating the past into the future.**

The analogy of warp and weft suffices. The failures in implementation I have seen happened because leadership either forced implementation by fiat (e.g., "I read the book and we are doing it") or mistakenly thought (consciously or subconsciously) that by introducing the tools, change would automatically happen. **They did nothing to change the context within which successful implementation occurs when leadership itself changes.**

This isn't about diluting the tool's effectiveness. It's about augmenting the tools' effectiveness with meaningful human connection. I strongly suggest that before beginning implementation of either set of tools, leadership sets the stage for positive change through your learning and modeling. Convene your team, which may be composed of a distinct set of individuals some who may not report directly to you but who are critical to your success and who influence other people, and start on a new journey with a new context. The steps for the first meeting are outlined in Chapter 14 and are not tied to either business model but to the type of possibility you can build as you move to the future; an organization different from the past; one that can achieve real possibilities collectively.

Accountability grows out of the act of co-creation. The essence of creating an alternative future different from the past comes from employee-to-employee engagement that focuses each step on the well-being of the whole.

With purposeful intent, accountability grows from this person-to-person engagement, and it will not happen accidentally. It may improve, perhaps marginally, through implementation of the tools by itself; some individuals just "get it" and step up. Real improvement is predicated on leadership not the command-and-control type, but by actively setting the stage to change the possibility of the organization.

Installation needs to be postponed (e.g., the implementation) until connectedness, relatedness, and language has started to shift. In this process, problem-solving becomes a means, not an end to itself. For the fabric (warp = community; weft = tools) of your organization to be truly effective, action needs to happen in a broader way. Prior to implementation of either model, I suggest gathering some trusted people together and asking for their input on these questions:

1. Would an initial meeting be worthwhile if all we did was strengthen our relationships?
2. Would a meeting be worthwhile if we learned something of value?
3. Suppose in a meeting we simply stated our requests of each other and what we were willing to offer. Would that justify our time together?
4. What if in the meeting we only discussed the gifts we wanted to bring to bear on the concern that brought us together? Would that be an outcome of value?

What would it be like to simply ask the questions, gather input, and listen?

I don't want to get all woo-woo here. This is not "group hug" time. Saying "Yes" to these questions opens and widens the possibilities for what constitutes action. When we name these as outcomes, it allows us to get completion for the investment we might make in the business model. With this expanded notion of action, we can bring a wider approach to visioning, problem-solving, and clearly defined outcomes into to our efforts.

Each business model is indeed focused on business performance and growth, rather than explicitly on building a "better" culture in terms of community.

Before implementation, I ask you to consider:

- focusing on conversations to build a stronger community;[36] and
- emphasizing practices like:
  ○ shifting the context for community from problem-solving to possibility;
  ○ changing the conversation from blame and entitlement to commitment and gifts; and
  ○ adjusting employees from consumer to owner or co-creator.

This implementation approach differs significantly from that of the two business models; success is predicated on commitment from all the people who live in, work in, and run the business model. Not forced, not mandated, not coerced. While the business models focus on organizational efficiency and growth, this work centers on creating meaningful connections and shared purpose within a community and therefore making the business model work at a deeper, more purposeful level. Many business models are designed with financial and operational success in mind but do not prioritize or have methodology to build a "better" organization in terms of community impact, employee well-being, or social responsibility. Let's bring "community" to the forefront.

As you weave the tools of your operating model (the weft) with the principles and practices of community (the warp), you'll gradually see a new fabric emerge, one in which every thread is valued, every voice is heard, and every

---

36. Chapter 14 has scripts for your use; one for each of six steps of developing your community-enhanced culture.

heart is invested. **You'll see the hard edges of hierarchy and competition soften into the fabric of collaboration and care.** You'll see the isolated silos of departments and divisions merge into vibrant networks of connection and co-creation. You'll see the mechanical gears of process and procedure come alive with the energy of passion and purpose.

This is the promise of community-enhanced culture. It is not just a better way of working, but a better way of being. A way of harnessing the full potential of every human being in service of something greater than themselves. A way of building organizations that don't just succeed but thrive not just in their outcomes, but in their essence. A way of shaping a world where every institution is a source of energy, every leader illuminates the paths of possibility, and every community is a catalyst for transformation. Be part of a movement of leaders who are proving every day that when we prioritize people and purpose, profit and performance will naturally follow.

Chapter Summary

This chapter challenged common leadership myths, particularly the belief that leadership is an innate trait rather than a learnable skill. It emphasized that successful implementation of business models depends not just on installing tools and systems, but on transformative leadership that builds community and connection. The chapter argued that traditional planning and command-and-control approaches often fail because they focus too much on problem-solving and metrics while neglecting human elements. Instead, it advocated for a "community-enhanced leadership" approach that starts with possibility thinking, emphasizes authentic relationships, and creates spaces for collective wisdom to emerge. The key message was that before implementing any business model, leaders must first create the right cultural context by shifting from a mindset of control to one of community-building, where accountability grows naturally from co-creation and shared purpose.

Key Chapter Takeaways

1. Leadership is learned, not innate and common myths about natural leadership abilities limit organizational growth.

2.   Business model success requires shifting from command-and-control to community-building.
3.   Planning should start with possibilities rather than problems.
4.   Implementation requires establishing community foundation before applying tools.
5.   True accountability emerges from co-creation and collective engagement.

Suggested Homework

1.   Gather key team members to discuss the four questions about relationship-building and collective learning presented in the chapter.
2.   Map current planning processes to identify where they focus on problems versus possibilities.

⚡ ⚡ ⚡ ⚡

CHAPTER 11

The Courage to be Real

Summary: When leaders have the courage to be genuinely human, sharing relevant struggles and inviting real dialogue, they create space for others to do the same. This shift from maintaining facades to thoughtful authenticity enables deeper collaboration and unexpected breakthroughs. Through structured practices like paired sharing, small groups, and regular reflection, organizations transform. People turn toward challenges together, feedback flows naturally, and conflict becomes a source of learning. Trust becomes most visible in difficult times, while individual growth intertwines with collective development, creating momentum that energizes the entire organization.

THE COURAGE TO BE REAL

In most organizations, vulnerability is seen as weakness and authenticity as unprofessional. People arrive at work wearing careful masks, sharing only what feels safe, hiding their doubts, struggles, and real experiences. This careful performance exacts a heavy toll not just on individuals, but on the organization's ability to learn, innovate, and adapt.

Yet the most powerful moments in organizational life often happen when someone has the courage to be real, to share a genuine struggle, to admit uncertainty, to express authentic emotion. These moments transform the quality of thinking and relationship in the room. They create openings for deeper understanding, more genuine collaboration, and unexpected breakthroughs.

Recognize
Vulnerability

Reflect and
Appreciate

Encourage
Open Sharing

Enhance
Innovation and
Learning

Foster Safe
Spaces

Build Trust and
Clarity

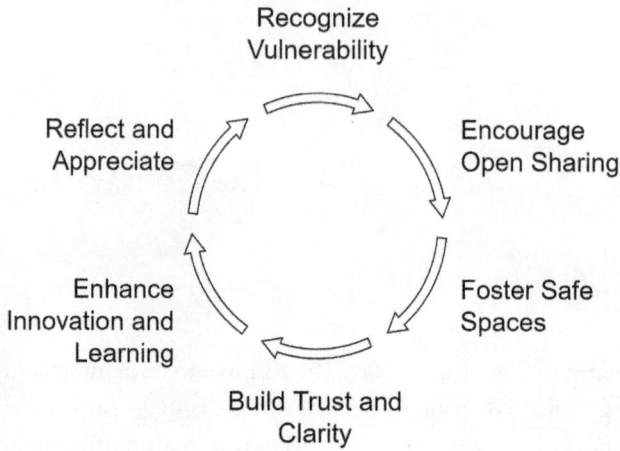

Figure 13—Building Meaningful Collaboration

LEADERSHIP'S CRITICAL ROLE

The journey toward authentic expression begins with leadership. When leaders maintain a facade of certainty and invulnerability, they create an implicit expectation that everyone else should do the same. But when leaders have the courage to be genuinely human, they change what's possible in the entire organization.

This doesn't mean inappropriate disclosure or emotional dumping. Rather, it means thoughtful sharing of relevant individual experiences and learning. A leader might share how they're wrestling with a difficult decision, acknowledge the emotional impact of a challenging situation, or express genuine uncertainty about the best path forward.

Consider the difference between these two leadership approaches:

- **Traditional**: "Here's what we need to do. Any questions?"

Or

- **Transformed**: "Here's what I'm wrestling with; I'd really value your perspectives."

The first closes the dialogue; the second invites genuine thinking together. The first maintains the leader's position of authority; the second creates space for collective wisdom to emerge.

ACKNOWLEDGING THE FULL HUMAN EXPERIENCE

Creating safety for vulnerability means acknowledging that work isn't separate from the rest of human experience. People bring their whole lives to work, their hopes, fears, struggles, and dreams. When we create space for this reality, several things become possible:

- Difficulties can be acknowledged and addressed rather than hidden and denied.
- Learning becomes more natural when people can admit what they don't know without fear.
- Innovation flows more easily when people can express unconventional ideas.
- Relationships deepen through shared understanding of real experiences.
- Emotions become sources of insight rather than disruptions to be managed.

This doesn't mean turning every meeting into a therapy session. It means creating appropriate spaces where people can be real with each other in service of the work they're doing together.

Supporting vulnerability requires thoughtful structure, creating safety for genuine connection. This emerges through several key practices:

- Paired sharing builds initial trust and clarity.
- Small groups (three to five people) enable deeper exploration and authentic expression.
- Regular reflection rituals support ongoing learning and development.
- Authentic appreciation encourages risk-taking and vulnerability.
- Celebrating learning rather than just achievement creates psychological safety.

Success comes from consistent attention to these practices, creating conditions where people feel safe to be genuine. When this happens, creativity, problem-solving, and satisfaction naturally flourish.

The Cultural Transformation

Trust in the Storm

When authentic relationships take root in organizations, several key transformations emerge. During challenges, people turn toward each other rather than away, with trust becoming most visible in difficult times.[37] In organizations, this same dynamic transforms feedback and conflict into sources of learning rather than threats to avoid.

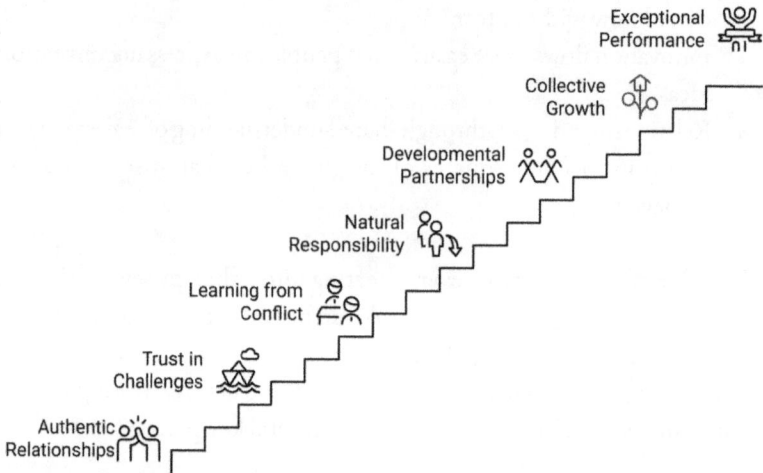

Figure 14—Cultural Transformation

37. As proof, in September 2024, large portions of the Appalachian Mountain region of Western Noth Carolina were devasted by Hurricane Helene. Our community was one of these. Despite recent political polarization, this community was repaired and strengthened by an incredible level of giving and outpouring of volunteers, food, supplies, and assistance. The hard times brought out the best in people.

The emergence of genuine relationships shifts ownership from assigned tasks to natural responsibility. People move beyond "that's not my job" to "how can I help," actively seeking ways to help, taking responsibility not just for tasks but for the health of team relationships and culture. Understanding deepens beyond surface-level roles to genuine appreciation of each other's hopes and challenges.

As these relationships mature, support evolves from simple task assistance to true developmental partnership. Individual growth becomes inseparable from collective development, creating momentum that energizes the entire organization. This represents an ongoing journey where human connection drives exceptional performance, not through mandate but through authentic care and shared purpose.

TRUTH TELLING

Ask yourself a challenging question: In our modern organizations whether small family businesses, major corporations, or nonprofits how often do we hear genuine, unvarnished truth? How frequently do people feel safe enough to speak with complete honesty about what matters most?

Then look deeper, into your own reflection. What truth are you holding back right now? What conversation are you avoiding with someone important in your life? Perhaps it's about your struggles as a business owner and changes you know are needed. Maybe you're overwhelmed with commitments but afraid to step back. The fear is real. Will speaking honestly damage relationships you value? Will others reject you for your truth?

We often find ourselves caught in this dance with truth-telling, weighing the risks against the need for authenticity. Sometimes prudence suggests waiting for the right moment. But when your inner wisdom signals it's time to speak, yet fear of losing connection holds you back, consider this: From our earliest years, we learned to shape our truths to maintain approval and acceptance. Think back to those childhood moments of pretending delight over unwanted gifts, teaching us that sometimes truth must yield to harmony.

This pattern follows us into professional life, where the stakes feel even higher. Yet perhaps the greatest risk isn't in speaking truth but in letting it remain unspoken, allowing barriers to authentic connection to quietly accumulate. The question becomes not whether to speak truth, but how to do so in ways that strengthen rather than sever the relationships we value.

> The success of an organization is inversely proportional to the number of its secrets.

EARN TRUST BY ACTING AND SPEAKING TRUTH

Speaking truth in organizations requires a fundamental shift in understanding. It isn't about accusation or judgment, declaring others incompetent or their decisions wrong. Instead, authentic truth-telling centers on owning your personal experience, clearly expressing your needs, desires, and perspectives without attacking others. It's the difference between "I think you're a terrible leader" and "I'm struggling to understand the direction we're taking." The first one is outward pointing, while the second is inward pointing.

The journey of truth-telling often involves careful discernment. There are moments when vulnerability serves a higher purpose, when sharing your honest perspective can open new possibilities for understanding and growth. Yet there are also times when holding your truth quietly, acknowledging it internally while choosing not to express it externally, represents the wiser path. The key lies in distinguishing between situations that call for vocal truth-telling and those that require internal truth-holding.

> Vulnerability is the birthplace of innovation, creativity, and change.
> —Brené Brown

Yet, it takes courage. As a leader, not only is truth-telling a prerequisite to success, but you also must model the very behavior you want from others around you. Speaking your truth from your heart without judgment or blame even if it's just to yourself in the mirror is an act of courage.

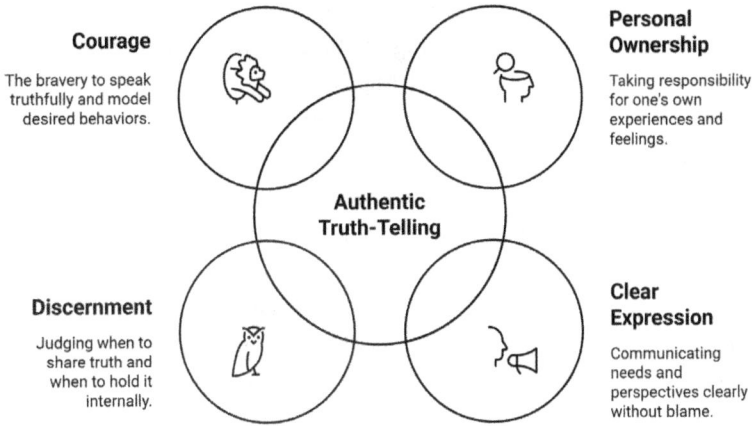

Courage
The bravery to speak truthfully and model desired behaviors.

Personal Ownership
Taking responsibility for one's own experiences and feelings.

Authentic Truth-Telling

Discernment
Judging when to share truth and when to hold it internally.

Clear Expression
Communicating needs and perspectives clearly without blame.

Figure 15—Speaking Your Truth

The tools can now become a more powerful source of truth. The business model does the heavy lifting on facts, allowing no space for equivocations, lying, obfuscation, CYAing, and other destructive behaviors.

> Transparency doesn't mean sharing every detail. Transparency means providing the context for the decisions we make. —Simon Sinek

It is the community you build while implementing a business model that ensures the success of your cultural shift. "Engagement is the means through which there can be a shift in caring for the well-being of the whole, and the task of the [leader] is to produce that engagement."[38]

Be the leader your people expect you to be. Engage your people in transformation.

Chapter Summary

In modern organizations, vulnerability and authenticity are often seen as weaknesses, with employees hiding behind professional masks. However, the

---

38. Block, *Community*, 87.

chapter argued that the most transformative moments in organizational life occur when people have the courage to be genuine. Leaders play a crucial role in this transformation by modeling authentic behavior not through inappropriate emotional disclosure, but through thoughtful sharing of relevant experiences and uncertainties. When organizations create safe spaces for acknowledging the full human experience, including struggles and emotions, it enables deeper learning, innovation, and genuine collaboration. This cultural shift leads to stronger relationships in which people turn toward each other during challenges, take natural ownership of responsibilities, and support each other's growth, ultimately driving exceptional organizational performance through authentic connection rather than mandate.

Key Chapter Takeaways

1. Authentic leadership sets the tone, when leaders show appropriate vulnerability, it transforms what's possible in the organization.
2. Vulnerability must be supported by thoughtful structure, not left to chance.
3. Small groups and paired sharing create safe spaces for genuine connection.
4. Cultural transformation happens when trust becomes visible during challenges, not just easy times.
5. Truth-telling requires courage but is essential for building real community.

Suggested Homework

1. Practice vulnerable leadership by sharing a current challenge you're wrestling with in your next team meeting, inviting others' perspectives.
2. Create structured opportunities for paired sharing before group discussions, allowing people to build trust in smaller settings first.

⚡⚡⚡⚡

CHAPTER 12

Community-Energized Engagement

Summary: Organizations thrive when we shift from viewing them as places of "work" to environments of energy exchange and community connection. Like physical energy, organizational energy cannot be commanded but only enabled through thoughtful conditions that support its natural flow. This transforms engagement—moving beyond programs and surveys to focus on authentic connections, purposeful alignment, and collective growth. Leaders must create spaces where energy flows naturally through meaningful dialogue and shared purpose, recognizing that performance and profits follow when human energy flourishes through authentic community connection.

The Language of Engagement

When someone asks, "Where do you work?" we respond automatically with practiced phrases: "I work at the bank" or "I work for a tech company." But what if this simple word, "work," undermines how we think about human contribution in organizations? The word "work" carries heavy historical baggage, evoking images of physical labor, strenuous effort, and often unwanted obligation. It suggests transaction rather than transformation, effort rather than energy, duty rather than possibility.

The traditional approach to employee engagement has seemingly reached its limits, particularly with the workplace shifts brought about by the recent pandemic. For decades, we've treated engagement as a problem to be solved through surveys, programs, and initiatives. While these tools have their place, they miss a fundamental truth and true engagement emerges from authentic community and the energy it creates.

Implementing a business system will not, single-handedly, improve employee engagement and may, if implemented by fiat or through a "canned" approach, exacerbate any engagement through resistance or "whiplash."

Consider instead the concept of "energy exchange" or "energy contribution." Instead of saying "I work at the bank," what if we said, "I contribute my energy at the bank" or "I'm part of the bank's community"? This isn't merely semantic wordplay. Language shapes how we think, and how we think shapes what we create.

THE POWER OF COMMUNITY-ENHANCED ENERGY

Organizations thrive when they function as both energy systems and communities. Rather than focusing just on employee satisfaction or commitment, successful organizations understand that real engagement comes from the energy created through authentic community connections.

What sets high-performing organizations apart isn't just their strategies or structure, it's their ability to build strong communities while effectively managing and multiplying energy throughout their system. In these organizations, employees contribute more than just their time. They bring their creativity, emotional investment, and intellectual capacity to a larger ecosystem where both people and organizations can flourish. This transformation happens when organizations move away from focusing on problems and scarcity, and instead embrace possibility and abundance, creating an environment where energy naturally flows through genuine connections and shared purpose.

THE PHYSICS OF ORGANIZATIONAL ENERGY

Organizational energy follows principles like physical energy: it can't be created or destroyed, only transformed and transferred through specific patterns and interaction points. Like physical energy, organizational energy flows best along natural pathways and multiplies through positive interactions. Small, focused interactions often create more impact than large, forced efforts.

Neither type of energy can be commanded, both must be enabled through environments that support their natural patterns. When the right conditions exist, both forms of energy can create dramatic effects, where small changes lead to transformative outcomes through amplification. Success comes not from trying to control energy directly, but from understanding and working with its natural tendencies to flow and multiply through authentic interactions.

UNDERSTANDING COMMUNITY-ENERGY DYNAMICS

Traditional approaches to engagement often miss how energy and community work together in organizations. Most leadership teams focus on analyzing engagement scores and launching programs to address problems. However, energy and community aren't states to achieve but flows to enable. They move through organizations via authentic relationships, meaningful work, and genuine connection to purpose. These flows strengthen when organizations focus on possibilities rather than problems, and on amplifying strengths rather than fixing weaknesses. This energy exchange works across multiple levels: Individual energy flows through personal creativity and growth, relational energy emerges through authentic connections, and collective energy develops when organizations align around shared purpose. These levels don't operate independently but reinforce each other, creating a multiplier effect that goes beyond traditional views of organizational life.

THE FRAMEWORK:
FOUR DIMENSIONS OF COMMUNITY-ENERGIZED ENGAGEMENT

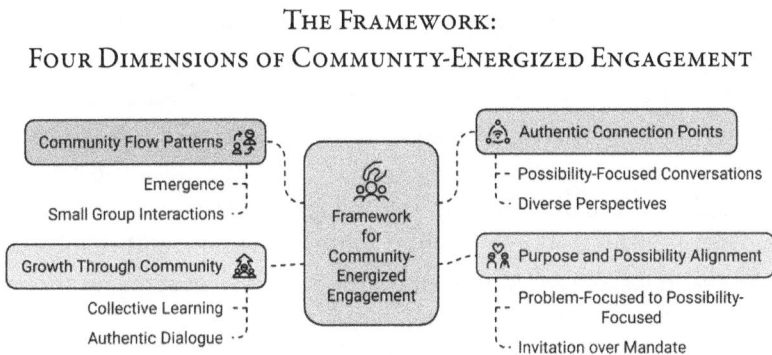

Figure 16—Dimensions of Community Involvement

Community Flow Patterns

Understanding and working with organizational flow patterns requires embracing the principle of emergence. Traditional organizations operate as if energy was unlimited and could be controlled from above by specifying work hours, schedules, output per timeframe, and other metrics. This approach inevitably leads to burnout and energy depletion. Instead, we must create conditions where energy can emerge naturally through authentic community interactions.

Several key practices shape these community flow patterns. Organizations must create open spaces where outcomes can emerge rather than being controlled from above, while embracing the transformative power of small groups engaged in brief but focused interactions, no task forces or standing committees. Success requires recognizing and working in harmony with natural community rhythms and formal meeting rituals, deliberately building in time for reflection and integration. Throughout this process, leaders must remain open to and welcome the collective wisdom that naturally emerges when communities are given the space to flourish.

Authentic Connection Points

Community is built through the quality of our interactions and the authenticity of our conversations. In organizations, these connection points amplify energy creating a multiplying effect that can transform entire systems. Energy feeds on energy.

These connection points are hindered in an environment that involves traditional problem-solving. When those environments embrace possibility-focused conversations and deliberately shift attention toward gifts and capacities, they stop dwelling on and discussing problems and deficits. Organizations must intentionally create spaces that foster authentic dialogue about what truly matters, while actively welcoming diverse perspectives and even constructive dissent. Through these practices, they can build vital bridges across traditional organizational boundaries, creating a more interconnected, interdependent, and dynamic community.

Purpose and Possibility Alignment

Purpose alignment takes on new depth when viewed through the community-enhanced lens. It becomes not just about aligning individual and organizational purposes, but about connecting to larger possibilities for the community we serve.

This alignment naturally emerges as organizations shift from problem-focused thinking to possibility-focused dialogue, while thoughtfully connecting individual gifts to broader community needs. Success depends on creating space where outcomes can emerge (rather than being controlled top down) and foster genuine ownership through invitation rather than mandate. Throughout this process, organizations must help individuals see how their daily work connects to and creates meaningful impact within the larger community.

Growth Through Community

Growth integration in a community context means moving beyond individual employee development to collective learning and emergence. It embraces the principle that the wisdom to solve our challenges already exists within the community.

This approach focuses on creating rich conditions for collective learning. It emphasizes building robust capacity for authentic dialogue, consistently embracing emergent outcomes.

IMPLEMENTATION: CREATING CONDITIONS
FOR COMMUNITY-ENERGIZED ENGAGEMENT

Instead of focusing on programs and initiatives, leaders need to create conditions where community can emerge, and energy can naturally flow and multiply. This requires a fundamental shift in how we think about organizational life not as a place where people "work," but as a space where energy is exchanged and amplified through authentic community connection.

This starts with asking the right questions. Instead of asking how to fix engagement problems, leaders must explore deeper inquiries. They must wonder about possibilities that haven't yet been imagined, consider what gifts are present in their community that haven't been fully welcomed, contemplate how to create spaces for authentic dialogue and emergence, and examine what small shifts might create large ripples of positive change throughout the organization. These small changes in the current situation can produce dramatically different outcomes.[39]

The role of leadership fundamentally shifts from controlling outcomes to enabling energy flow. Leaders must learn to ask powerful questions rather than simply providing answers, while deliberately creating spaces for authentic dialogue throughout the organization. This new approach requires welcoming diverse perspectives and even dissent, maintaining a steadfast focus on possibilities rather than problems, and building genuine ownership through invitation rather than mandate.

Measuring What Matters

While traditional metrics have their place, community-enhanced engagement requires different indicators. Leadership must look carefully for signs that reveal the quality of conversations and connections taking place, while encouraging the emergence of new possibilities throughout the system. Leaders should track the natural flow of energy and ideas.

Looking Forward: The Community-Energized Future

As organizations face increasingly complex challenges, the ability to build authentic community and sustain energy becomes ever more critical. Understanding and working with organizational energy through a community-enhanced lens is about creating the conditions for sustainable performance and meaningful impact, performance and profits follow.

The path forward doesn't require more programs or initiatives. It requires a fundamental shift in how you think about and work with your community. This means developing new capabilities, adopting different leadership

---

39. Allison Rauch, "Butterfly effect (chaos theory)," Britannica, December 21, 2024. https://www.britannica.com/science/butterfly-effect.

approaches, and creating an environment that supports, rather than hinders, natural community emergence and energy flow.

The organizations that thrive in the future will be those that master this new approach to engagement managing satisfaction. The choice facing leaders isn't whether to make this shift but how quickly and effectively they can embrace the power of community-enhanced engagement.

Chapter Summary

The chapter explored a fundamental shift in how we view organizational engagement, moving away from traditional "work" language and metrics toward the concept of "energy exchange" within communities. It argued that true engagement emerges from authentic community connections rather than formal programs or initiatives. The chapter presented a framework with four dimensions: Community flow patterns, authentic connection points, purpose alignment, and collective growth. Rather than trying to control outcomes, leaders should create conditions where energy naturally flows and multiplies through genuine community interactions. This approach emphasizes the importance of asking powerful questions, welcoming diverse perspectives, and measuring the quality of conversations and connections rather than traditional engagement metrics.

Key Chapter Takeaways

1. The language we use shapes our reality, shifting from "work" to "energy exchange" opens new possibilities for engagement.
2. Energy flows through authentic relationships and meaningful exchange, shifting focus from fixing weaknesses to amplifying gifts.
3. Small groups with a possibility-oriented mindset create more energy and engagement than large-scale programs.
4. Leaders must shift from controlling outcomes to creating conditions for energy flow through powerful questions and invitations.
5. Success requires new metrics focused on energy quality, flow patterns, relationship depth, and collective learning.

Suggested Homework

1. Map Your Energy Patterns: Over the next two weeks, observe and document where energy naturally flows in your organization.

2. Practice Possibility Questions: In your next three leadership or team meetings, replace problem-focused questions with possibility-focused ones:
    o Instead of "What's wrong?" ask "What possibilities haven't we explored?"
    o Instead of "How do we fix this?" ask "What gifts could we amplify?"
    o Instead of "Who's responsible?" ask "What small shifts might create positive ripples?"
    o Track how these different questions change the quality of conversation and energy in the room.

$$\not{f}\not{f}\not{f}\not{f}$$

CHAPTER 13

Organizational Readiness

Summary: This chapter outlines the path to authentic organizational transformation, starting with leadership vision that goes beyond metrics to purpose. It presents ten key steps for transformational leadership, including establishing clear purpose, developing facilitation skills, deep listening, powerful questioning, and pattern recognition. The chapter emphasizes that success requires both structural elements (support systems, rituals) and human elements (community building, enabling collective wisdom). It concludes that transformational leadership is cyclical rather than linear, requiring consistent practice and attention to both structure and emergence, with success measured through increased collective capacity, engagement, and community strength.

THE ART OF READINESS

Leadership Vision and the Path to Authentic Change

True organizational transformation begins with leadership vision, but not in the traditional sense of top-down directives or carefully crafted mission statements. Instead, it starts with leaders embarking on a deeper journey of understanding, one that reaches beyond quarterly targets and strategic plans to touch the very heart of organizational purpose.

This journey demands that leaders first achieve profound clarity about why their organization exists and what difference it seeks to make in the world. It requires you to look past the comfortable metrics of financial success to grapple with deeper questions about meaning and impact. What truly matters in the work we do? What difference are we called to make in the world? What future are we trying to create together? How does our daily work and energy serve something larger than ourselves? What legacy do we hope to leave? How do we open up to our energy?

These questions aren't philosophical luxuries but practical necessities, creating the North Star that will guide all transformation efforts. Without this clarity, even the most well-designed change initiatives risk becoming mere exercises in restructuring rather than true transformation.

The journey then demands a fundamental shift in how leaders view their organizations. The traditional view of organizations as collections of individuals performing tasks (in silos) must give way to understanding organizations as living communities capable of collective wisdom, energy, and shared purpose and energy. This shift fundamentally changes how leaders approach their role and their relationship with the organization.

True transformation requires leaders to commit genuinely to building authentic community. This means valuing relationships as deeply as results, investing deliberately in connection and belonging, and creating space for real dialogue. It requires honoring the whole person rather than just the role they play and actively building collective capacity beyond individual skills.

This commitment challenges leaders to examine whether they're truly ready to prioritize community building alongside traditional performance metrics. Are they willing to invest time and resources in building relationships? Will they protect space for dialogue even when pressing tasks demand attention? Can they value the intangible aspects of community (such as its energy) as much as tangible results?

Perhaps most demanding is the requirement for leaders to hold the mirrors up to themselves and examine their own openness to change. This goes far beyond supporting others through change. It requires leaders to question their own assumptions, adapt their leadership style, and learn new ways of being. They must be willing to let go of control and embrace uncertainty, understanding that true transformation often emerges in unexpected ways.

Leaders must embody a genuine learning orientation that goes beyond proclamations. This means demonstrating real curiosity about new possibilities, showing comfort with not knowing all the answers, and willingly experimenting with new approaches. It requires openness to feedback not just accepting it but actively seeking it and finding joy in the discovery process itself.

Critical to this journey is developing the capacity to see energy and unique gifts each person brings to the organization. This means looking beyond roles and titles to see whole persons, valuing diverse contributions even when they don't fit standard metrics, and creating space for these gifts to emerge. It involves actively matching gifts with opportunities and celebrating the unique contributions each person makes.

The journey requires leaders to develop strong facilitation skills and create conditions in which authentic dialogue can flourish. This means learning to create safe spaces for real conversation, guiding collective thinking without directing it, and navigating difficult conversations with grace. It requires mastering the delicate balance between providing structure and allowing emergence.

All these elements come together in a new understanding of leadership; one built on creating conditions where people and possibilities can flourish.

TEN STEPS FOR TRANSFORMATIONAL LEADERSHIP

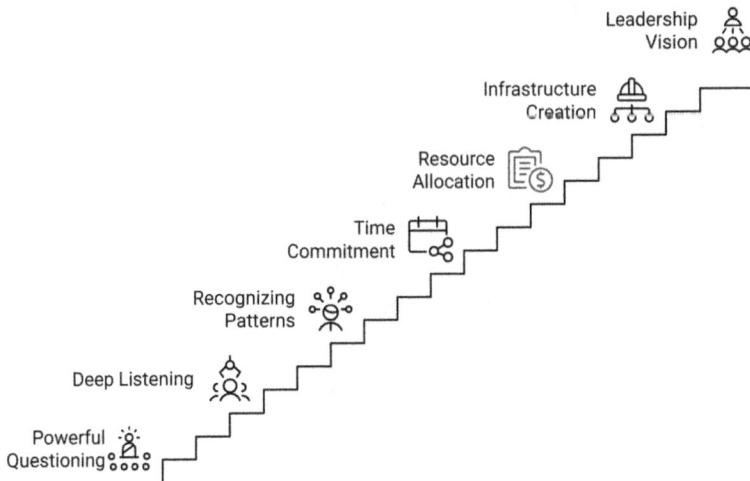

Figure 17—Organizational Readiness

1. Establish Vision and Purpose Clarity

Leadership begins with clear purpose. Before initiating any transformation, leaders must deeply understand why their organization exists beyond the pursuit of profit. This understanding goes to the heart of purpose not just what we do, but why it matters in society. Leaders must clearly articulate the difference they seek to make, painting a vivid picture of the future they want to create.

Each role, each task, each decision must connect to this broader meaning, creating a web of purpose that engages and energizes everyone in the organization.

2. Develop Core Facilitation Mastery

True facilitation mastery means creating conditions where authentic dialogue can flourish naturally. Leaders learn to hold space for emergence rather than controlling outcomes, guiding collective thinking processes with a light but skilled touch.

This capacity includes navigating complexity with grace, helping groups find their way through uncertainty while maintaining focus on purpose. The goal is enabling groups to access their collective wisdom, creating spaces where the whole becomes greater than the sum of its parts.

3. Cultivate Deep Listening Capacity

Moving beyond mere hearing to deep understanding transforms leadership effectiveness. This involves practicing full presence in all interactions.

This deeper listening enables understanding of systemic implications, seeing how each conversation connects to larger patterns and possibilities. Perhaps most importantly, it creates space for others' full expression, allowing authentic voice and contribution to emerge.

4. Master the Art of Powerful Questions[40]

Rather than providing answers, leaders learn to ask questions that open new possibilities. These aren't just any questions, but ones that challenge assumptions through genuine curiosity and evoke accountability, enabling breakthrough thinking in individuals and groups.

Through powerful questions, leaders help access collective wisdom that remains untapped in more directive approaches. The art lies in knowing which questions to ask when, and how to hold space for the answers to emerge.

5. Build Pattern Recognition Intelligence

Developing capacity to see larger patterns transforms leadership effectiveness. This intelligence goes beyond recognizing recurring themes to understanding the relationships that shape organizational life. Leaders learn to anticipate emerging trends, identifying strategic implications before they become obvious to others. Pattern recognition becomes a key leadership tool for navigating complexity and change.

6. Create Support Structures

Transformation requires infrastructure such as thoughtfully designed spaces and systems that enable sustained development. This includes creating regular learning rhythms, from daily practices to annual reviews. Feedback mechanisms help maintain course corrections while celebration practices maintain energy and momentum.

7. Foster Community and Connection

Leaders learn to value relationship quality as much as traditional results, creating space for authentic connection throughout the organization. This enables genuine dialogue across traditional boundaries. Honoring the whole person's development means seeing beyond roles to the full humanity of everyone.

---

40. See also Appendix 3: It's the Questions You Ask.

8. Enable Collective Wisdom

This involves designing processes that enable truly collaborative thinking, integrating diverse perspectives into richer understanding. Innovation flows naturally when people connect authentically around meaningful challenges. Building collective sensemaking capacity enables the organization to navigate complexity with greater wisdom.

9. Maintain Rituals

Daily reflection and learning capture the pieces for the foundation for growth. Weekly skill development focus maintains momentum, while monthly pattern recognition enables course correction. Quarterly capability assessment provides a bigger picture perspective, while annual vision renewal ensures alignment with evolving purpose.

10. Lead Transformative Integration

Bringing all these elements together requires artful leadership. Modeling continuous learning and development sets the tone for others. Connecting individual growth to organizational evolution creates sustainable transformation. The art of transformational leadership lies in holding all these elements in dynamic balance.

Remember:

- Start where you are with what you have.
- Build capacity progressively over time.
- Focus on consistent practice rather than perfection.
- Learn through action and reflection.
- Adjust based on emerging needs and opportunities.

**Support
Structures**

Creating systems
and processes that
support sustained
organizational
growth.

**Vision and
Purpose**

Establishing a clear
organizational
purpose to guide
actions and
decisions.

**Transformational
Leadership**

**Powerful
Questions**

everaging strategic
questioning to
challenge
assumptions and
evoke insights.

**Facilitation
Mastery**

Mastering
facilitation to foster
authentic dialogue
and collective
wisdom.

Deep Listening

Enhancing
leadership
effectiveness
through profound
understanding and
presence.

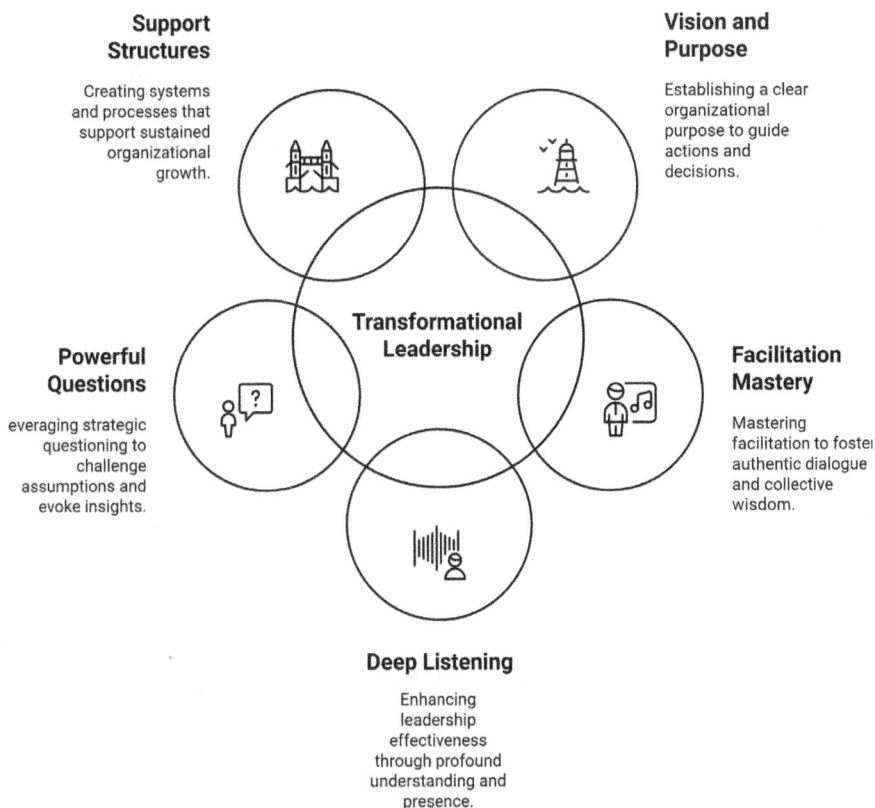

Figure 18—Success Indicators

These steps are not linear but cyclical. They support and reinforce each other, creating an upward spiral of developing capacity for transformational leadership.

Chapter Summary

The chapter explored transformational leadership, emphasizing that true organizational change begins with leaders developing deep clarity about organizational purpose beyond financial metrics. It presented ten key steps for transformational leadership, from establishing vision to implementation, focusing on building authentic community, developing facilitation skills, and creating conditions for collective wisdom to emerge. The chapter emphasized that leaders must shift from viewing organizations as collections of individuals to seeing them as living communities capable of shared purpose and energy. Success requires leaders to invest in relationship-building, master the art of powerful questioning, and create supportive structures while maintaining regular rituals for sustained development and learning.

Key Chapter Takeaways

1. True transformation requires leader commitment to building authentic community alongside performance.
2. Deep listening and powerful questioning are essential leadership skills for enabling change.
3. Pattern recognition intelligence helps leaders anticipate and navigate transformation.
4. Support structures and rituals maintain momentum for sustained development.
5. Success emerges through consistent practice rather than sporadic inspiration.

Suggested Homework

1. Document your organization's purpose beyond metrics and draft responses to "What difference are we called to make?"
2. Practice deep listening in your next three meetings, note patterns and insights that emerge when fully present.

⚡⚡⚡⚡

CHAPTER 14

Six Critical Conversations

Summary: This chapter outlines six essential leadership tasks for building community before implementing business models: gathering allies, exploring possibilities, creating ownership, providing space for dissent, facilitating commitment, and recognizing gifts. For each task, it provides detailed scripts to guide leaders through structured conversations that transform organizational culture. It concludes that organizational transformation emerges from combining business tools with meaningful human connection.

Conversations that Lead to a Different Culture

The power of conversation has been studied for centuries. The philosopher Plato famously weighed in on the subject, saying wise men speak because they have something to say; fools speak because they have to say something. Starting with conversation is the logical first step to transforming a community and culture.

> Leadership is about shaping the conversation. —Peter Block

Peter Block's book *Community* outlines essential principles for conversations that strengthen community bonds. This framework is particularly relevant for organizational leaders, since every organization is fundamentally a community that you shape through your leadership.

> We are a community of possibilities, not a community of problems. Community exists for the sake of belonging and takes its identity from the gifts, generosity, and accountability of its citizens. It is not defined by its fears, its isolation, or its penchant for retribution. —Peter Block, *Community*

Block argues that the real challenge lies in fostering genuine connections with your team members that enable them to release old patterns. He emphasizes that building community can only create meaningful change when it offers a distinct alternative to conventional organizational structures and traditional ways of working together.

Your role as a leader is to transform the isolation within your workplace into connectedness and caring for the whole by "building the social fabric."[41] Recall that Block's work in *Community* forms the warp (i.e., the strength) of the fabric.

This fabric can be one of leaders creating leaders who create leaders with full accountability, using not only the key tools of either model but also the sources of truth and rituals. **Leadership has the capacity to initiate an alternative, accountable future**. The models provide the tools and serve as the sources of truth; you provide the leadership, enabling full accountability.

Who Are Your People?

As you set about to transform your organization, you need to understand your people. Most leaders are typically surrounded by the five types of people shown here, with trust level plotted against agreement level.

---

41. Peter Block, *Community*, 54.

	High Trust	Low Trust
High Agreement	Allies	Skeptics
Unknown Agreement		**Fence Sitters** (low trust; no sense of agreement)
Low Agreement	Resisters	Adversaries

Figure 19—Trust/Agreement Matrix

- Allies both have high trust and high agreement with you.
- Skeptics have high agreement, accompanied by lower trust, and change must be proven to them.
- Resisters have high trust but don't agree with the change. They'll go along but at a much slower pace.
- Fence Sitters have lower trust, but you are simply unsure of their level of agreement. Proceed carefully until they are better understood.
- Finally, Adversaries have both low trust and low agreement. They will likely passively work against change.

SIX LEADERSHIP TASKS TO BUILD COMMUNITY

One of the first tasks on your journey to transforming your workplace is to gather Allies who support you. These are typically, but not always, those who are directly accountable to you.

Take a few minutes to reflect on how you might gather your Allies on your path through work and life. Grab your journal and a pen. Even better, find a friend with whom you can reflect on the questions. When you're ready, pause, feel your breath, and write down what comes up in response to the following questions.

Ask yourself:

- Who in your organization really believes in you?
- Who might push you to move past fear and grow into the person you want to be?
- Who might you like to check in with regularly about your progress?

If you want to go fast, go alone. If you want to go far, go together.
—African Proverb

The First Task of Leadership Is to Gather Allies

I encourage you, then, to reach out to the people you thought of (likely those closest to you), share that you are working on implementing the business model, and discuss the possibility of setting up regular conversations to support each other. Taking the time to create a team of support now will help you progress much faster with the work ahead. Getting implementation started and ultimately institutionalized in your organization will be easier.

The larger portion of this chapter is devoted to six example scripts, each presented in detail. Don't "blow off" reading them, because an understanding of the process in each script is essential to a better understanding of the effort to start an alive community.

What follows is a suggested script for the Invitation to Allies.

INVITATION SCRIPT

Setting

Small group discussions (5–10 people) following this initial company-wide Invitation Conversation script.

Facilitator (senior leader or trained facilitator)

Good morning/afternoon, everyone. Thank you for being here today. I've called this meeting because we're at a pivotal moment in

---

our organization's journey, and I want to invite each of you to be part of shaping our future.

Opening

We've achieved a lot together, and I'm proud of what we've built. But I believe we have the potential to create something even more remarkable not just a successful business, but a thriving community that makes a real difference in the world.

To help us realize this potential, we're considering implementing a business model. But before we dive into the details, I want to pause and reflect on why we're here and what we truly want to create together.

The Invitation

So, I'm extending an invitation to each of you. This isn't just an invitation to learn about a new business model. It's an invitation to co-create the future of our organization. It's an invitation to build not just a more efficient company, but a more vibrant, purposeful community.

What if we could create a workplace where:

- Every person feels a deep sense of belonging and purpose?
- We consistently achieve our business goals while also making a positive impact on each other and our wider community?
- We have the structures to operate efficiently, but also the flexibility to innovate and adapt?
- Each of us feels empowered to contribute our unique gifts and perspectives?

This is the possibility I see for us, and I believe that by combining a robust business model with strong community-building practices, we can make this vision a reality.

Introducing the Business model

The business model offers us tools to streamline our operations, clarify our goals, and align our efforts. But I don't see this as just another management tool. I see it as a framework that, with the right approach, can help us build a stronger sense of community and shared purpose. For example:

- The business model's focus on clear communication and regular meetings can help us have more meaningful conversations and build stronger relationships.
- Its emphasis on defining core values and purpose can help us articulate and live our shared beliefs.
- The goal setting and accountability structures can empower each of us to take ownership of our collective success.

The Ask

Here's what I'm asking of you today:

1. Be open to the possibility of what we could create together.
2. Engage fully in the process as we learn about and implement this business model.
3. Bring your whole self to this endeavor, your ideas, your doubts, your hopes, and your unique gifts.
4. Help us shape this implementation in a way that strengthens our community, not just our bottom line.

Your Voice Matters

I want to stress that this is not a top-down initiative. Your voice, your insights, and your commitment are crucial to making this work. Over the coming weeks, we'll have conversations about possibilities, ownership, commitments, and the gifts we each bring to our community. We'll also seek your input on how to tailor this business model to our unique culture and needs. Your feedback and ideas will be essential in ensuring that this business model serves our community, not the other way around.

Closing

So, I extend this invitation to each of you: Will you join me on this journey? Will you help us create both a more successful business and a more vibrant, purposeful community? I believe that together we can create something truly extraordinary, something that fulfills our potential both as a business as well as a community of talented, passionate individuals working towards a shared purpose. Thank you for your attention. I look forward to embarking on this journey with all of you.

Next Steps

- Open the floor for initial questions and reactions.
- Announce upcoming smaller group discussions for more in-depth conversations.
- Provide resources for employees to learn more about the chosen business model and community-building principles.
- Set a timeline for the next steps in the implementation process.

Figure 20—The Invitation Script

The Second Task of Leadership Is to Jointly Determine the Possibility

Most of us have been to meetings where it wasn't quite clear why we were there or that focused on the problems and didn't seem to lead anywhere new. Far too often, we lose our way by trying to define or fix a problem instead of imagining an alternative future, or by jumping straight to the how without first getting clear on our why.

Block suggests beginning meetings with a *declaration of possibility*, e.g., a statement of why you are gathered; not to start to implement a new business model but to set the stage for success before starting. **Focusing on a clear and shared purpose can open our vision to a wide range of possibilities for a different future**. This shift in perspective itself can be transformative.

Once a group has built trust and connection, we can use powerful questions such as these to discover communal possibility:

- What can we create together that will make a difference?
- How can we use the tools of the business model to create a new future?
- How do we look and feel differently?

These are not idle questions. Ask them of your Allies and others to gain a common sense of connection.

Following is suggested script for the second task:

POSSIBILITY SCRIPT

Setting

A company-wide meeting or series of departmental meetings

Speaker

CEO, senior leader, or outside facilitator

Welcome and Introduction

Welcome, everyone. Thank you for joining this important conversation about our future. In our last meeting, we introduced the idea of implementing our business model to not only improve our business operations but also strengthen our community. Now, we're here to explore the possibilities this could create for us.

Setting the Context

Before we begin, I want to remind us of the purpose of this conversation. We're not here to problem-solve or to focus on past challenges.

Instead, we're here to imagine and articulate the future we want to create together. We're here to dream big and to consider possibilities we may not have thought of before.

Framing Questions

[Put these questions on prepared flip chart.]
    To guide our discussion, I'd like us to consider these questions:

1. What new possibilities could this business model open for us?
2. How might this business model help us create a workplace that we're truly excited to be part of each day?
3. In what ways could this business model help us make a more significant positive impact on each other and our wider community?
4. How might this business model allow us to better use our individual and collective strengths?
5. What could our organization look like in three years if we successfully implement this business model in a way that also strengthens our community?

Small Group Discussions

Let's break into smaller groups of three to four people. In your groups, please discuss these questions. Remember, at this stage, there are no wrong or bad answers. We're here to imagine possibilities, not to evaluate feasibility. Be bold in your thinking!
    [Allow 20–30 minutes for small group discussions.]

Sharing Possibilities

Now, let's come back together and share some of the possibilities we've envisioned. Who would like to start?
    [Facilitate sharing from each group, capturing key ideas on a whiteboard or shared screen.]

Exploring Shared Themes

Looking at all these ideas, I'm noticing some common themes. Let's explore these further: [examples only for illustrative purposes but pay attention to the embedded questions]

1. Improved Clarity and Alignment
   - How might greater clarity on our goals and roles create new possibilities for collaboration and innovation?
   - What could we achieve if everyone in the organization was fully aligned with our priorities?
2. Enhanced Personal and Professional Growth
   - How might the structured approach of our business model create new opportunities for learning and development?
   - What possibilities open up when each of us has a clear path for growth within the organization?
3. Stronger Sense of Community
   - How might the regular rhythm of meetings and check-ins foster deeper connections among us?
   - What could our workplace feel like if we all had a stronger sense of belonging and shared purpose?
4. Increased Agility and Adaptability
   - How might a better business model and processes allow us to be more responsive to changes in our industry?
   - What possibilities emerge if we can quickly align our efforts to new opportunities or challenges?
5. Greater Impact on Our Wider Community
   - How might improved business performance allow us to contribute more to causes we care about?
   - What possibilities arise if we integrate community impact into our core business goals?

Personalizing the Possibilities

[Put these questions on prepared flip chart or a one-page handout beforehand.]

Now, I'd like each of you to take a moment to reflect personally:

- What possibility most excites you?
- How do you see yourself contributing to and benefiting from this future we're envisioning?
- What gifts or strengths do you have that could help bring these possibilities to life?

[Allow a few minutes for personal reflection, then invite volunteers to share.]

Connecting Possibilities to Implementation

As we consider these exciting possibilities, let's also start thinking about how the business model might help us realize them:

1. The business model's emphasis on defining core values and purpose can help us articulate and live our shared vision.
2. Its focus on setting and achieving short-term goals, 90-day efforts (priorities) can help us make consistent progress towards our bigger goals.
3. The regular meeting pulse can provide opportunities for ongoing communication and community-building.
4. The emphasis on the right people in the right seats can help each of us find where we can contribute most effectively.
5. The measurables can help us focus not just financial performance, but also our impact on our community and employee satisfaction.

Closing and Next Steps

Thank you all for your enthusiastic participation. The possibilities we've discussed today are truly inspiring. They show that implementing this business model isn't just about improving our business metrics, it's about creating a future where we can all thrive and make a meaningful impact.

In our next conversation, we'll discuss ownership or how each of us can take responsibility for bringing these possibilities to life. Before then, I encourage you to continue reflecting on the possibilities we've discussed and to share your thoughts with your colleagues.

Remember, the future we create will be shaped by the possibilities we can envision together. Let's keep dreaming big and supporting each other as we work to make these possibilities a reality.

Thank you again for your time and insights. I'm excited about the journey ahead!

Next Steps

- Compile and distribute a summary of the possibilities discussed.
- Announce the date and topic (ownership) of the next conversation.
- Provide resources for employees to learn more about specific aspects of the business model that resonated with them.
- Encourage ongoing informal discussions about these possibilities.

Figure 21—The Possibility Script

The Third Task of Leadership Is to Create Ownership

Finger-pointing is rampant in our culture. **It can be easier to focus on what others should change than to accept responsibility for how we contribute to our problems.** Focus on how we create a better future. The problem is, as Block writes, "Without this capacity to see ourselves as cause, our efforts become either coercive or wishfully dependent on the transformation of others."[42] Simply put, we are the cause of our current situation and are accountable for the change we want.

Block suggests that each successful meeting serves two functions. The first,

---

42. Block' *Community,* 127.

as we discussed above, is to address its stated purpose to design a better future. The second is to be an opportunity for each person to decide to become more engaged as an "owner." The ultimate question of ownership is:

What have I done to contribute to the very thing I complain about or want to change?

How powerful can this discussion alone be? However, facing the idea that we're causing our own challenges can be difficult to take on immediately. It can be easier to explore the ownership that people feel for a particular gathering. One way to do this is to personally ask people to rate on a five-point scale, from low to high, their responses to four questions.

- How valuable an experience (or project, or community) do you plan for this to be?
- How much risk are you willing to take?
- How participative do you plan to be?
- To what extent are you invested in the well-being of the whole?

Rather than offering advice or trying to cheer up people who struggle with these questions, just be compassionately interested in whatever answers arise. You don't have to "fix" anyone or anything at this stage.

A suggested script for your use in this Third Task:

OWNERSHIP SCRIPT

Setting

Small group discussions (10–15 people) following the Possibility Conversation

Facilitator

Senior leader or trained facilitator

Welcome and Introduction

Welcome, everyone. Thank you for joining this crucial conversation

---

about ownership as we move forward with implementing our business model. In our previous meetings, we invited participation and explored exciting possibilities for our future. Now, we're here to discuss how each of us can take ownership of this process and our collective future.

Setting the Context

The purpose of this conversation is to shift our perspective from what others or the organization should do to what *each of us* can do to contribute to the change we want to see. This is about personal responsibility and commitment.

Remember, ownership isn't about blame. It's about recognizing our power to influence outcomes and acting accordingly.

Framing Questions

[Put these questions on prepared flip chart or single handout page beforehand.]

To guide our discussion, let's consider these key questions:

1. What have I done, perhaps unintentionally, that might be contributing to the very issues I hope this new business model will address?
2. In what ways have I been waiting for others to solve problems that I could address myself?
3. How might my current attitudes or behaviors need to shift to fully embrace and benefit from this new business model?
4. What unique strengths or perspectives do I bring that could contribute to the successful implementation of this business model?
5. What personal commitments am I willing to make to ensure the success of this initiative?

Personal Reflection

Let's start with some individual reflection. Please take a few minutes to consider these questions silently. Jot down your thoughts if you find that helpful.

[Allow 5–10 minutes for personal reflection.]

Paired Discussions

Now, let's pair up. Share with your partner one or two key insights from your reflection. Listen carefully to each other. Remember, this is about honest self-reflection, not criticism of others.

[Allow 10–15 minutes for paired discussions.]

Group Sharing

Thank you for those thoughtful discussions. Now, let's open up to the larger group. Who would like to share an insight about how they can take more ownership in this process?

[Facilitate group sharing, capturing key themes on a whiteboard or shared screen.]

Exploring Common Themes

Looking at what's been shared, I'm noticing some common themes. Let's explore these further: [examples only for illustrative purposes]

1. Proactive Problem-Solving
   - How can we shift from a "that's not my job" mindset to a "how can I help" approach?
   - What small, daily actions can each of us take to address issues proactively?
2. Embracing Accountability
   - How can we hold ourselves and each other accountable in a supportive, non-judgmental way?
   - What would it look like if we all took full ownership of our roles, responsibilities, and accountabilities?
3. Continuous Learning and Adaptation

- How can we take ownership of our own learning as we implement this new business model?
- In what ways can we be more open to feedback and willing to adapt our behaviors?
4. Collaborative Ownership
    - How can we balance individual ownership with teamwork and mutual support?
    - What could our organization achieve if everyone felt a keen sense of ownership?
5. Leading by Example
    - How can each of us, regardless of our position, lead by example in taking ownership?
    - What ripple effects might we see if we all stepped up our ownership?

Connecting Ownership to Business Model

As we consider these aspects of ownership, let's think about how they connect to the business model we're implementing:

1. The Accountability Chart® in the business model clearly defines roles and accountabilities. How can we use this to increase our sense of ownership?
2. The business model's emphasis on measurable goals [Rocks in Traction/EOS, or Critical Numbers in Scaling Up] provides clear targets. How can we take ownership of achieving these goals?
3. The regular meeting ritual provides opportunities for consistent communication. How can we use these to reinforce our commitments and support each other's ownership?
4. The focus on core values and purpose can guide our actions. How can we take ownership of living these values every day?
5. The business model's emphasis on identifying and solving issues encourages proactive problem-solving. How can we embrace this approach in our daily work?

Personal Commitments

Now, I'd like each of you to consider making a personal commitment. What specific action or change are you willing to commit to that will demonstrate your ownership in this process?

Please take a moment to write down your commitment. Be as specific as possible.

[Allow a few minutes for writing commitments.]

Would anyone like to share their commitment with the group?

[Invite volunteers to share their commitments.]

Closing and Next Steps

Thank you all for your honesty, insights, and commitments today. The level of ownership you've demonstrated is truly inspiring. Remember, taking ownership isn't a one-time event; it's an ongoing practice. Let's support each other in honoring these commitments and continuing to step up our ownership.

In our next conversation, we'll discuss dissent and voicing our doubts and concerns as a way of deepening our commitment. Your honest engagement in that conversation will be crucial.

Before we close, I want to acknowledge that taking ownership can sometimes feel challenging or uncomfortable. If you need support in fulfilling your commitments or in navigating this change, please don't hesitate to reach out to me, your manager, or HR.

Thank you again for your participation and your commitment to our shared future.

Next Steps

- Compile (anonymously) and distribute a summary of the commitments made.
- Announce the date and topic (dissent) of the next conversation.
- Provide resources or support for employees to fulfill their ownership commitments.

- Encourage managers to follow up with their team members on their individual commitments.

Figure 22—The Ownership Script

The Fourth Task of Leadership Is to Provide Space for Dissent

Organizations flourish when we welcome dissent rather than suppress it. This insight, central to Block's work, reframes dissent from a problem to be managed into an expression of deep commitment to the organization's wellbeing. When people feel safe to voice authentic doubts, e.g., owning their concerns without blame or complaint, the entire environment becomes more real and trustworthy. The transformative power of expressed dissent lies in its ability to free us from being controlled by our doubts and fears. By giving voice to concerns, we gain choice about them, turning what might have been underground resistance into opportunities for genuine dialogue and growth. When someone disagrees with your proposal, thank them and then listen. Hold space for doubt, and work toward understanding the needs and intentions that the person is expressing. **Block reminds us that as leaders, we have a responsibility to listen and protect space for people's doubt, but we don't necessarily need to respond to each doubt.** Some questions for the expression of dissent:

- What doubts and reservations do you have?
- What is the "no," or refusal, that you keep postponing?
- What have you said "yes" to that you no longer really mean?
- What is a commitment or decision that you have changed your mind about?
- What forgiveness are you withholding? What resentment do you hold that no one knows about?

A suggested script for this fourth task follows:

DISSENT SCRIPT

Setting

Small group discussions (10–15 people) following the Ownership Conversation

Facilitator

Senior leader or trained facilitator

Welcome and Introduction

Welcome, everyone. Thank you for joining this crucial conversation about dissent as we continue our journey of implementing your business model. In our previous meetings, we've invited participation, explored possibilities, and discussed personal ownership. Today, we're here to voice our doubts, concerns, and reservations about this process.

Setting the Context

The purpose of today's conversation might seem counterintuitive. We're going to openly discuss our doubts and concerns about implementing our business model. This isn't about complaining or trying to derail the process. Instead, it's about deepening our commitment by honestly addressing potential obstacles and challenges.

Remember, dissent is not disloyalty. It's a valuable part of any change process. By voicing our concerns, we can address them proactively and strengthen our approach.

Framing Questions

[Put these questions on prepared flip chart or single handout page beforehand.]
To guide our discussion, let's consider these key questions:

1. What doubts or reservations do you have about implementing this business model?
2. What potential negative consequences, if any, do you foresee from this implementation?
3. What aspects of our current culture or operations do you worry might be lost or compromised?
4. What personal concerns do you have about how this change might affect your role or work?
5. What do you think is the biggest risk we face in this implementation process?

Ground Rules for the Conversation

Before we begin, let's establish some ground rules:

1. Speak honestly and respectfully.
2. Listen to understand, not to debate or refute.
3. Acknowledge that all concerns are valid, even if we don't all share them.
4. Focus on issues, not individuals.
5. After voicing a concern, try to suggest a possible solution or mitigation strategy.

Small Group Discussions

Let's break into small groups of three or four people. In your groups, please discuss these questions openly. Remember, the goal is to surface concerns so we can address them, not to convince others or defend the business model. *[Allow 20–30 minutes for small group discussions.]*

Sharing Concerns

Now, let's come back together and share some of the key concerns that emerged in your discussions. Who would like to start?

[Facilitate sharing from each group, capturing key concerns on a whiteboard or shared screen.]

Exploring Common Themes

Looking at all these concerns, I'm noticing some common themes. Let's explore these further: [examples only for illustrative purposes]

1. Fear of Increased Workload or Complexity
   - How might we ensure that this business model simplifies rather than complicates our work?
   - What support or resources might we need to manage any initial increase in workload?
2. Concerns About Cultural Shift
   - How can we preserve the positive aspects of our culture while embracing this new business model?
   - What specific cultural elements are we most concerned about losing, and how might we intentionally maintain them?
3. Doubts About Long-term Sustainability
   - What factors might cause us to abandon this business model over time?
   - How can we build in mechanisms to ensure ongoing commitment and adaptation?
4. Worries About Individual Roles and Job Security
   - How might roles change with this new business model and how can we support people through these changes?
   - How can we ensure that the "right people in the right seats" philosophy doesn't lead to unnecessary anxiety?
5. Skepticism About Leadership Commitment
   - How can leadership demonstrate ongoing commitment to this process?
   - What transparency measures can we put in place to maintain trust throughout the implementation?

Addressing Concerns

[Put these questions on prepared flip chart or single handout page beforehand.]

Now that we've identified these concerns, let's start thinking about how we might address them:

1. For each major concern, let's brainstorm potential solutions or mitigation strategies.
2. What additional information or resources might help alleviate some of these concerns?
3. How can we incorporate addressing these concerns into our implementation plan?
4. What ongoing feedback mechanisms can we establish to continue surfacing and addressing concerns?

[Facilitate a problem-solving discussion, capturing proposed solutions.]

Connecting Dissent to Commitment

It might seem paradoxical, but voicing our doubts and concerns can deepen our commitment. By addressing these issues openly:

1. We demonstrate trust in each other and in the process.
2. We improve our implementation plan by anticipating and addressing potential pitfalls.
3. We create a culture of openness that will serve us well beyond this specific implementation.
4. We take ownership of the challenges, not just the benefits, of this new business model.

Personal Reflection

[Put these questions on prepared flip chart or single handout page beforehand.]

Now, I'd like each of you to take a moment for personal reflection:

- How has voicing or hearing these concerns affected your perspective on the implementation?
- What commitment can you make to help address one of the concerns raised today?
- How can you use this practice of constructive dissent in your day-to-day work?

[Allow a few minutes for personal reflection, then invite volunteers to share.]

Closing and Next Steps

Thank you all for your honesty and courage in voicing your concerns today. Your willingness to engage in this difficult conversation demonstrates your commitment to our organization and to this process.

Remember, dissent isn't a one-time event. We need to continue having open, honest conversations throughout this implementation process and beyond. Your ongoing feedback will be crucial to our success.

In our next conversation, we'll discuss specific commitments to action. The concerns and solutions we've discussed today will inform those commitments, ensuring that we move forward with a clear-eyed view of both the challenges and opportunities ahead.

Thank you again for your participation and your commitment to making this implementation successful.

Next Steps

- Compile and distribute a summary of the concerns raised and proposed solutions.
- Incorporate addressing key concerns into the implementation plan.
- Announce the date and topic (commitment) of the next conversation.

- Provide resources or support for employees to learn more about how the business model addresses common concerns.
- Establish an ongoing feedback mechanism for surfacing and addressing concerns throughout the implementation process.

Figure 23—The Dissent Script

The Fifth Task of Leadership Is to Facilitate Commitment

After you have set the context of ownership, explored possibility, and held space for doubt, it comes time for participants to declare their commitment to action. Block writes that honoring our word is the emotional and relational essence of community, and he suggests the following questions to help participants deepen commitment:[43]

- What promises am I willing to make?
- What measures have meaning to me?
- What price am I willing to pay?
- What is the cost to others for me to keep my commitments or to fail in my commitments?
- What is the promise I am postponing?
- What is the promise or commitment I am unwilling to make?
- What is the promise I'm willing to make that constitutes a risk or major shift for me?

A suggested script for the fifth task follows:

---

43. Block, *Community*, 138.

COMMITMENT SCRIPT

Setting:

Company-wide or departmental meeting following the Dissent Conversation

Facilitator:

CEO, senior leader, or trained facilitator

Welcome and Introduction

Welcome, everyone. Thank you for joining this pivotal conversation about commitment as we move forward with implementing this business model. We've journeyed through invitation, possibility, ownership, and dissent. Now, we're here to make specific commitments that will turn our discussions into action.

Setting the Context

The purpose of today's conversation is to solidify our collective commitment to this implementation process. We've explored exciting possibilities, taken ownership of our roles in this change, and voiced our concerns. Now, it's time to commit to specific actions that will make our vision a reality.

Remember, commitment is not about perfection. It's about taking meaningful steps, learning from our experiences, and supporting each other along the way.

Recap of Previous Conversations

Before we make our commitments, let's briefly recap our journey:

1. We invited everyone to be part of shaping our future with our business model.

2. We explored the possibilities this business model could create for our organization and community.
3. We discussed how each of us can take ownership of this process.
4. We voiced our doubts and concerns, strengthening our approach by addressing potential challenges.

All of these conversations have led us to this moment of commitment.

Framing Questions

[Put these questions on prepared flip chart or single handout page beforehand.]

As we prepare to make our commitments, let's consider these key questions:

1. What specific actions am I willing to take to support the implementation of this business model?
2. How can I use my unique strengths and position to contribute to our success?
3. What support do I need to fulfill my commitments, and how will I ask for it?
4. How will my commitments address the concerns we discussed in our last conversation?
5. How will I hold myself accountable for these commitments?

Personal Reflection

Let's start with some individual reflection. Please take a few minutes to consider these questions and jot down your thoughts.
[Allow 10 minutes for personal reflection.]

Small Group Sharing

Now, let's form small groups of three or four people. Share your commitments with your group members. Offer each other feedback and suggestions for making these commitments specific, measurable, and impactful.
[Allow 20 minutes for small group discussions.]

Large Group Commitments

Thank you for those thoughtful discussions. Now, let's share some of our commitments with the larger group. Who would like to start?
[Facilitate group sharing, capturing key commitments on a whiteboard or shared screen.]

Exploring Commitment Themes

Looking at the commitments shared, I'm noticing some common themes. Let's explore these further: [examples only for illustrative purposes]

1. Learning and Skill Development
   - What resources can we provide to support these learning commitments?
   - How can we create a culture of continuous learning throughout this implementation?
2. Cross-Functional Collaboration
   - How can we facilitate collaboration across departments to fulfill these commitments?
   - What structures or processes might we need to put in place to support this collaboration?
3. Communication and Transparency
   - How can we ensure open and consistent communication about our progress?
   - What channels or forums can we create for ongoing dialogue?

4. Process Improvement
   - How can we purposefully and regularly gather and implement improvement ideas?
   - How will we balance adherence to the business model with flexibility for improvement?
5. Accountability and Measurement
   - How will we track and celebrate progress on these commitments?
   - What mechanisms can we put in place for peer support and accountability?

Connecting Commitments to Business Model

Let's consider how our commitments align with key aspects of the business model:

1. How do our commitments support the implementation of the accountability chart?
2. Which commitments will help us in setting and achieving our rocks / key results or critical numbers?
3. How do these commitments enhance our ability to identify and solve issues?
4. Which commitments will help us live our core values and purpose more fully?
5. How do these commitments support the establishment of our meeting rhythm?

Leadership Commitments

As leadership, we also will make specific commitments to support this implementation:

1. [Leader 1] commits to . . . [specific action]
2. [Leader 2] commits to . . . [specific action]
3. [Leader 3] commits to . . . [specific action]

We invite you to hold us accountable for these commitments, just as we'll support you in fulfilling yours.

Formalizing Commitments

[Have a Commitment Card ready to hand out.]
To formalize these commitments:

1. Please write down your primary commitment on the commitment cards provided.
2. We'll collect these cards and create a "Commitment Wall" in a common area.
3. Take a photo of your commitment card to keep with you as a reminder.

[Allow time for writing commitments and collecting cards.]

Supporting Each Other

Commitment is not a solitary act. Let's discuss how we can support each other:

1. How can we create a culture of encouragement and positive accountability?
2. What should we do if we see someone struggling with their commitment?
3. How can we celebrate progress and small wins along the way?

Closing and Next Steps

Thank you all for your thoughtful and courageous commitments today. The specificity and enthusiasm of your pledges give me great confidence in our ability to successfully implement our business model and create the future we've envisioned together.

Remember, commitment is an ongoing process. We'll revisit and renew these commitments regularly as we move forward.

Our next and final conversation in this series will focus on gifts—recognizing the unique contributions each of us brings to this process. Your commitments today are already a testament to those gifts. Thank you again for your dedication to our shared success.

Next Steps

- Create and display the "Commitment Wall."
- Incorporate key commitments into the business model implementation plan.
- Announce the date and topic (gifts) of the next conversation.
- Establish regular check-ins on commitment progress.
- Provide necessary resources and support for employees to fulfill their commitments.
- Begin implementing the business model, guided by these commitments.

Figure 24—The Commitment Script

The Sixth Task of Leadership Is to Recognize Gifts

Block writes, "Community is built by focusing on people's gifts rather than their deficiencies. In the world of community and volunteerism, deficiencies have no market value; gifts are the point. Citizens in community want to know what you can do, not what you can't do."[44]

In a world in which we are taught to ignore and underappreciate our gifts, our work is to recognize, honor, and bring our gifts into the world. To help each other offer our gifts more fully and deepen our connection to each other, it's important to take time in a gathering to honor our gifts. In fact, a focus on strengths and gifts can permeate an entire gathering.

You can ask participants to share what they are receiving from another participant or the group, or you can invite individuals to reflect on their own gifts. These questions can help:

---

44. Block, *Community*, 142.

- What is the gift you currently hold back?
- What is it about you that no one knows about?
- What are you grateful for that has gone unspoken?
- What is the positive feedback you receive that still surprises you?
- What is the gift you have that you do not fully acknowledge?

This is the script suggested for your use in the final task before starting to implement the chosen business system:

GIFTS SCRIPT

Setting

Company-wide or departmental meeting following the Commitment Conversation

Facilitator

CEO, senior leader, or trained facilitator

Welcome and Introduction

Welcome, everyone, to our final conversation in this series as we prepare to fully implement our business model. We're here to recognize and celebrate the gifts each of us brings to this process and to our organization.

Setting the Context

The purpose of today's conversation is to acknowledge the unique strengths, talents, and contributions that each person brings to our community. As we embark on this implementation journey, it's crucial to recognize that our collective gifts are what will make this process successful and meaningful.

Remember, gifts aren't just about skills or expertise. They're about the unique perspectives, experiences, and qualities that make each of us valuable to our community.

Recap of the Journey

Before we dive into today's topic, let's briefly recap our journey:

1. We invited everyone to be part of shaping our future with our business model.
2. We explored the exciting possibilities this business model could create.
3. We discussed how each of us can take ownership of this process.
4. We voiced our doubts and concerns, strengthening our approach.
5. We made specific commitments to action.

Now, we're here to recognize the gifts that will make all of this possible.

Framing Questions

[Put these questions on prepared flip chart or single handout page beforehand.]

As we prepare to discuss our gifts, let's consider these key questions:

1. What unique strengths or talents do you bring to our organization and this implementation process?
2. How has our community (our organization) helped you discover or develop your gifts?
3. What gifts have you recognized in your colleagues that you'd like to acknowledge?
4. How can your unique gifts contribute to the successful implementation of our business model?
5. What gifts do you see in our organization that will support this process?

Personal Reflection

Let's start with some individual reflection. Please take a few minutes to consider these questions and jot down your thoughts.
  [Allow 10 minutes for personal reflection.]

Paired Appreciations

Now, let's pair up with someone we don't often work with directly. Take turns sharing one gift you see in your partner and how you think that gift will contribute to our business model implementation. Remember, gifts can be qualities like empathy, attention to detail, creative thinking, or the ability to build consensus.
  [Allow 10 minutes for paired discussions.]

Small Group Sharing

Let's form small groups of four or five people. In your groups, please share:

1. a gift you bring to this process,
2. a gift you've recognized in someone else in the organization, and
3. how you think these gifts will support our business model implementation.

[Allow 20 minutes for small group discussions.]

Large Group Sharing

Thank you for those thoughtful discussions. Now, let's share some of the gifts we've recognized with the larger group. Who would like to share a gift they've recognized in someone else?
  [Facilitate group sharing, capturing key gifts on a whiteboard or shared screen.]

Exploring Gift Themes

Looking at the gifts shared, I'm noticing some powerful themes. Let's explore how these gifts align with key aspects of the business model: [examples only for illustrative purposes]

1. Innovative Thinking
   - How do our innovative thinkers support the creation and communication of our long-term goals?
   - How can we nurture this gift to keep our organization forward-thinking?
2. Operational Excellence
   - How do those gifted in operations help us in implementing the practical aspects of business model?
   - How can we leverage this gift to streamline our processes?
3. Relationship Building
   - How do our relationship builders help in creating the strong teams necessary for the business model?
   - How can we use this gift to enhance our meeting rhythms and communication?
4. Analytical Skills
   - How do our analytical thinkers support the data-driven aspects of this business model?
   - How can we use this gift to improve our scorecards and metrics?
5. Adaptability and Resilience
   - How do those gifted with adaptability help us navigate the changes that come with implementing business model?
   - How can we nurture this gift to create a more agile organization?

Connecting Gifts to the Business Model Components

Let's consider how our collective gifts align with key components of business model:

1. How do our gifts support creating and communicating a sharp vision?
2. How do our gifts contribute to getting the right people in the right seats?
3. How do our gifts help in leveraging data for better decision-making?
4. How do our gifts support effective problem-solving?
5. How do our gifts contribute to defining and improving our core processes?
6. How do our gifts help create discipline and accountability?

Organizational Gifts

[Put these questions on prepared flip chart or single handout page beforehand.]

Now, let's zoom out and consider the gifts of our organization as a whole:

1. What unique strengths does our organization possess?
2. How have these organizational gifts contributed to our success so far?
3. How can we leverage these organizational gifts in implementing the business model?

[Facilitate a brief discussion on organizational gifts.]

Nurturing and Leveraging Our Gifts

[Put both of these sets of questions on prepared flip chart or single handout page beforehand.]

As we recognize these gifts, let's discuss how we can nurture and leverage them:

1. How can we create opportunities for people to use their gifts more fully in their roles?

2. How can we foster a culture that continually recognizes and appreciates these gifts?
3. How can we ensure our implementation of the business model allows these gifts to flourish?

Personal Commitments to Gifting

To conclude, I'd like each of you to consider:

1. How will you more fully bring your gifts to our business model implementation?
2. How will you help create space for others to shine with their gifts?

Please take a moment to write down your reflections.
[Allow a few minutes for writing, then invite volunteers to share.]

Closing and Next Steps

Thank you all for your openness and generosity in recognizing and sharing your gifts. The array of talents, perspectives, and strengths we've discussed today gives me immense confidence in our ability to successfully implement the business model and achieve our vision.

Remember, recognizing gifts is not a one-time event. As we move forward with our implementation, let's continue to acknowledge and appreciate the unique contributions each person brings to our community.

As we conclude this series of conversations, we're now ready to fully embark on our business model journey. We do so with a shared vision, a sense of ownership, an understanding of our challenges, clear commitments, and a deep appreciation for our collective gifts.

Thank you for your engagement throughout this process. I'm excited to see how we'll use our gifts to create something extraordinary together.

Next Steps

- Create a "Gift Map" showcasing the diverse talents in the organization.
- Incorporate recognition of gifts into regular business model meetings.
- Begin the formal implementation of business model, leveraging the insights from all six conversations.
- Establish a regular "Gifts Check-In" as part of your business model ritual.
- Provide opportunities for employees to further develop and apply their unique gifts.
- Celebrate early wins in the implementation process, highlighting how different gifts contributed to the success.

Figure 25—The Gifts Script

When you have the courage to reach out for support from people who care, you'll remember that stress and suffering are normal parts of our human experience. The support you receive will make it easier for you to meet your goals. In turn, this will build momentum, which helps you reach out again, increasing your odds of success even more. The cycle carries forward.

Either of these two business models are simply a set of tools. Your people must own the use of the tool in a community of others. It cannot be decreed. It cannot effectively be implemented by fiat. Use the opportunity to truly build a transformed, community-enhanced organization.

Chapter Summary

This chapter outlined six essential leadership tasks for building organizational community and implementing business models effectively. It provided detailed scripts for each task: gathering allies, exploring possibilities, creating ownership, providing space for dissent, facilitating commitment, and recognizing gifts. Each script offered structured guidance for facilitating conversations that transform workplace culture from traditional hierarchical structures to authentic, engaged communities. The focus was on creating genuine dialogue, building trust, and fostering collective ownership rather than imposing change through top-down mandates. The chapter emphasized that successful implementation depends on leaders' ability to create spaces for authentic conversation, welcome diverse perspectives, and recognize each person's unique contributions to the organization's success.

Key Chapter Takeaways

1. Building community requires structured conversations before implementing business models.
2. True engagement comes from sequential tasks: Invitation, possibilities, ownership, dissent, commitment, gifts.
3. Leaders must create safe spaces for authentic dialogue, including dissent.
4. Truth-telling and vulnerability from leadership enables organizational transformation.
5. Implementation success depends on community building rather than command-and-control.

Suggested Homework

1. Map your organization using the Trust/Agreement Matrix to identify allies and potential resistance.
2. Draft your invitation script, personalizing the template to address your organization's specific context.

⚡⚡⚡⚡

CHAPTER 15

The Keys to Success

Summary: This chapter outlines four fundamental leadership efforts essential for successful business model implementation: Changing leadership style and language to focus on powerful questions rather than answers; embracing true accountability rather than merely "holding" people accountable; establishing clear sources of truth; and creating organizational rituals that institutionalize change. It emphasizes that while tools can create improvement, lasting transformation requires leaders to move beyond basic implementation to build organizational community, comparing this approach to the Japanese concept of *shokunin*—craftsmanship that serves the greater good.

How to Successfully Implement

The four hidden benefits of both business models were presented in Chapter 10: Embracing Transformation.

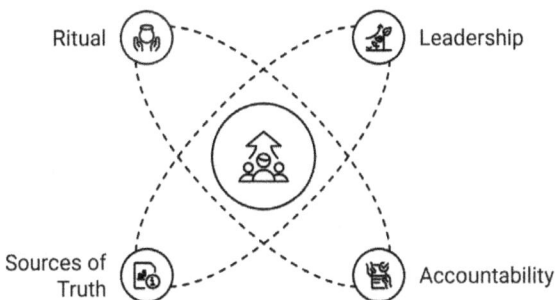

Figure 26—Hidden Benefits

Most of the benefits that result from implementation are not about using the tools; the true, lasting benefits accrue because the business model tools provide you with a way to change your approach to leading your firm.

Earlier, the analogy of a hammer as a tool was used. Let's build on that here. Simply put, a hammer can be used to tear something apart or to build something. In building something, the same hammer can be used by a novice or a craftsman, and each will get different results from the same tool. When you move from simply using a tool (e.g., by installing either system) to being a craftsperson, the benefits can include something much larger, benefits that serve a greater community.

Shokunin means "artisan" or "craftsman" in Japanese, but it embeds a larger context. Toshio Odate states that beyond technical abilities, *shokunin* "implies an attitude and social consciousness . . . a social obligation to work his best for the general welfare of the people . . . this obligation is both material and spiritual."[45]

What is being suggested here is that you, as owner/CEO of your organization, can also use the tools (e.g., either model) to merely put them to use or to use them to go beyond improving efficiency to building a better organization, your community.

The challenge there is to rise above the thought that by merely implementing the tools (by yourself or using an outsider), you'll get all you wish for. Don't get me wrong. Based on my own experience, you will make improvements, perhaps even remarkable improvements. You will receive some benefits through increased efficiency and consistency. The new tools will work at some level for you and will produce some results.

But do you really purposefully change the culture or merely add these tools to the existing culture, hoping for change?

Consider, though, the *shokunin* who creates something for the general welfare of the people. What if, by starting the implementation in a unique way, a more inclusive way, you begin to build a different culture and further extend the benefits?

Implementing in a unique way starts also with your behavior and language, the first of four fundamental leadership efforts.

---

45. Toshio Odate, *Japanese Woodworking Tools: Their Tradition, Spirit and Use* (Taunton Press, 1984), viii.

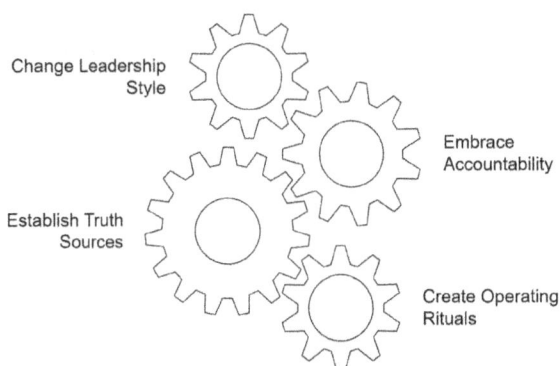

Figure 27—Four Fundamental Leadership Efforts

While these four efforts are presented sequentially, the fundamental leadership efforts are undertaken concurrently.

I.   **During implementation, the *first fundamental leadership effort* is to change leadership style and language.**

Demonstrating leadership is about creating the culture you want, and that typically requires a shift and growth. First, a shift in perspective; you are not most effective when telling people what and when to do something. **Shift the perspective from *answering* questions to *asking* questions.** Ask tough questions embedded with accountability. Ask people to join you in growing both as a person and as an employee. Use the scripts from the previous chapter.

The power is in the questions you ask; questions are more transforming than answers. Without accountability woven into dialogue, relationships may form, but the fundamental structure and dynamics of the community remain unchanged.

Most leaders know how to ask questions but do not consider how far their questions can go. Yet, questions alone are insufficient. **Context matters,** the organization matters, the people matter, the "social structure" of how people are interdependent matters. "Powerful questions are those that, in the answering, evoke a choice for accountability and commitment."[46] But not every question has the power to transform. Here are some examples of questions that have hidden agendas, have little power (but a lot of force), and perhaps cause the

---

46. Block, *Community*, 101–103.

very fragmentation we are trying to avoid. These questions include (and face it, you have either said or heard these questions before), but are not limited to:

- How can we create conditions where accountability naturally emerges?
- What structures enable people to choose and embrace accountability?
- How might we develop a shared vision that resonates deeply with everyone?
- What resources, both financial and non-financial, will fuel this transformation?
- Which organizations have successfully navigated similar challenges, and what principles can we learn from their journey?
- How do we find and develop better leaders?

These are **not** powerful questions; in fact, they lean toward manipulation. Reread the six questions above. In isolation, it is easy to see why those questions can be manipulative; they are focused externally, towards someone else, as if pointing a finger at them. Yet, we ask those questions regularly. Further, most of our questions have embedded answers or implied blame. **These are all** *designed to change other people* **and encourage a response to create a known, predicable future based on the past**, to take uncertainty out of the future and direct the organization backwards, prolonging the past into the future. That's precisely what we are working to avoid.

On the other hand, questions with power engage your staff in a unique way, inviting them to create a new future possibility. "Powerful questions cause you to become an actor as soon as you answer them."[47] They open the conversation, and the resulting dialogue becomes constructive.

- What mistakes have we as a team made?
- What part of our dissatisfaction is ours to own?
- What is our contribution to the very thing we are complaining about?
- How valuable do we plan for this effort to be?

Again, reread this second set of questions, especially in comparison with the previous set. These tend to be inwardly focused and within your control.[48]

---

47. Block, *Community*, 106.
48. See Appendix 3: It's the Questions You Ask.

If you are answering questions, you are managing, e.g., managing things, tasks, deadlines, etc. If you are asking questions, you are becoming a leader.

2. **During implementation, the** *second fundamental leadership effort* **is to embrace accountability.**

Accountability is not about "holding" someone accountable. The desire to be accountable is within most people, and it is your role, as leader, to set them up to succeed and to be accountable for their behavior and their actions. You and your leadership team set (and reset) the expectations; your people will be or will not be accountable. You then own the consequences, both positive (e.g., more roles and promotion) and negative (poor performance evaluation and, perhaps, an exit from the organization).[49]

Again, it starts and ends with you.

> It is easy to fool yourself. It is more difficult to fool the people you work for. It is still more difficult to fool the people you work with. And it is almost impossible to fool the people who work under your direction.
> —Henry Bates Thayer

As a leader you must not only exemplify the personal accountability you expect in others, but you must also be the one asking others for their accountability, not merely the "completion" of the effort (e.g., done/not done). This is not a nuance. When accountability exists, tasks get done without undue pressure on the task itself. Your role in embracing accountability is about the other individual "owning" the accountability, the task is simply the carrier of personal accountability.

For example, when a team member misses a self-selected deadline (such as a task or to-do), you must be there to help them identify where they went wrong (e.g., overcommitment, unrealistic timeframe, etc.) and ask them to put together a plan to prevent from happening again. For example, in a case of underperformance, when tempted to say, "Why didn't you do this?" (focusing on the task) ask instead, "What could you have done differently to ensure you got it done in time?" (focusing on accountability).

---

49. See Chapter 17, EAC diagram.

Remember, accountability is not punishment; it is meant to be an opportunity for learning and growth.

Accountability doesn't just happen; you create it. Using the tools of either business model and the questions of leadership will help you produce a fully accountable organization.

3. **During the implementation, the** *third fundamental leadership effort* **is to establish and embed sources of truth.**

Organizations are fraught with half-truths, untruths, "alternative facts," misleading information, disinformation, lies, and so forth. It all simply serves to hinder performance. It doesn't have to be this way.

If we maintain the same conversations, we will be gaining the same results, committees, functions, silos, etc., all work against themselves as vigorously as they try to move forward. Egos will be in the way. Guarding turf is both energy extractive and counterproductive. CYA is unfortunately too pervasive.

Change the nature of the conversations. As the leader, you are the "architect" providing a framework for the changing conversations. For the future to be different from the past,[50] you must (1) set the standard for the behaviors you expect, and (2) set the context for the future.

You are the business model, the guide of your organization that all will follow and emulate. If you don't speak the truth or act the truth, you won't get it from your people.

Use the sources of truth to create a shift in thinking and behaving.

4. **During implementation, the** *fourth fundamental leadership effort* **is to create rituals, an operating rhythm, to enhance and institutionalize change.**

Rituals form the operating rhythm and are crucially important to the success you have with transformation. A ritual is simply a repeated behavior (such as holiday season dinners with the family or regular participation at a house of faith) that becomes part of one's life. Rituals vary greatly, but we engage in rituals with the belief that we will achieve known outcomes. Some research

---

50. Which isn't working for you; remember those frustrations from Chapter 3.

has shown that "performing rituals with the intention of producing certain results appears to be sufficient for that result to come true."[51]

The best place for establishing an operating ritual is at the annual planning session, which should be more expansive than the traditional strategic annual planning process. Start by exploring high-level company plans (ten years or more) as your primary targets/goals. Look for big, ambitious goals (BHAGs) and consider different possibilities that come from years of execution. Review the long-term goals/targets and redo the near-term plan (e.g., the next several years), then review the past year/current year financial and other metrics.

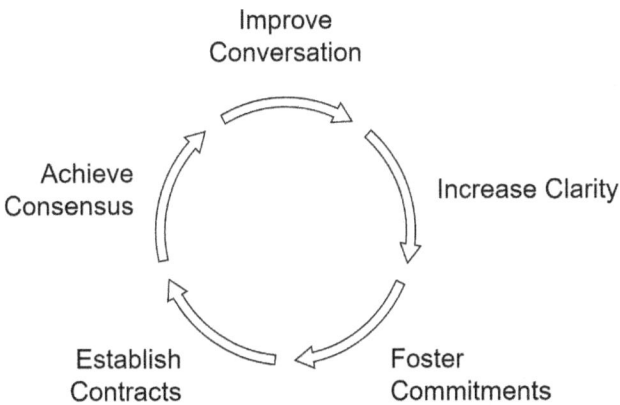

Figure 28—Elements of Effective Communication

By you and your leadership team actively exploring possibilities, discussing them, and planning accordingly, this process results in the Five Cs:

- Improved **Conversation** among your people →
- More **Clarity** as to what is to happen, bringing →
- Personal **Commitments**, made by speaking out, which create →
- Verbal **Contracts**, among all, finally building →
- Team **Consensus**

The key to your success certainly lies in creating a community that uses the

<hr>

51. Francesca Gino and Michael I. Norton, "Why Rituals Work," Scientific American, May 14, 2013. https://www.scientificamerican.com/article/why-rituals-work/.

tools, not from an implementation point of view, but from the perspective of building the culture you desire: a community.

Chapter Summary

The chapter outlines four fundamental leadership efforts crucial for successful business model implementation: Changing leadership style and language (emphasizing powerful questions over answers), embracing accountability (focusing on personal ownership rather than task completion), establishing sources of truth (to combat misinformation and promote transparency), and creating operational rituals (to institutionalize change). It emphasizes that while business models provide useful tools, the true benefits come from how leaders use these tools to transform organizational culture. The chapter stresses that implementation success depends on leaders taking a craftsperson's approach (*shokunin*), not just using tools mechanically, but applying them thoughtfully to build better organizations and serve the broader community.

Key Chapter Takeaways

1. Leadership requires shifting from giving answers to asking powerful questions.
2. True accountability emerges from ownership, not from being "held accountable."
3. Sources of truth combat organizational half-truths and misinformation.
4. Rituals create operating rhythm that institutionalizes change.
5. Implementation success depends on craftsmanship mindset (*shokunin*) over tool usage.

Suggested Homework

1. Audit your current questions and document which are externally focused (manipulation) versus internally focused (transformation).
2. Map your organization's current rituals and identify gaps in operating rhythm.

⚡⚡⚡⚡

CHAPTER 16

A Deeper Dive into the Benefits

Summary: This chapter dives deep into how leadership and accountability manifest in community-enhanced organizations. It emphasizes that effective leadership is not mysterious but practicable, centered on creating other leaders and asking powerful questions rather than providing answers. The chapter redefines accountability, moving beyond the concept of "holding people accountable" to creating environments where accountability emerges naturally through clear expectations, commitment, and consequences. It introduces a structured operating rhythm at three speeds (annual, quarterly, weekly/daily) supported by sources of truth and rituals, noting that these practices typically require only four to six percent of your annual time but yield significant returns. The chapter concludes with practical strategies for igniting accountability, emphasizing the importance of shifting focus from internal problem-solving to external opportunities, and celebrating progress over success.

What Can Be Done Differently?

In this chapter we will further dive into the specific four benefits that accrue to you and your organization through an implementation that embraces your employees, not just leadership.

To restate: The four main benefits inherent in the business models, none of which are specifically addressed in either model, are depicted:

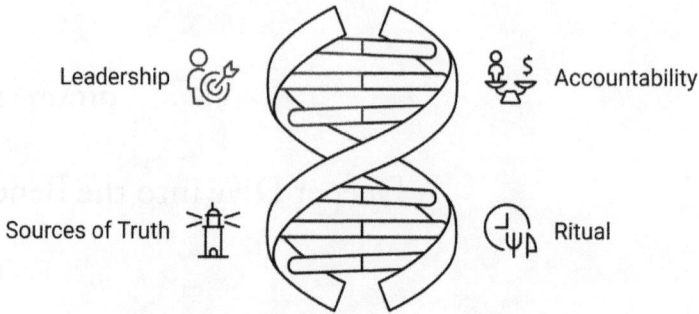

Figure 29—Four Hidden Benefits

IMPLEMENTATION GUIDANCE

Leadership

Leadership is neither difficult, ethereal, nor out of reach, but it is simply practicable. Let's summarize some of the points made earlier on leadership for your reference.

In organizations today, leadership is too important and too significant to be left to one person. Create a culture where, as the leader, you create leaders who create leaders. Consider the strength and resiliency of an organization where everyone is a leader. No one person should have the "exclusive capacity to lead the organization."[52]

Your journey as a leader begins with self-development, the most challenging aspect of leadership growth. To become the leader others will follow, focus on setting a clear direction through purposeful action, embodying the qualities you admire in others, maintaining a commitment to continuous learning, and cultivating an inspiring vision that resonates with your community.

"Leading yourself is the most difficult thing that you do every day and yet it is the only thing that will help you achieve your goals and then understand how to help others to do that for themselves."[53] Leaders creating leaders who create leaders.

Leaders ask great questions. A weakness I often see in people in executive

---

52. Banks, LinkedIn.
53. Randy Hall, "Self-Leadership—The Toughest Kind," 4thGearConsulting.com. 2009.

positions is their belief that their job is to supply all the answers. They tend to dominate discussions ("the loudest voice in the room") and always want to have the last word. *The problem is that no matter how smart and capable those people are, they will always be limited by their own thinking and life experiences.* Worse yet, they create an environment where everyone looks to them for the answers. Leaders have trained the other people that they don't have to think, they simply ask the leader. Not only does this practice hinder growth and development, but it also leads directly to mediocre effort, commitment, and results, while you lose the opportunity to leverage your people.

Leadership is not about "telling," nor is it about managing things or tasks. Your leadership is directly proportional to your ability to ask the tough questions, the questions others won't ask. "What mistakes have we as a team made?" Ask with the intent to just identify and write down the issue. "What part of our dissatisfaction (say, for results) is ours to own?" Not to blame, but to identify issues. If two of your leadership team members are raising performance concerns with each other, ask either one, "What is your contribution to the very thing you are complaining about?" That always raises eyes that were averted and calls the question.

Leadership is about the questions you ask, not the answers you give.

Two traits I see in exceptional leaders are (1) an above average ability to listen to what someone has to say and (2) an aptitude for asking great follow-up questions. The best leaders intuitively know that success lies in identifying and asking the right questions, rather than jumping to quick conclusions based on personal hunches or faulty assumptions. You never lead a high-performing organization by using "seat of the pants" or "gut level" decision-making.

Asking good questions does not come easily to everyone. I encourage you to make a concerted effort to ask better questions.[54] Don't take intellectual shortcuts or cover up, for the sake of your ego, a lack of knowledge with simple head-nodding and acquiescence. Don't let your pride get in the way of fully understanding what you need to know to be successful.

---

54. I have often asked leaders I coach to start a list of ten questions and learn to use them. Add to the list. There are many other great questions in this book to use, with some reproduced in Appendix 3.

Leadership begins with a shift in mindset. By recognizing the importance of community-enhanced leadership and its link to long-term success, leaders can create a culture that supports and encourages creativity. Give a gift of encouraging managers to see beyond the immediate fires and embrace the value of observing (scanning) opportunities which will be instrumental in overcoming this challenge and developing future leaders.

Business owners/CEOs must broaden their perspective when identifying leadership for projects. By recognizing the gifts of individuals who proactively identify potential challenges and propose innovative solutions, organizations can nurture a culture of forward-thinking and learning. Rewarding proactive behavior is key to breaking the cycle of firefighting; aka, tyranny of the urgent.

Accountability is not accidental nor is it automatic. Everyone in the organization "owns" accountability. Accountability is woven throughout the tools of either business model, as we saw in Chapter 4. For example, accountability for the marketing team is to use the strategy as defined by leadership in their implementation efforts. Accountability is each member of your team completing the key metrics. Accountability is for attainment of high priority activities.

The vernacular of business gets us into a murky situation. We have all been trained to use the phrase, "hold accountable" as in, "Go hold that person accountable." Anyone have teenagers? You understand.

"Fewer words in corporate vernacular induce a tighter wince than 'accountability,'" according to Ron Carucci, and for good reason. Eighty-two percent of managers "acknowledge they have 'limited to no' ability to hold others accountable successfully."[55]

You simply cannot "hold" someone accountable; **when you are faced with that decision/discussion, the other person is already not accountable** (or why have the conversation anyway?).

Dwight Mihalicz, CMC, in his blog on high performance cultures, writes:

Accountability isn't the easiest term to grasp, and there's often a tendency to confuse it with responsibility. Here's how the two are differ-

---

55. Ron Carucci, "How to Actually Encourage Employee Accountability," Harvard Business Review, November 23, 2020. https://hbr.org/2020/11/how-to-actually-encourage-employee-accountability.

ent. With accountability, someone is held to account and the action must result. By contrast, responsibility is more values driven, coming from within. In other words, one who is accountable must complete something. But one who feels responsible genuinely believes that what they need to do is important. To be clear, responsibility is essential in organizations. Workers should feel responsible for doing excellent work and completing tasks. Nevertheless, there is a clear difference between responsibility and accountability. In organizational account-ability, we have been able to measure the difference between *Clarity of Accountability* as delegated by a manager, and *Felt Accountability* as taken on by the individual.[56]

The employee will, hopefully, feel accountable. As a leader, though, you "own" the setting (and resetting) of expectations, the *clarity of accountability*. Be clear and concise and listen for understanding and commitment. Here is a simple "formula":

Expectations	Accountability	Consequences
Setting standards and goals	Taking responsibility for actions	Outcomes resulting from actions

Figure 30—EAC: Accountability

Expectations yield **Accountability**, which yields **Consequences** (plus or minus).

---

56. Dwight Mihalicz, "Building High-Performance Cultures with the Effective Point of Accountability," Effective Managers, October 8, 2024. https://effectivemanagers.com /dwight-mihalicz/building-high-performance-cultures-with-the-effective-point-of-acco untability/.

Your role as a leader is to set, and reset, the *clarity* of expectations. If you do a respectable job of setting (and resetting) expectations, that person will show up as accountable or not. You then "own" the consequences, both positive and negative. **Personal accountability is being willing to answer for the outcome resulting from your choices, behaviors, and actions.**[57]

Accountability is the glue that ties commitment to results assisted by the sources of truth and rituals. It is the conversations we have that create accountability.

> It is easy to dodge responsibilities, but you cannot dodge the results of your dodging. —Sir Josiah Stamp, Kingston Daily Freeman, Kingston, NY, January 3, 1928.

Accountability feels like an attack when you're not ready to acknowledge how your behaviors harm others. Yet, accountability is simply being reliable. Ask yourself periodically, "Can people count on me to do what I say I'll do, as I said I would do it?"

Humans want to be accountable; Unfortunately, and especially in the workplace, they do not know the results for what they are accountable. Asking someone to be accountable is an act of generosity and compassion but can be perceived as being uncomfortable.

Author and educator bell hooks famously said, "How do we hold people accountable . . . yet at the same time remain in touch with their humanity enough to believe in their capacity to be transformed?"[58] This is, in essence, one core predicate for effective leadership and for building community.

Two suggestions to foster accountability:

- Don't ask "Why?" or "Why not?" when someone surprises you or disappoints you with non-performance; ask who, what, when, where,

---

57. Mark Samuel, "8 Behaviors that Help Develop Personal Accountability," B State, March 3, 2021. https://bstate.com/2021/03/03/behaviors-that-help-develop-personal-accountability/.

58. Melvin McLeod, "There's No Place to Go but Up: bell hooks and Maya Angelou in conversation," Lion's Roar, January 1, 1998. https://www.lionsroar.com/theres-no-place-to-go-but-up/.

and how questions instead. It is difficult to challenge the answer from a "Why" question.

- Don't accept "I'll try" or "I'll give it my best." Say "Of course you will try, that's why I hired you. Now what will you do and when?"

As we've seen earlier, each business model provides several sources of truth to measure behavior and performance, The measurement is very binary; for example, something is done or it is not done. The usefulness of these business models, therefore, is in:

- creating a consistent methodology for recording, tracking, and prioritizing efforts (the sources of truth),
- creating an environment (e.g., a ritual) where no surprises are allowed,
- creating a culture where you stop giving and accepting excuses, and
- creating and tracking the facts of progress, not opinions.

All this works to increase accountability, although not automatically. You must be actively involved.

Also consider how each business model provides the tools to foster a different level of conversation about accountability:

- The community-enhanced model identifies who is *accountable* to whom, not *reports* to whom.
- The tools identify the key roles (tied to results) in each organization/accountability box, not responsibilities, skills, or knowledge.
- The tools provide clarity regarding roles and help you remove overlaps or gaps.

In Chapter 4, we addressed the similarities and differences of accountability as evidence in each business model. From that analysis, a synthesized view of accountability can be derived.

Accountability is a fundamental organizational principle that creates clarity, drives performance, and enables growth by:

- clearly defining and communicating roles and expectations for individuals, functions, and processes throughout the organization;

- establishing measurable objectives and key performance indicators at all levels, from individual tasks to overarching strategic goals;
- implementing regular rituals of review and communication to track progress, address issues, and maintain alignment;
- fostering a culture where individuals take ownership of their commitments and outcomes, both in terms of results and behaviors;
- linking individual and team performance to the organization's broader strategic objectives and financial health;
- providing mechanisms for feedback, coaching, and continuous improvement to support ongoing development and success;
- extending beyond internal operations to encompass key external relationships and stakeholder management; and
- balancing a focus on short-term execution with long-term strategic alignment and growth.

Accountability is not difficult but is also practicable.

To repeat, neither of the two business models defines accountability; yet both create the tools for you to develop accountability in all.

The critical issue of accountability among managers cannot be understated. Remember that research has shown that a staggering 82 percent of managers feel they aren't good at leading people and therefore lack the necessary skills and mindset to effectively uphold accountability in their teams.[59] This creates a pressing problem within organizations, where the consequences of neglecting accountabilities can burden team members and hinder overall success.

Extensive experimental studies have consistently unveiled the dire consequences that arise when some team members neglect their responsibilities and impose a burden on their colleagues.[60] These studies have demonstrated a distressing reality that free-riders and cheaters often manage to thrive within a group, while hard-working contributors are left to bear the brunt of addi-

---

59. Randall J. Beck and Jim Harter, "Why Great Managers Are So Rare," Gallup. 2016. https://www.gallup.com/workplace/231593/why-great-managers-rare.aspx.

60. Darren Overfield and Rob Kaiser, "One Out of Every Two Managers is Terrible at Accountability," Harvard Business Review, November 8, 2012. https://hbr.org/2012/11/one-out-of-every-two-managers-is-terrible-at-accountability.

tional workload. These individuals shamelessly enjoy the benefits of group membership without making any personal sacrifices.

However, the paradigm shifts dramatically when groups consist of community-enhanced contributors who are committed to the success of the team. It should come as no surprise that such groups outperform those plagued by cheating free riders. **What may be astounding, though, is the discovery that enforcing consequences for the lack of accountability leads to even better group performance**. The presence of consequences ensures that everyone pulls their weight and contributes to collective success.

The importance of tackling accountability cannot be stressed enough. By understanding the implications and complexities of this issue, organizations can work toward creating an environment that fosters accountable behavior while ultimately driving group performance.

Appropriate use of the tools of either business model will help you unlock the power of accountability. Here are a few strategies to improve accountability:

- You stand for what you tolerate. Lead by example.
- Clarity is a foundational element of accountability. Clearly define the expectations, objective(s), and key results/outcomes.
- Develop a culture of open communication, where each employee feels comfortable in expressing their concerns and providing suggestions.
- Provide timely and specific feedback. More than "job well-done," be specific in your description and praise.
- Recognize that people prefer the problem they have to the solution they don't know. Embrace a culture of possibilities.

We have our stories. We created them and we believe them, but don't let stories undermine the actions required to improve accountability.

Here are some questions that may help you start with raising accountability:

- In what ways are your folks avoiding being accountable?
- In what ways do we support their behavior or avoid addressing it?
- What are the symptoms that someone is not going to be accountable?
- Are there any "early warning" signals?
- What environment must be created to foster accountability?

Accountability Is . . . Simply . . . Caring for the Group

And this is the best place to start: Own your own accountability, get it out there. Once you have taken the courageous step of acknowledging your own lack of accountability, it is important to communicate your intent to change and actively seek support from those around you. Engaging your colleagues, team members, and superiors in your accountability journey not only demonstrates your commitment but also creates a network of individuals who can provide guidance and ask you to be accountable.

Transitioning from a culture defined by a lack of accountability to a community-enhanced culture where its ownership is celebrated can be perceived as a daunting task. However, embracing accountability is not as painful as it may seem. In fact, we often underestimate the eagerness of people to be accountable. By opening up about our desire to improve, we create an environment where others are motivated to do the same.

Sources of Truth are also found throughout the tools: The goals, key results, Rocks, To-Dos, etc. The items on most of the tools become "truth" around which behaviors, and therefore accountability, is expected.

Sources of truth allow for success to be defined in clear, quantifiable, succinct ways. **Don't allow squishy descriptions, especially for quarterly goals/key results and To-Dos.** They must be succinct and truth based.

Both business models provide some very good, tested tools which, when used appropriately, provide information which becomes sources of truth.

Rituals define the consistent pattern to review that source of truth and build accountability. The ritual is what creates accountability.[61] Whether in daily, weekly, quarterly, or annual meetings, all will know that they will review their progress for the other members of their team(s) and they will also know they will be asked to be accountable by their peers.

Set up an operating rhythm, with three speeds, each with two parts.

Speeds:
  ◦ Annual
  ◦ Quarterly
  ◦ Weekly/Daily

---

61. Kevin Fishner, First Round.

Fundamental Dimensions:
- Source of truth
- Ritual

The purpose of this operational rhythm isn't to dogmatically stick to goals set at the beginning of the year; it's to create a new future.

	Weekly Meetings	Quarterly Meetings	Annual Meeting
The Truth	Weekly reporting	Key Results, Rocks	Goals, Objectives
The Rituals	Daily or Weekly Team Meeting	Quarterly Team Meetings and Quarterly State of the Company	Goals, Objectives
	Meetings	Business Reviews	Annual Planning Summit
	Daily or 90+/- minutes weekly	One-day/quarter	Two–three days Annual

Figure 31—Sources of Truth and Rituals

It's hard to change annual performance week-to-week or even quarter-to-quarter. A change (or renewal) happens or doesn't happen based on the past year of experience with your existing products or services, and it is your review of the scorecard or key numbers that will help you identify the trends. We need to track leading indicators that create a robust growth rate. For every lagging indicator (e.g., revenue), I recommend two leading indicators that you review on a weekly basis, your source of truth.

And if one leading indicator acts up and it is **not** tied directly to goal, it isn't necessary to act on it but be aware and track and do not act immediately.

This operating rhythm (e.g., ritual) also is a time management tool. It saves you two to three times the amount of time you invest. There's an annual ritual (two or three days), focused on new pictures and plans with annual goals. There's a quarterly meeting (one day, four times per year) focused on short-term goals. And there is a weekly meeting (for 1½ hours per week) or a daily meeting (about 10 minutes). In all three, it's the established and maintained ritual that is important. It is equivalent to approximately four to six percent of your annual time (assuming only 2,000 work hours/year). **Four to six percent of your annual time working *on* your business, not *in* your business.** It is certainly worth that small percentage of your time to make an investment in the future, isn't it?

Don't lock your annual goals in after the first quarter, as others have suggested. Use each quarterly meeting to do a thorough analysis of the changes in both your internal and external environments and if something critical has changed, either rewrite or replace the affected goal with another. I have not ever seen the world wait for nine months simply because we were told to lock in your annual goals. Have you?

Use your business model and its tools to do the heavy lifting for sources of truth and ritual; they are designed with that in mind. "Oftentimes companies will focus on the source of truth and not the ritual and that's one of the biggest mistakes that you can make." [62] Focus on what matters.

Providing your best people with the best culture creates a better leader in you. They look to you for guidance and direction. Show them how, through your behavior and questions, they can create and sustain a culture of accountability backed up by a source of truth and ritual (including rituals of reflection and introspection).

Where to Start?

With you and your leadership:

- Ask questions; stop providing all the answers.
- Model the behavior(s) you want.
- As goes leadership, so does the rest of the organization.
- Change your everyday language:
  - Use E→A→C$^{+/-}$—Expectations, Accountability, and Consequences, both positive and negative.
  - Change "reports to" to "accountable to."

---

62. Fishner, First Round.

- ○ Change "responsible for" to "accountable for."
- ○ Change "responsibilities" to "accountabilities."
- ○ Change "job duties" to "accountabilities."

Three Ways to Ignite Accountability While Focused on a Sense of Urgency

Offer clarity to get them on track: Success is not solely reliant on your talented people. It demands a vision that not only guides but empowers your team to excel. As a leader, you communicate this vision, ensuring alignment and a sense of direction among your team members. Now is the time to reflect on community-enhanced strategies that have the potential to propel your business to new levels within the next six to 12 months.

You can inspire greatness and drive transformation. You and your team embrace this opportunity, seize the moment, and together conquer the challenges and pave the way for the future you desire.

Shift from internal to external line of sight: It is all too common for owners/CEOs to be consumed by the urgent demands and pressing challenges that arise. Indeed, it is crucial to address these internal issues promptly and effectively. However, there is a danger for those who become fixated on extinguishing these immediate fires and/or solving issues/problems.

The market is ever-changing and dynamic, constantly presenting opportunities that open and close in quick succession. Yet, without an outward possibility focus, these opportunities will simply not be observed.

Use your rituals to ensure an open forum for discussion of possible market moves, innovations, or changes. Emphasize the elements; don't emphasize issue processing or fixing problems, yet don't overlook problem resolution. By fostering a culture that encourages employees to proactively seek out and discuss market opportunities, you move your organization along a journey of growth and innovation. The time has come to break free from the constraints of an inward focus.

Don't emphasize continued success, emphasize continued progress: As the leader, it is crucial that you actively support the development of these ideas, providing a solid foundation for their implementation. Equally significant is the unwavering support you offer, regardless of the ultimate outcome, whether a triumphant success, a humbling failure, or even a necessary change in direction. Embracing this mindset of community-enhanced leadership will enable you to recognize that every attempt, regardless of its result, contributes invaluable knowledge to your organization.

It is through exploration that success is born. Embrace the unknown, learn from each endeavor, and perhaps transform every attempt into triumph. Trust in the power of embracing both successes and failures, as they are the building blocks to a better future.

It begins with you and your leadership team. **After all, you are what you accept!**

- It's okay to demonstrate and encourage vulnerability.
- A leadership team's struggles are in direct proportion to its secrets.
- It starts at top: Stop having all the answers and own the questions.
- Let the sources of truth do the "heavy lifting," but you develop and "own" accountabilities.
- If your fly is down, acknowledge it, apologize, and keep moving.

Building a culture of accountability is an ongoing journey. Stick with it. Build and enforce your organization's rituals that enable accountability.

Chapter Summary

The chapter focused on practical implementation of leadership principles, emphasizing four key areas: Leadership through asking questions rather than providing answers, embracing accountability as a cultural norm rather than a punitive measure, using sources of truth from business models to guide decisions, and establishing operational rhythms through rituals. It stressed that effective leadership starts with self-development and creating an environment where everyone can become a leader. The chapter provided specific guidance on fostering accountability through clear expectations, consequences, and regular review cycles, while emphasizing that success requires approximately four to six percent of annual time invested in working on the business rather than in it.

Key Chapter Takeaways

1. Leadership success comes from asking powerful questions rather than providing answers.

2. Accountability follows a formula: Expectations yield Accountability which yields Consequences.
3. Leaders must create other leaders who create leaders.
4. Operating rhythm requires three speeds (annual, quarterly, weekly/ daily) with consistent rituals.
5. Sources of truth must be clear, quantifiable metrics that eliminate excuses.

Suggested Homework:

1. Audit your current leadership language; document instances of giving answers versus asking questions.
2. Map your operating rhythm against the Sources of Truth and Rituals matrix (figure 31) to identify gaps in your review process.

⚡ ⚡ ⚡ ⚡

CHAPTER 17

What's In It for All?

Summary: While command-and-control methods may offer some positive results, they leave significant value unrealized. The community-enhanced approach transforms implementation from a top-down directive into a collaborative journey, inviting all levels of the organization to participate in adapting the business model to their context. This shift yields multiple benefits: deeper employee engagement, stronger accountability through voluntary ownership, safe spaces for constructive dissent, and recognition of individual gifts. For owners and CEOs, this approach offers ten key advantages, from improved employee engagement and cultural strength to enhanced decision-making and sustainable growth. The key insight is that success comes not from perfect execution of procedures but from creating conditions where authentic community connections can flourish.

WHAT'S IN IT FOR YOUR PEOPLE?

Typically, businesses implement one of these models through the command-and-control/fiat approach. "I've read the book, now we will do it." Often this top-down approach results in limited employee input and, likely, an amount of passive-aggressive resistance. Sometimes, the installation is done by an outside resource using a "cookbook," following specific steps with "canned" language (e.g., one size fits all) without regard to your specific or unique needs or wants. Both top-down and cookbook approaches offer some positive results, but tend to leave a lot on the table, unfulfilled. Consider building a community to help improve the results you get through either process.

The community-enhanced approach invites all levels of the organization to participate in the implementation process and creates forums for employees to contribute energy and ideas on how to adapt the business model to their context, fostering a sense of co-creation rather than imposition.

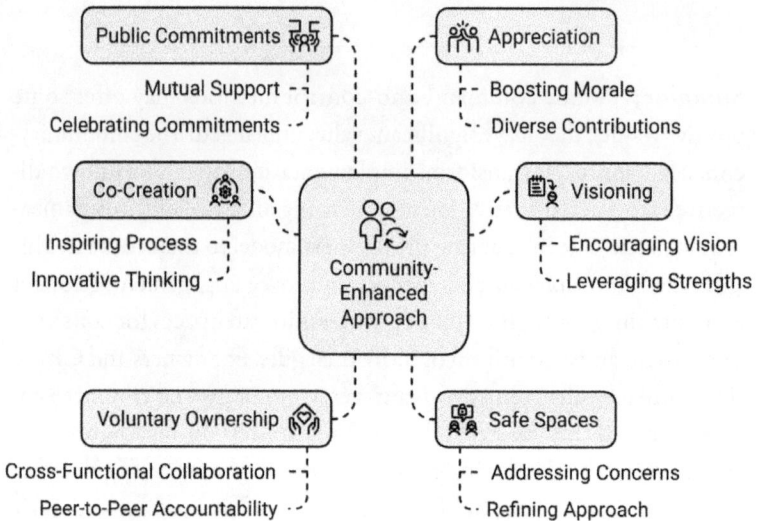

Figure 32—Community-Enhanced Benefits

The traditional implementation approach (top-down) also often focuses on solving current problems or issues. While problems may indeed require fixing, the community-enhanced approach frames the implementation as an opportunity to create a desired future, encouraging visioning sessions that go beyond the standard tools, and integrating possibility-oriented language into all communications.

Your added benefits will include:

- a more inspiring and motivating implementation process,
- increased innovative thinking and creativity, and
- a shift in focus from fixing weaknesses to leveraging strengths.

Traditional implementation assigns responsibilities based on roles. In contrast, the community-enhanced approach encourages voluntary ownership of aspects of the implementation, creates opportunities for cross-functional collaboration, increases energy, recognizes gifts, and implements peer-to-peer accountability.

Further benefits include:

- deeper sense of personal investment in the success of the business model,
- more organic adoption of new practices, and
- enhanced cross-departmental understanding and cooperation.

Traditional implementation may discourage or overlook expressions of doubt, while the proposed community-enhanced approach will create safe spaces for expressing concerns about the implementation, use dissent as a tool for refining and improving the approach, and acknowledge and address fears and reservations openly.

This results in additional benefits, such as:

- early identification of potential issues,
- increased trust and psychological safety, and
- more robust and resilient implementation.

Traditional implementation relies on assigning tasks to individuals and KPIs; a community-enhanced approach to implementation encourages public commitments to specific actions supporting the implementation, facilitates peer-to-peer promises of mutual support, and celebrates fulfilled commitments regularly.

This community-enhanced approach results in:

- stronger personal accountability,
- enhanced sense of community and mutual support, and
- more meaningful and intrinsically motivated actions.

Finally, while traditional implementation focuses primarily on outcomes and performance, a community-enhanced approach will regularly acknowledge unique contributions of team members to the implementation process, create opportunities for employees to apply their distinct energy, gifts, and talents, and integrate appreciation practices into regular meetings and reviews.

Community-enhanced approach to implementation results include:

- boosting morale and engagement,
- encouraging diverse contributions, and
- fostering a culture of appreciation and mutual respect.

Integrating community-building principles into the implementation of either business model can significantly enhance the effectiveness and sustainability of these business models. This community-enhanced approach addresses many of the familiar challenges in implementing new management business models, such as resistance to change, lack of engagement, and difficulties in sustaining new practices.

By focusing on invitation, possibility, ownership, dissent, commitment, and gifts, organizations can create a more inclusive, engaging, and ultimately more successful implementation process. This community-enhanced approach not only helps in better adoption of the chosen business model but also contributes to building a stronger, more cohesive organizational culture.

The key is to view the implementation not just as a process of adopting new tools and practices, but as an opportunity to strengthen the fabric of the organizational community. This approach can help bridge the gap between the structured, tool-based approaches of either business model and the human, relational aspects of organizational life.

WHAT'S IN IT FOR YOU, THE OWNER/CEO?

Why would you, a CEO/business owner of a small- to mid-sized privately held organization, implement either business model using community-based leadership?

The answer should be readily apparent by now. Let's restate the ten specific benefits to accrue to you:

Figure 33 – What's in it for the CEO?

1. **Employee Engagement:** Higher ownership and commitment across all levels, leading to smoother implementation with less resistance
2. **Cultural Strength:** Improved sense of belonging and relationships, resulting in better retention and talent attraction
3. **Problem-Solving:** Enhanced diverse perspectives and collaborative thinking, leading to better innovation and adaptability
4. **Leadership Development:** Broader leadership capabilities throughout organization, reducing dependency on top-down management
5. **Strategic Alignment:** Better shared understanding and commitment, improving execution while reducing miscommunication
6. **Sustainable Growth:** More adaptable and resilient structure, creating stronger foundation for scaling
7. **Decision Quality:** More informed choices through multi-level input, balancing data with human insights
8. **Customer Connection:** Stronger customer relationships leading to improved satisfaction and organic growth
9. **Leadership Growth:** Personal development for owner/CEO, resulting in reduced stress and higher satisfaction
10. **Market Distinction:** Unique combination of structure and community creating competitive advantage

Implementing business models with community-enhanced leadership creates more engaged, adaptable organizations, particularly benefiting small- to mid-sized companies by addressing both structural and human needs.

This approach accelerates implementation by involving employees in decision-making early, fostering open dialogue, and distributing accountability. The result is clearer understanding, collaborative problem-solving, and early issue identification.

Benefits include enhanced learning, stronger relationships, higher satisfaction, and improved resilience. The model develops leaders at all levels while creating a customer-centric workforce. Internal silos dissolve, improving operations and innovation.

The result is not just smoother adoption of practices, but lasting organizational benefits that support sustainable growth.

The community-enhanced method transforms the implementation from a top-down directive into a collaborative journey, fostering a sense of ownership and commitment among employees. This results in not just the adoption of new business practices, but the development of a stronger, more cohesive, community-enhanced organizational culture.

Shift from Responsibility-Focused Environment	Shift to Community-Focused Environment
Characteristics • Task-oriented approach • Emphasis on following instructions • Hierarchical decision-making • Individual role focus • Success measured by task completion	**Characteristics** • Proactive engagement • Outcome-oriented • Self-driven improvement • Collaborative problem-solving • Emphasis on learning and growth

Shift from Responsibility-Focused Environment	Shift to Community-Focused Environment
Advantages • Clear chain of command • Predictable workflows • Easy-to-measure individual performance • Clear job descriptions and roles • Efficient in stable, unchanging environments	**Advantages** • Higher levels of innovation and creativity • Increased employee engagement and satisfaction • More agile and adaptive organization • Stronger alignment between individual actions and organizational goals • Enhanced problem-solving capabilities

Figure 34—Traditional vs. Community Accountability

It's your choice, of course, but what if you simply implement the business models without considering using this approach to implementation? To summarize, here are the types of things you would consciously leave on the table:

- Depth of employee engagement
- Valuable insights and perspectives
- Organizational adaptability
- Cultural strengthening
- Leadership development opportunities
- Trust and open communication
- Cross-functional collaboration
- Implementation efficiency
- Sustained momentum
- Employee retention
- Customer-centric focus
- Innovation potential
- Holistic organizational growth
- Your own personal growth
- Your leadership reputation and legacy

Is it worth it to leave these profound benefits unfulfilled?

By not adopting a community-enhanced leadership business model for implementation, you risk more than just a less efficient adoption of a business model. You miss a significant opportunity to transform the implementation process into a catalyst for broader positive change within the organization.

These potential losses span from tactical (slower implementation, missed insights) to strategic (reduced adaptability, missed innovation opportunities). Perhaps most critically, you lose the chance to use the implementation to strengthen the organization's culture, develop its people, and build a more resilient, adaptive business. This is an error of commission, not omission.

While a traditional top-down approach might seem faster or more controllable in the short term, it often leads to superficial change and missed opportunities for deep, lasting organizational improvement. In today's dynamic business environment, these missed opportunities can have significant long-term impacts on the organization's competitiveness and success.

But, again, how you implement the business model you choose is your decision.

Woven together, the principles behind the community-enhanced leadership gradually transform the fabric of an organization. **They replace the language of deficits with the language of possibilities, the posture of defensiveness with the posture of openness, the energy of resistance with the energy of commitment.** They create a space where every person feels seen, heard, and valued, not for fitting a mold, but for bringing their authentic self to the table. **Leadership happens in the spaces between people**, in the quality of our conversations, in the authenticity of our commitments, and in the depth of our connections.

Build Connections

Establish strong
interpersonal links to
facilitate communication
and collaboration.

Strengthen Field

Enhance the overall
energy environment to
support sustained
leadership effectiveness.

Design Channels

Create pathways for
energy flow to ensure
efficient interaction.

Measure Quality

Assess the effectiveness
of energy interactions to
ensure they meet
leadership goals.

Manage Flow

Identify and address
obstacles to maintain a
smooth energy flow.

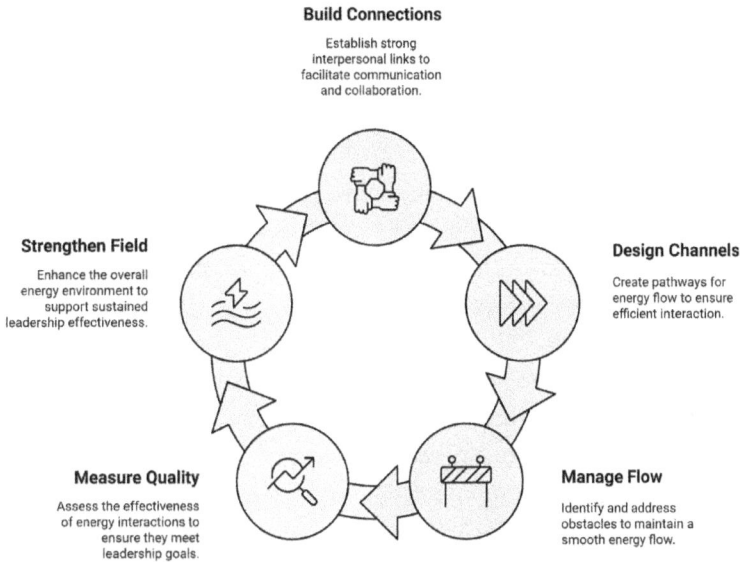

Figure 35—Leadership as Energy Architect

Leadership lies not in position or authority but in the quality of connections and interactions that emerge between people. Just as we learned in our high school science classes, energy in physics flows through natural channels and cannot be commanded but only enabled. Similarly, leadership influence operates through authentic community connections rather than traditional hierarchical structures. This understanding fundamentally transforms how we view and practice leadership in organizations.

Creating these conditions for authentic leadership begins with thoughtful attention to space, including physical, temporal, and psychological spaces. Leaders must deliberately design environments where genuine dialogue can emerge naturally. This means rethinking traditional meeting structures, moving beyond rigid agendas to include time for authentic conversation and emerging insights. Physical spaces need to support both focused work and spontaneous collaboration, while psychological safety must be consistently maintained through leadership behavior that welcomes diverse perspectives and acknowledges emotions.

Leaders must identify and remove barriers that block natural collaboration while creating rituals that support sustainable energy exchange. This includes rituals such as daily practices with brief stand-up meetings, weekly team sessions that celebrate progress, and regular renewal opportunities that allow for natural work rhythms rather than constant push.

Leaders must consistently frame conversations around possibility rather than problems, build trust through reliable presence and attention, and create cultural reinforcement mechanisms that support community building. Success comes through steady, thoughtful attention to context rather than dramatic interventions.

Equally important is leadership's role in minding the gaps, identifying and addressing places where connections are missing or weak. The goal isn't to eliminate all gaps but to ensure they don't impede the organization's ability to function as a cohesive community.

Through all these dimensions, leadership manifests most powerfully through questions rather than answers. Leaders must master the art of asking questions that create productive tension and foster accountability while remaining open-ended enough to invite genuine dialogue. These questions shape the quality of interaction between people, influencing how energy flows and multiplies throughout the organization.

This understanding transforms how we implement organizational initiatives. Success comes not from perfect execution of procedures but from the authentic community connections that emerge in the spaces between formal structures.

The future belongs to organizations that understand these natural leadership dynamics, creating environments where both people and performance thrive through authentic connection. Leaders must develop new capabilities to work effectively with these spaces such as becoming skilled at creating conditions for emergence, nurturing authentic connections, enabling natural energy flow, shaping supportive contexts, and minding organizational gaps. This represents a fundamental shift from leadership as position to leadership as the art of creating spaces where people and possibilities can flourish.

This understanding of "leadership in the spaces between people" is critically important for several key reasons:

Integration with Community-Enhanced Implementation

The concept directly supports the core premise that implementing business systems through community-building rather than command-and-control creates more sustainable transformation. Recognizing that leadership happens in interactions rather than positions provides a practical framework for how to build community while implementing business systems.

Bridging Tools and Culture

These business tools alone aren't enough. Success comes from weaving them into a vibrant community culture; the very fabric of the organization. Understanding leadership as happening in the spaces between people explains how this weaving occurs. It happens through the quality of interactions that bring tools to life rather than just their mechanical installation and implementation.

Energy and Engagement

The physics parallel about organizational energy finds practical application through this leadership understanding. Just as energy flows through connection points in physics, organizational energy flows through the quality of interactions leaders create. This helps explain why community-enhanced implementation produces better results than traditional approaches.

Transforming Implementation

Traditional implementation focuses on installing tools and processes. Understanding leadership as occurring in spaces between people provides the "how" of this transformation by focusing leader attention on creating conditions where authentic community can emerge through quality interactions.

Supporting the Six Conversations

The six critical conversations scripted in Chapter 14 (Invitation, Possibility, Ownership, Dissent, Commitment, and Gifts) all depend on leadership that can create spaces for authentic dialogue. This leadership understanding provides practical guidance for how to create those spaces effectively.

Creating Sustainable Change

Seeing leadership as occurring in interaction spaces explains how sustainable change happens through the ongoing quality of connections rather than just initial installation and subsequent implementation efforts.

Leadership, then, is about creating and nurturing the connections that enable authentic community to emerge. Just as energy in physics transfers through the space between atoms, leadership energy flows through the quality of interactions between people.

Five Efforts to Consider for Implementation Guidance:
1. Creating Quality Spaces

Leadership begins with thoughtful attention to how we structure interactions. Rather than filling every moment with activity or content, effective leaders deliberately design spaces that invite genuine dialogue and unexpected discoveries. This means rethinking traditional meeting rituals, moving beyond rigid agendas to include time for authentic conversation and emerging insights. By creating these quality spaces, leaders allow space for possibilities conversations and for natural energy flows to develop, fostering deeper connections and more meaningful outcomes than typically emerge from tightly controlled interactions.

2. Focusing on Connections

The heart of leadership lies in nurturing relationships, not just managing tasks. Leaders must develop the ability to sense the quality of connections within their organizations, actively looking for signs of both vitality and strain. This requires asking questions that invite people to share their authentic experiences and insights, while creating safe spaces for meaningful dialogue.

3. Enabling Energy Flow

Just as energy in physics requires clear channels, organizational energy needs open pathways to flow effectively. Leaders must become skilled at identifying and removing barriers that block natural communication and collaboration. This involves creating consistent rituals that support regular meaningful interaction while remaining alert to signs of energy depletion or blockage.

4. Shaping the Context

Leadership's primary role is creating conditions where people and possibilities can flourish. This means thoughtfully shaping the environment in which interactions occur, consistently framing conversations around possibility rather than problems. Leaders build trust through reliable presence and attention, demonstrating through their actions that authentic engagement matters more than superficial compliance.

5. Minding the Gaps

Effective leaders develop keen awareness of where connections are missing or weak within their organizations. They actively seek opportunities to bridge silos through intentional cross-functional dialogue. This attention to organizational gaps isn't about controlling interaction but about enabling new possibilities to emerge through enhanced connection.

Shift leadership from a position of "doing to" people to one of "creating with" people. Success comes not from directing activity but from nurturing the quality of connections that enable collective wisdom and energy to emerge naturally.

The key insight is that by attending to the quality of these "spaces between people," leaders can create conditions where both people and performance naturally thrive.

Chapter Summary

The chapter contrasted traditional top-down implementation of business models with a community-enhanced approach, emphasizing the benefits of the latter. It explained that while traditional implementation focuses on problem-solving and task assignment, the community-enhanced approach encourages co-creation, voluntary ownership, open discussion of concerns, and recognition of individual gifts. The chapter outlined ten specific benefits for CEOs who adopt this approach, including higher employee engagement, stronger culture, better problem-solving, and sustainable growth. It warned that failing to use a community-enhanced approach means missing opportunities for organizational transformation, deeper employee engagement, and lasting cultural change. The chapter concluded by explaining that effective leadership happens in the "spaces between people" through quality interactions rather than hierarchical structures.

Key Chapter Takeaways

1. Community-enhanced implementation creates deeper engagement than command-and-control approaches.
2. Traditional top-down implementation leaves significant benefits unrealized.
3. The shift from responsibility-focused to community-focused environment transforms organizational culture.
4. CEOs gain ten specific benefits including stronger leadership pipeline and sustainable growth.
5. Successful implementation requires balancing structured tools with human relationships.

Suggested Homework

1. Map current implementation approach against the Traditional vs. Community Accountability chart to identify gaps.
2. Document specific benefits your organization would gain from community-enhanced implementation versus traditional approach.

⚡⚡⚡⚡

CHAPTER 18

What's Holding You Back?

Summary: This chapter addresses the emotional barriers CEOs face when considering community-enhanced leadership, identifying seven key fears, including loss of control, leadership insecurity, distrust in employees, impatience for results, fear of vulnerability, attachment to traditional power structures, and fear of chaos. It acknowledges these emotions as valid while arguing that avoiding community-enhanced leadership for emotional comfort ultimately leads to unrealized potential for both the leader and organization. The chapter concludes that addressing these emotional barriers requires patience and self-reflection, emphasizing that the goal isn't to abandon traditional leadership skills but to expand one's leadership capacity for creating a more dynamic organization.

GETTING OVER YOURSELF

You may be wrestling with the decision on how to move ahead. After all, don't all CEOs have emotions and fears that might prevent one from adopting a community-enhanced leadership business model despite its benefits? Giving additional change-oriented roles to employees can be anxiety-producing, if for no other reason than the embedded unknowns and perhaps taking you out of your own comfort zone.

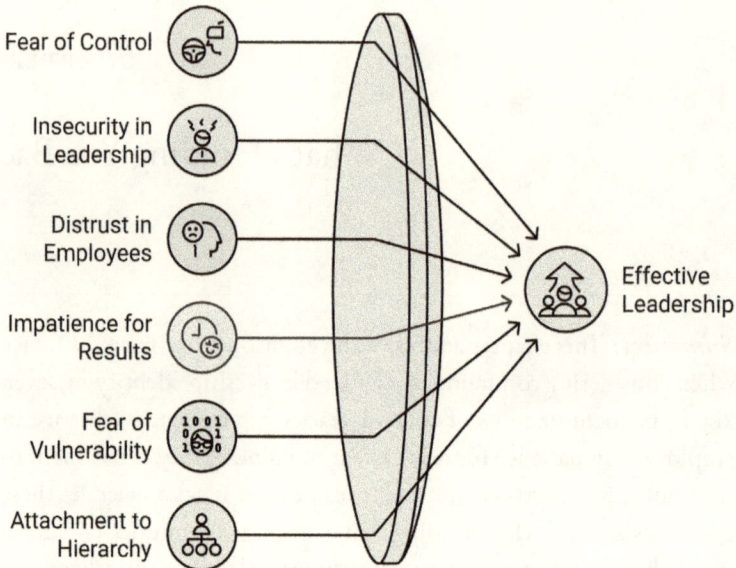

Figure 36—Leadership Challenge Lens

Let's explore this from an emotional perspective. It is highly reasonable and understandable to have certain emotions with the potential impact of this type of decision. These are not squishy emotions, they are real.

Fear of Losing Control: Anxiety about relinquishing tight control over the organization's direction and its underlying belief: "If I'm not controlling everything, things will fall apart."

Insecurity About Leadership Abilities: Self-doubt about ability to lead in a more collaborative, open environment caused by its underlying belief: "My authority is what makes me a good leader."

Distrust in Employees' Capabilities: Skepticism about employees' ability to contribute meaningfully and its underlying belief: "Only I (and perhaps my top executives) truly understand what's best for the company."

Impatience for Quick Results: Frustration with the perceived slowness of collaborative processes, with its underlying belief: "We don't have time for all this 'community' stuff; we need results now."

Fear of Vulnerability: Discomfort with showing uncertainty or admitting to not having all the answers, supported by the underlying belief: "Leaders must always appear strong and all-knowing."

Attachment to Traditional Power Structures: Comfort and security in familiar "command and control" hierarchical business models, with its underlying belief: "This is how business leadership has always worked; why change it?"

Fear of Chaos or Losing Focus: Anxiety about the messiness of participatory processes, supported by its underlying belief: "Too many voices will lead to confusion and lack of direction."

These emotions are very real and can, at times, keep you awake at night.[63] Our underlying belief system amplifies and augments our emotions. And the potentially crushing responsibilities in your role as the owner/CEO can, and do, affect your decision-making.

The emotional reasons for avoiding community-enhanced leadership often stem from deep-seated fears, insecurities, and attachments to traditional notions of power and control. **However, the opportunity costs of this avoidance are profound and touch on the very essence of what it means to be a leader.**

By choosing a more traditional, top-down approach, a CEO may maintain a sense of control and familiarity but at the cost of deeper, more meaningful leadership experiences. The lost opportunities for connection, growth, and transformative impact can leave a lasting void, not just in the organization's performance, but in the leader's own sense of fulfillment and legacy.

In essence, while avoiding community-enhanced leadership may feel safer emotionally in the short term, it risks leaving both the business owner/CEO and the organization in a state of unrealized potential, missing out on the rich, rewarding experience of leading a truly engaged, innovative, and united team.

Addressing these emotional barriers is a journey that requires patience, self-reflection, and a willingness to step out of one's comfort zone. Implement strategies to address the emotion barriers now to gradually build your comfort and confidence in a more collaborative leadership style.[64]

The key is to approach this journey as a learning process, where both successes and setbacks provide valuable insights. As you begin to experience the benefits of increased engagement, innovation, and shared purpose that come with community-enhanced leadership, the emotional rewards often outweigh the initial discomfort.

---

63. As a business owner coach, I have experienced in private conversations with clients that all of these fears are real.

64. See Appendix 8 for some suggested strategies to help you push ahead.

Chapter Summary

The chapter addressed the emotional barriers CEOs/business owners may face when considering a community-enhanced leadership approach, focusing on seven key fears: Losing control, leadership insecurity, distrust in employees, impatience for results, vulnerability, attachment to traditional power structures, and fear of chaos. While acknowledging these emotions as valid, the chapter argued that avoiding community-enhanced leadership for emotional comfort leads to significant opportunity costs in organizational potential and leadership fulfillment. It emphasized that addressing these emotional barriers requires patience and self-reflection, but the benefits of increased engagement and innovation ultimately outweigh the initial discomfort.

Key Chapter Takeaways

1. Fear of losing control and vulnerability are natural emotional responses to community-enhanced leadership.
2. Underlying beliefs amplify emotional barriers to change.
3. Avoiding community-enhanced leadership for emotional comfort leads to unrealized potential.
4. Traditional command-and-control feels safer but limits organizational growth.
5. Transition requires expanding leadership skills rather than abandoning traditional approaches.

Suggested Homework

1. Self-reflect on which emotional barriers most affect your leadership decisions.
2. Map your underlying beliefs about leadership and how they might limit organizational potential.

⚡⚡⚡⚡

CHAPTER 19

Bringing It All Together

Summary: This chapter argues that while business model tools alone can improve organizational efficiency by 50 to 80 percent, they are insufficient for true cultural transformation. It contrasts traditional metrics-based success with deeper measures of organizational thriving, including authentic engagement, collective wisdom, natural ownership, and alignment of individual gifts with purpose. The chapter emphasizes that true success emerges when organizations move beyond managing performance to creating environments where people feel truly seen, where innovation flows from collective thinking, and where ownership emerges naturally rather than being assigned. It concludes that combining business tools with community-building principles creates organizations that don't just succeed but thrive, transforming both outcomes and organizational essence.

As previously mentioned, the tools embedded in either business model are especially useful for transforming the small- to mid-size business. They are predicated on sound business principles. Whether you implement them yourself or use an outside hired resource, when used by themselves, your organization likely will come out for the better. These effectiveness and efficiency gains, typically after two years, may be in the 50 to 80 percent range, which I have witnessed. The organization is running better.

The problem is that the tools alone are insufficient and do not provide a way to shift the culture. One must start by developing an enhanced community. Using the tools within a "container" of community ensures a more successful, lasting change. With emphasis on building an enhanced community you can strengthen your leadership (and that of all your people) and increase accountability through having a source of truth and rituals.

My experience with both business models is that they are very appropriate for small- to mid-sized organizations and they also provide generally unrecognized additional benefits of combining a set of rituals with the sources of truth. Together you have a good leadership business model increasing accountability. Then there are additional hidden benefits from implementing either business model:

- Clarified accountabilities and roles
- An abundance of pros; "amateur hour" ends upon implementation
- Greater visibility of what's working and what's not working
- Identification of key outcomes/results
- Improvement in cash flow, and therefore shareholder value
- More time and energy for the toughest/biggest value activities
- Reduced frustration and improved culture and values
- Growth in valuation because of scalability and cashflow

Reread and focus on the last bullet point above, if you will, especially in context with the box below.

Would you be okay with getting 175 times return on your investment to transform your organization?

One client's experience was that for every \$1 invested in [the business model's implementation], the client realized a return of \$175 in increased, incremental shareholder value in only five years.

Beyond Metrics to Meaning

Being Truly Seen and Valued: True success begins when team members experience the profound difference between being "managed" and being truly seen. This manifests in daily moments where people feel their whole selves, not just their job titles or deliverables, are welcomed and valued.

In these organizations, you'll notice people sharing personal stories naturally during meetings, not because it's mandated, but because they feel safe bringing their full selves to work. You will notice the energy in the room energizing each person. Conversations extend beyond tasks to include hopes, concerns, and dreams. Leaders ask questions that demonstrate genuine curiosity about team members' perspectives and lives.

The difference is palpable in performance discussions, which transform from evaluations into explorations of contribution and purpose. Instead of focusing solely on what people deliver, these conversations center on how individuals are growing, what gives them energy, and where they see possibilities for deeper impact.

Innovation Through Collective Wisdom: When an organization truly succeeds at building community, innovation becomes a natural outcome of people thinking together. You'll see it in the way solutions emerge not from lone geniuses but from the interplay of diverse perspectives and experiences, each building upon the other.

The magic happens in everyday moments: A casual conversation that sparks a new idea, a team meeting where different viewpoints collide to create unexpected insights, or a problem-solving session where everyone's unique perspective contributes to a breakthrough solution.

Such organizations don't just brainstorm they create spaces where people can think together deeply, challenge assumptions safely, and build on each other's ideas naturally. Innovation becomes less about individual brilliance and more about collective discovery. Energy begets energy.

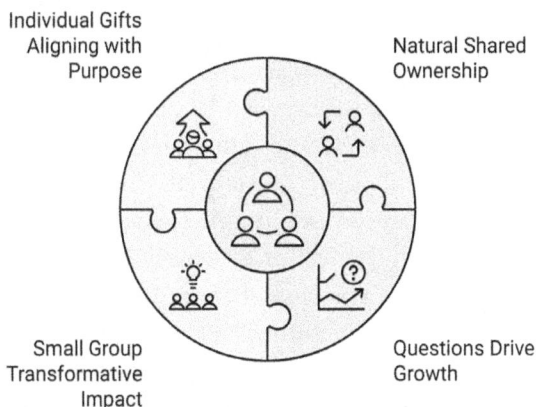

Figure 37—Synergy in Organizational Success

Natural Shared Ownership: In thriving communities, ownership shifts from being assigned to emerging naturally. You recognize this transformation when people stop saying "That's not my job" and start asking "How can I help?" The change is evident in the way team members naturally pick up tasks that need doing, not because they're told to, but because they feel genuine responsibility for the collective success.

This manifests in meetings where people actively engage in discussions outside their formal roles, offering insights and support across traditional boundaries. You see it in spontaneous collaboration, where team members driven by their individual and collective energy come together to solve problems without waiting for formal assignments or authority.

The energy is different; instead of pushing for accountability, leaders find themselves creating space for the natural ownership that comes from people feeling deeply connected to work and each other.

Questions Drive Growth: Success becomes visible when organizations shift from having all the answers to getting curious about better questions. You notice this in meetings that begin not with status updates but with genuine inquiry about what matters most right now.

These organizations create space for questions that don't have immediate answers, but rather that make people think differently. Doing so challenges assumptions and that opens new possibilities. Leaders model this by asking more than telling, by showing comfort with uncertainty, by demonstrating that not knowing can be the start of important discoveries.

Learning becomes less about formal training and more about collective exploration. Team members naturally ask, "What if?" and "Why not?" Their curiosity drives continuous growth and innovation.

Small Group Transformative Impact: True success reveals itself in the power of small groups to create significant change. Rather than relying on large-scale initiatives, these organizations understand that transformation happens in intimate circles where people can connect deeply and think together effectively.

You see this in the way work naturally organizes into small, cross-functional, interdependent teams that take on challenges with energy and creativity. These groups become more than task forces; they become communities of practice where deep learning and innovation naturally occur.

The energy and impact of these small groups ripples outward, influencing the larger organization through natural networks of relationships and shared learning. Their successes aren't just measured in deliverables but in how they transform both the work and the people doing it.

Individual Gifts Aligning with Purpose: Perhaps the most profound sign of success is when individual gifts naturally align with organizational purpose. This happens when people feel free to bring their unique talents and perspectives to work, and when the organization creates spaces where these gifts can flourish.

You recognize this alignment in the joy people bring to their work, in the natural way they step into responsibilities that match their talents, and in the creative solutions that emerge when people operate from their strengths.

This manifests in role accountabilities that flex to accommodate unique contributions, in project assignments that consider not just skills but sources of energy and gifts, and in development paths that honor individual calling alongside organizational needs, all not constrained by rigid job descriptions.

The Integrated Picture of Success: When all these elements come together, you find organizations in which:

- authenticity replaces compliance,
- curiosity overcomes certainty,
- natural ownership supersedes assigned accountability,
- collective wisdom surpasses individual expertise,
- small group energy transforms large system challenges, and
- personal calling aligns with organizational purpose.

Success becomes less about hitting targets and more about creating conditions where people and purpose naturally flourish together. The metrics still matter, but they become natural outcomes of something deeper, a community where everyone can contribute their best to something that matters.

True success isn't a destination but a continuing journey of creating spaces where people can be fully themselves, think together effectively, take natural ownership, learn continuously, work intimately, and align their gifts with purpose. When these elements come together, extraordinary results emerge, not as goals to be achieved but as natural outcomes of a healthy community.

As you weave the tools of your operating model (the "weft") with the principles and practices of community (the "warp"), you'll gradually see a new fabric emerge, one in which every thread is valued, every voice is heard, and every heart is invested. You'll see the hard edges of hierarchy and competition soften into collaboration and care. You'll see the isolated silos of departments and divisions evolve into vibrant networks of connection and co-creation. You'll see the mechanical gears of process and procedure come alive with the energy of passion and purpose.

This is the promise of Supercharge, not just a better way of working, but a better way of being. A way of harnessing the full potential of every human being in service of something greater than themselves. A way of building organizations that don't just succeed but thrive, not just in their outcomes, but in their essence. A way of shaping a world where every institution is a source of aliveness, every leader is an embodiment of possibility, and every community is a catalyst for transformation.

Chapter Summary

The chapter emphasized that while the business models' tools can improve organizational efficiency by 50 to 80 percent, implementing them alone is insufficient for true transformation. It argued that embedding these tools within a community-focused approach leads to more lasting change through strengthened leadership, accountability, and cultural shifts. The chapter concluded by describing what success looks like in organizations that effectively combine business tools with community building where innovation emerges naturally, ownership is shared, questioning drives growth, and individual gifts align with organizational purpose.

Key Chapter Takeaways

1. Business tools alone can improve efficiency but can't transform culture.
2. True success comes when employees feel seen and valued beyond their job titles.
3. Innovation emerges from collective wisdom rather than individual brilliance.
4. Natural ownership replaces assigned accountability in thriving communities.
5. Individual gifts must align with organizational purpose for lasting success.

Suggested Homework

1. Audit how your current meetings balance task discussions with space for authentic connection and collective thinking.
2. Map where natural ownership already exists in your organization versus where it's purely assigned accountability.

⚡⚡⚡⚡

CHAPTER 20

What Now?

Summary: This concluding chapter synthesizes the core message that true organizational transformation requires integrating business tools with community building. It argues that while both paths can lead to good results, extraordinary outcomes emerge only when organizations view tools not just as performance frameworks but as platforms for human development and connection. The chapter outlines how this integration transforms every aspect of implementation from meetings becoming spaces for both achievement and connection to metrics evolving into catalysts for learning and growth. It concludes with six practical steps for leaders to begin this transformation, emphasizing that success comes when organizations prioritize people and purpose alongside profit and performance, creating workplaces that don't just succeed but truly thrive, supercharged.

After all this reading, you may be thinking about what your first step should be. You can begin by fighting institutional inertia and adopting a new bias for action, a new operating business model will be leveraged and, in doing so, build an accountable community.

Either business model is simply that, a different operating model; a set of proven, effective, yet simple tools for use in small- to mid-size organizations. Each guides the culture to become one of accountability and performance, through sources of truth and practicable rituals. You must have all. Supercharged transformation means to *create a future distinct from the past*, no tweaking, modifying, or building on the past. The work is in small groups (likely your leadership team, initially). A shift in thinking equals transformation. **Bring new healthy conversations into every corner of your organization.**

> Living systems outperform mechanical ones. When we breathe life into our implementations through genuine human connection, results exceed expectations.

Instead of seeing tools as mere performance frameworks, we recognize them as platforms for growth and possibility. They become catalysts not just for directing effort but for developing potential. Quarterly goals transform into opportunities for both achievement and capability building.

Weekly meetings evolve from monitoring sessions into spaces where people thrive through meaningful connection and collective learning.

In thriving organizations, achievement emerges from engagement rather than enforcement. Innovation flows from exploration, not mandates. Accountability springs from commitment rather than compliance. Growth becomes woven into the organization's fabric rather than imposed through initiatives.

When organizations create conditions for thriving, people bring their energy and whole selves to work. Innovation flourishes in an environment of trust. The organization develops resilience, adapting quickly to challenges. Performance becomes sustainable, driven by inspiration rather than exhaustion.

This transformation requires purposeful connection, embedded growth opportunities, quality relationships, and energy management. Leadership shifts from driving performance to nurturing thriving thus creating safe spaces while maintaining high standards.

Business tools become frameworks for human development: Scorecards evolve into learning tools, issues become growth opportunities, and planning sessions transform into collective visioning. This creates organizations where innovation and excellence emerge naturally.

The key insight is that highest performance emerges through human flourishing. Community-enhanced leadership creates organizations where people grow while delivering extraordinary results, measuring success not just in outcomes, but in how people thrive. This is the new frontier where performance becomes the natural outcome of human development.

The Choice Before Us Is to Go from Good to Extraordinary

We stand at a crossroads in organizational leadership. One path leads to increasingly sophisticated tools and systems pushing efficiency and effectiveness. The other integrates these tools with the deeper wisdom of human community. The choice isn't between success and failure; both paths can lead to good results. The choice is between good and extraordinary.

Your current EOS or Scaling Up implementation likely delivers solid results. The tools work. The models function. The metrics improve. But there's a gnawing sense that something more is possible. This isn't just intuition. It's recognition of a fundamental truth about organizations that tools and systems, no matter how sophisticated, are just the beginning.

The journey from good to extraordinary begins with a profound shift in how we think about organizational life. Instead of seeing our business systems primarily as performance tools, we recognize them as frameworks for human connection and development. This isn't about choosing between structure and community: It's about weaving them together into something more powerful than either alone.

Consider how this integration transforms every aspect of your implementation:

- Traditional meetings shift to become containers for both achievement and connection. While maintaining their focus on results, they create space for real dialogue and genuine engagement.
- Standard metrics evolve into catalysts for both performance and learning. Beyond tracking numbers, they spark conversations about growth and possibility.
- Regular planning sessions transform from goal-setting exercises into opportunities for collective wisdom to emerge. While maintaining clear direction, they tap into the power of shared insight and commitment.

This shift reveals itself in several key dimensions:

- **From mechanical to alive:** Organizations move beyond mere efficiency to genuine vitality, where energy flows naturally rather than being forced.
- **From transactional to relational:** Interactions shift from simple exchanges to meaningful connections that build both capability and commitment.
- **From controlling to co-creating:** Leadership evolves from directing activity to fostering conditions where extraordinary results can emerge naturally.

The energy and impact of this transformation ripples throughout the organization. Innovation emerges naturally from an engaged and energized workforce rather than through mandated programs. Engagement flows from genuine human connection and shared purpose, not through compliance mechanisms. Excellence springs from intrinsic motivation rather than external pressure, while growth evolves organically through curiosity and meaningful challenges rather than formal programs. These elements reinforce each other, creating a self-sustaining cycle that leads to an organization that's not just higher performing but more vitally alive.

Your existing tools, vision documents, meeting rhythms, metrics, and key objectives become more powerful when reimagined. They transform into frameworks for discovery rather than just direction, creating spaces for dialogue rather than discussion, enabling development rather than just deployment, and fostering connection rather than mere coordination.

Making this shift requires attention to several key elements:

- **Building community:** Creating the conditions where genuine connection can flourish alongside focused execution
- **Fostering dialogue:** Moving beyond surface communication to real exchange of ideas and perspectives
- **Nurturing growth:** Seeing every activity as an opportunity for both achievement and development
- **Enabling emergence:** Creating space for unexpected possibilities while maintaining clear direction

Leadership's role transforms from managing systems to nurturing potential. This means:

- creating conditions where people can bring their energies and full selves to work,
- building structures that support both performance and possibility,
- fostering relationships that enable both accountability and growth, and
- maintaining standards while encouraging exploration.

The journey from good to extraordinary is about enhancing what works through deeper understanding of the human community. Every tool, every process, every practice can either contribute to or detract from this integration. Consider what this might mean for your organization:

- What if your implementation created both results and relationships?
- How might performance improve if it emerged from connection rather than control?
- What would change if every tool served both structural and human needs?

The promise of community-enhanced leadership is the creation of organizations that don't merely:

- achieve goals, but nurture growth;
- measure metrics, but create meaning;
- manage performance, but inspire purpose; and
- coordinate action while building community.

The choice isn't whether to use sophisticated business systems; they're essential. The choice is whether to limit yourself to their mechanical application or to enhance them through the power of the human community.

The future of organizational leadership is about better ways of being together. It's about creating organizations where structure enables rather than constrains, where discipline supports rather than suffocates, where every person can bring their full potential to work those matters.

This is the promise of community-enhanced leadership, not just good organizations, but extraordinary ones. Not just successful enterprises, but transformative ones. Not just effective systems, but fully alive ones.

Your new journey begins with a simple choice: Will you be satisfied with good, or will you reach for extraordinary? Will you settle for effective tools, or will you seek to infuse them with the power of genuine community?

The tools are ready. The potential is waiting. The only question is: Are you ready to begin?

Be the leader your people expect you to be, because magic happens at the intersection of entrepreneurship and a culture of discipline.

Focus on your peoples' potential. Here's how to start, in Six Steps:[65]

- Issue the invitation and invest in those who show up.
- Forestall problem-solving and stay focused on the possibility (until it is spoken with passion).
- Confront people with their freedom (What are you concerned about? What do you complain about?).
- Seek dissent. A team member must have the right to say "No" before saying "Yes."
- Demand authentic commitment from those who say "Yes."
- Bring the gifts (i.e., strengths, skills, knowledge) from the margin to the center.

Summary

The intention herein is to extoll the virtues of using a simple yet effective system as a business model for your organization and to weave those tools onto the warp of building a community.

Assuming you do build that community-enhanced culture you so deeply desire, consider the major changes:

- First, truth doesn't flow from the top down. It emerges through dialogue and collective experience. Leaders become facilitators of discovery rather than sources of all answers.
- Second, accountability isn't enforced, it's inspired. When leaders create

---

65. Derived from Block, *Community*.

conditions of genuine belonging and shared purpose, people naturally step up to their own outcomes.

- Third, sources of truth aren't absolute, they are guidance. They exist to provide a solid foundation for behaviors and performance.
- Fourth, rituals matter. Whether it's how you run meetings, make decisions, or celebrate successes, conscious attention to organizational rituals shapes culture and behavior.

This shift requires courage to be vulnerable, to admit uncertainty, to trust in the wisdom of the group. But the rewards are extraordinary: Higher engagement, more innovation, better decisions, and sustainable performance.

This is about enhancing the tools' power through meaningful human connection.

The question is how quickly you can begin. Your organization's future depends on it.

The most successful transformations begin with leaders who understand that their role is not to have all the answers, but to create the conditions where answers can emerge from the collective intelligence of the organization.

This is the promise of *Supercharge*; not just a better way of working, but a better way of being. A way of harnessing the full potential of every human being in service of something greater than themselves. A way of building organizations that don't just succeed, but thrive and not just in their outcomes, but in their essence. A way of shaping a world in which every institution is a source of vitality, and every leader illuminates the paths of possibility, and every community is a catalyst for transformation.

As you continue on this path, know that you are part of a growing movement of leaders and organizations who are daring to reimagine what's possible; choosing to lead not from transaction, but from trust; not from control, but from co-creation and not from scarcity, but from abundance; and proving every day that when we prioritize people and purpose, profit and performance will naturally follow.

In the preface, I wrote about the combination of the tools and *Community: The Structure of Belonging* and that by using each concurrently, business owners can achieve more complete, lasting results than by either alone. In doing so, you leverage the advantages of each to supercharge your journey to your desired future.

Chapter Summary

The chapter concludes the book by emphasizing the transition from traditional tools-based implementation to a community-enhanced approach, presenting six concrete steps to begin this transformation. It argues that successful organizations integrate business systems with human community, where truth emerges through dialogue, accountability is inspired rather than enforced, and rituals shape culture. The chapter emphasizes that this integration leads to extraordinary results rather than just good ones, transforming standard business tools into frameworks for human development and connection. It concludes that prioritizing people and purpose naturally leads to improved profits and performance.

Key Chapter Takeaways

1. Business model tools must be seen as platforms for nurturing growth, not just directing performance.
2. True transformation shifts truth from top-down to emerging through dialogue.
3. The choice isn't between structure and community but how to weave them together.
4. Leadership's role transforms from having answers to creating conditions for solutions to emerge.
5. Success requires moving beyond mechanical implementation to creating truly alive organizations.

Suggested Homework

1. Map your organization's shift using the three key changes framework: how truth flows, how accountability emerges, and how rituals shape culture.
2. Document where your current implementation leans, mechanical versus alive, using specific examples from meetings, metrics, and planning sessions.

⚡⚡⚡⚡

Appendices

Summary: The core thesis outlines that while business models like Traction and Scaling Up provide effective tools, lasting transformation requires integrating these tools with community-building principles to create a "supercharged" approach combining structural benefits with authentic human connection.

Appendix 1 compares *Traction* and *Scaling Up* through four key benefits: Leadership, Accountability, Sources of Truth, and Ritual, highlighting how each model approaches these elements differently while sharing common foundational principles.

Appendix 2 examines how Peter Block's six conversations (Invitation, Possibility, Ownership, Dissent, Commitment, and Gifts) transform organizational culture during business model implementation, detailing specific benefits for both organizations and employees.

Appendix 3 provides a comprehensive collection of powerful questions designed to enhance leadership effectiveness and build community, emphasizing the importance of asking questions rather than providing answers.

Appendix 4 compares leadership conceptualization in both models, identifying 12 dimensions in Traction and 15 in Scaling Up, highlighting their shared elements while noting Traction's simpler approach versus Scaling Up's complexity.

Appendix 5 examines how accountability is structured in both models, with Traction offering ten tools focused on clear organizational structure and Scaling Up providing ten areas with a broader scope.

Appendix 6 compares how rituals are structured in both models, with *Traction* embedding six key rituals and *Scaling Up* featuring seven, differing in their approach to structure and flexibility.

Appendix 7 explores how sources of truth manifest in both models, with Traction employing nine key elements focused on fundamental practices and Scaling Up offering 11 tools for managing growth complexity.

Appendix 8 provides nine practical strategies to help leaders transition from traditional to community-enhanced leadership styles, addressing specific fears and challenges leaders face when moving away from command-and-control approaches.

⚡⚡⚡⚡

Four Benefits

Summary: Appendix 1 presents a detailed comparison of Traction and Scaling Up by examining how their tools and frameworks support four fundamental benefits: Leadership, Accountability, Sources of Truth, and Ritual. While both models aim to improve organizational performance, they differ in their approach and complexity. Traction emphasizes simplicity with clear Visionary/Integrator roles, straightforward accountability tools, and structured meetings, making it ideal for establishing foundational business practices. Scaling Up offers a more sophisticated framework with detailed tools for leadership development, multiple accountability layers, comprehensive planning documents, and a more elaborate meeting rhythm, designed for managing growth complexity. Despite their differences, both models share core elements like structured meetings, clear accountability mechanisms, defined metrics, and regular planning sessions, allowing organizations to choose the approach that best fits their needs and growth stage.

LEADERSHIP, ACCOUNTABILITY, SOURCES OF TRUTH, AND RITUAL

Let's recast the two models by placing their respective tools into the framework of the four benefits. You will note that on many occasions, a tool ends up in more than one benefit area, which is not surprising.

Traction	Scaling Up
Traction/EOS provides a comprehensive, structured approach to business management. It emphasizes clear leadership roles, strong accountability mechanisms, well-defined sources of truth for decision-making, and consistent rituals to maintain alignment and drive execution. The business model is designed to create clarity, focus, and discipline throughout the organization, with a particular emphasis on simplicity and practical application.	Scaling Up provides a comprehensive framework for growing businesses, emphasizing leadership development, clear accountability, well-defined sources of truth, and consistent rituals. The business model is designed to help organizations manage the complexities of rapid growth while maintaining alignment and driving performance. It offers a more detailed and nuanced approach compared to some other business models, reflecting its focus on scaling businesses through various growth stages.

Traction	Scaling Up
Leadership: • **Visionary vs. Integrator Roles:** Distinguishes between big-picture thinking (Visionary) and day-to-day execution (Integrator). • **Leadership Team Dynamics:** Emphasizes a strong, cohesive leadership team of three to seven members. • **Accountability:** Leader's model; enforces accountability throughout the organization. • **Clarity and Communication:** Helps leaders provide clear direction and effectively communicate vision and issues. • **Issue Solving:** Leads to identification, discussion, and prompt solution of issues. • **Data-Driven Decision-Making:** Emphasizes the use of a scorecard for informed decision-making. • **Core Focus:** Maintains alignment with the company's purpose and niche. • **Simplicity and Focus:** Encourages simplifying complex business concepts.	**Leadership:** • **The Four Decisions:** Must excel in People, Strategy, Execution, and Cash decisions. • **Face Time with Employees:** Emphasizes significant interaction with employees at all levels. • **Continuous Learning and Teaching:** Expected to be lifelong learners and actively teach others. • **Setting the Pace:** Leaders' energy and focus directly impact company performance. • **Clarity of Vision and Purpose:** Must articulate and reinforce vision, purpose, and values. • **Data-Driven Leadership:** Emphasis on using KPIs and metrics to guide decisions. • **Balancing Short-term and Long-term:** Must balance immediate performance with long-term value creation. • **Developing Future Leaders:** Focus on identifying and nurturing leadership talent within the organization.

Traction	Scaling Up
Accountability: • **Accountability Chart:** Clearly defines who is accountable for what in the organization. • **Rocks:** Quarterly priorities that individuals commit to achieving. • **Measurables:** Key performance indicators for each role. • **Level 10 Meetings:** Weekly meetings to review scorecards and maintain accountability. • **Scorecard:** Weekly metrics providing a pulse on the business. • **To-Do Lists:** Action items assigned and reviewed weekly. • **Core Values:** Basis for accountability in behavior and decision-making.	**Accountability:** • **Function Accountability Chart:** Clearly defines who is accountable for what functions and associated KPIs. • **Process Accountability Chart:** Outlines accountability for core processes in the organization. • **Rockefeller Habits Checklist:** Ten habits that drive accountability and execution. • **One-Page Strategic Plan:** Aligns the entire organization around key goals and metrics. • **Critical Numbers:** Key metrics focused on quarterly and annually. • **Cash Acceleration Strategies:** Specific focus on financial accountability. • **Coaching and Feedback:** Regular sessions for performance accountability.

Traction	Scaling Up
Sources of Truth:	**Sources of Truth:**
• **Vision/Traction Organizer:** Comprehensive document capturing long-term vision and strategy.	• **One-Page Strategic Plan:** Comprehensive reference for strategic direction and goals.
• **Accountability Chart:** Defines organizational structure and responsibilities.	• **Core Values and Purpose:** Fundamental guides for organizational culture and decision-making.
• **Rocks:** Quarterly priorities guiding short-term focus.	• **Function Accountability Chart:** Clear reference for roles, responsibilities, and functional KPIs.
• **Scorecard:** Key metrics for tracking business performance.	• **Process Accountability Chart:** Reference for core processes and their owners.
• **Level 10 Meeting Agenda:** Structured agenda for weekly team meetings.	• **Rockefeller Habits Checklist:** Guide for execution discipline and leadership behaviors.
• **Issues List:** Compilation of obstacles, problems, and opportunities.	• **Cash Acceleration Strategies:** Primary reference for financial decision-making and cash management.
	• **Key Performance Indicators (KPIs) and Critical Numbers:** Objective metrics for assessing organizational health and performance.
	• **BHAG (Big Hairy Audacious Goal):** Long-term visionary goal guiding strategy.
	• **Brand Promise and Brand Promise Guarantee:** Clear statement of customer value proposition and commitments.

Traction	Scaling Up
Rituals: • **Weekly Level 10 Meetings:** 90-minute structured meeting with a specific agenda. • **Quarterly Rocks Setting:** Establishing three to seven priorities for the next 90 days. • **Quarterly Conversations:** One-on-one meetings between leaders and direct reports. • **Annual Planning Session:** Two-day offsite meeting to review and set direction for the coming year. • **Quarterly Meeting Checks:** Review overall company performance and rocks. • **5-5-5 Communication Structure:** Five minutes each of personal sharing, performance review, and feedback in weekly leader-direct report check-ins.	**Rituals:** • **Daily Huddle:** Five to 15-minute stand-up meeting for daily alignment. • **Weekly Meeting:** 60- to 90-minute meeting focused on tactical issues. • **Monthly Management Meeting:** Half-day meeting to address key strategic issues. • **Quarterly Planning Session:** One- to two-day offsite to review progress and set priorities. • **Annual Planning Retreat:** Two- to three-day offsite to set strategy for the coming year. • **One-on-One Coaching:** Regular meetings between leaders and team members. • **Theme Implementation:** Quarterly or annual themes to focus the entire organization.

⚡ ⚡ ⚡ ⚡

Key Points or Conversations for Community-Enhanced Leadership

Summary: Appendix 2 explores how Block's six conversations (Invitation, Possibility, Ownership, Dissent, Commitment, and Gifts) can transform organizational culture when implementing business models. It outlines specific benefits of this community-enhanced approach, including five organizational benefits (enhanced buy-in, improved alignment, increased adaptability, enhanced problem-solving, and stronger culture) and four employee benefits (increased satisfaction, psychological safety, personal growth, and stronger community). The appendix then contrasts traditional command-and-control leadership with community-enhanced leadership, demonstrating how accountability shifts from being externally imposed to intrinsically motivated. It concludes by describing key elements of community-enhanced leadership that foster authentic accountability through shared purpose, transparent communication, and continuous learning.

SIX CONVERSATIONS

In *Community: A Structure of Belonging*, Peter Block provides a six-part process using conversations to build an effective community, an organization for this effort. What are the Six Conversations?

1. **Invitation Conversation:** Invite people to participate in creating possibility with the key question: *"What invitation can we make that has the power to engage people?"*

2. **Possibility Conversation:** Focus on what we want our future to be, as opposed to problem-solving the past, with the main question: *"What possibility can you see in this situation that we have not yet considered?"*

3. **Ownership Conversation:** Foster a sense of responsibility and commitment with the key question: *"What have I done to contribute to the very thing I want to change?"*

4. **Dissent Conversation:** Voice doubts and reservations as a way of deepening commitment with the main question: *"What doubts and reservations do you have?"*

5. **Commitment Conversation:** Make promises to fellow community members about our contribution to the success of all with the main question: *"What promise am I willing to make to this enterprise?"*

6. **Gifts Conversation:** Acknowledge the gifts and strengths of the community and its members with the key questions: *"What has this community done for you? What has it made possible for you? What gifts do I bring?"*

These conversations are designed to be transformative, shifting the context from one of deficiencies and problems to one of possibility and gifts. They aim to build a sense of ownership, commitment, and shared responsibility among community members.

Benefits of Community-Enhanced Leadership Implementation of Your Business Model

On Leadership: Create the culture you want or get the culture you deserve. By implementing either business model within the "container" of creating a community-enhanced community, your organization benefits in five direct ways:

1. **Enhanced Buy-in and Commitment:** By engaging employees through the six conversations, organizations create a sense of ownership and shared responsibility. This leads to higher levels of engagement in the

implementation process, reduced resistance to change, and more sustained effort in adopting new practices.

2. **Improved Alignment:** The six conversations help create a shared understanding of the organization's vision and goals, how the business model supports these objectives, and each individual's role in the process. This alignment can lead to more coordinated efforts and faster achievement of organizational objectives.

3. **Increased Adaptability:** By encouraging open dialogue, including dissent, organizations identify potential obstacles early, develop more robust implementation plans, and create a culture of continuous improvement.

4. **Enhanced Problem-Solving Capabilities:** The diverse perspectives surfaced through these conversations can lead to more creative solutions to implementation challenges, better utilization of collective intelligence, and improved cross-functional collaboration.

5. **Stronger Organizational Culture:** The process of community-building strengthens trust between leadership and employees, interpersonal relationships across the organization, and a sense of belonging and shared purpose.

In addition to the five benefits above accruing to the organization, employees directly feel four additional benefits:

1. **Increased Employee Satisfaction:** Employees who feel heard and valued through this process are likely to experience higher job satisfaction, improved sense of purpose and meaning in their work, and greater alignment between personal and organizational values.

2. **Enhanced Psychological Safety:** The open conversations, particularly around dissent and gifts, can foster a culture where people feel safe expressing ideas and concerns, have an increased willingness to take calculated risks, and share more open and honest communication throughout the organization.

3. **Personal Growth and Development:** Engaging in these conversations can lead to increased self-awareness, development of communication and leadership skills, and a greater sense of agency and empowerment.

4. **Stronger Sense of Community:** The process naturally builds deeper

connections among team members, a shared sense of journey and accomplishment, and increased empathy and understanding across separate roles and departments.

Not only does the organization itself directly benefit (in at least five ways) from wrapping implementation in the "container" of building a community-enhanced culture, the individuals within that community do as well. Combined, they yield the following explicit benefits:

- **Improved Implementation (of the Business Model) Outcomes:** Compared to command/fiat implementation, this approach is likely to result in higher adoption rates of your chosen business model practices, more consistent application of the business model across the organization, and better long-term sustainability of the implementation.
- **Enhanced Organizational Performance:** The combination of aligned efforts and engaged employees can lead to improved productivity and efficiency, better financial performance, and enhanced innovation and adaptability in the marketplace.
- **Reduced Turnover:** The community-enhanced approach, with its resulting job satisfaction, can result in lower employee turnover rates, reduced costs associated with hiring and training, and retention of institutional knowledge.
- **Improved Customer Satisfaction:** As employees become more engaged and aligned, this often translates to better customer service, improved product/service quality, and stronger customer relationships.
- **Enhanced Employer Brand:** The positive internal culture created through this process can lead to improved reputation as an employer, easier recruitment of top talent, and positive word-of-mouth in the industry.

The community-enhanced leadership approach to implementing business models like these represents a significant shift from traditional, top-down leadership models. This innovative approach not only facilitates more effective implementation but also cultivates a leadership style that is more suited to the complexities and dynamics of modern organizations. Let's look at the shifts in dynamics:

Command-and-Control Way	Shifts to	Community-Enhanced Way
Directive	→	Facilitative
Monologue	→	Dialogue
Control	→	Influence
Uniformity	→	Diversity
Reactivity	→	Proactivity
Positional Power	→	Personal Power
Scarcity Mindset	→	Abundance Mindset

Figure 38 —Shift from Traditional to Community-Enhanced Leadership

This community-based leadership style represents a significant evolution from command/fiat structures. It is particularly well-suited for implementing comprehensive business models, which require organization-wide engagement and alignment. By fostering a sense of shared ownership, open communication, and collective intelligence, this leadership approach not only facilitates more effective implementation of these business models but also creates a more resilient, adaptive, and innovative organizational culture.

Leaders who adopt this style are likely to see improved employee engagement, more effective problem-solving, increased organizational agility, and ultimately, better business outcomes. Moreover, this approach is more aligned with the values and expectations of modern workforces, particularly younger generations who seek meaning, involvement, and personal growth in their work.

As organizations continue to navigate increasingly complex and rapidly changing environments, the ability to lead through community-building and collective engagement will become not just an advantage but a necessity for sustained success.

On Accountability

In the context of community-based implementation of business models, accountability takes on a new dimension. Unlike traditional top-down business models, where accountability is often conflated with blame, this approach fosters a culture where accountability is intrinsic, shared, and viewed as a pathway to collective success.

Self-Directed Accountability: In a community-based approach, accountability primarily comes from within as employees take ownership of their roles and outcomes, seeing themselves as integral to the organization's success. The drive to meet commitments comes from a sense of personal integrity and commitment to the community, rather than fear of punishment. Individuals actively seek solutions when faced with challenges, rather than waiting for direction.

Peer-to-Peer Accountability: The community aspect fosters a culture of mutual accountability. Team members support each other in meeting commitments, offering help and resources. There's an open exchange of feedback among peers, focused on improvement rather than criticism. Success and failure are seen as collective outcomes, encouraging mutual support.

Transparent Communication: Accountability thrives in an environment of openness. Teams have frequent, open discussions about progress, challenges, and needs. Key performance indicators and goals are openly shared and discussed. There's a culture of addressing issues directly and constructively.

Alignment with Organizational Goals: Accountability is tied directly to the organization's vision and objectives. Everyone understands how their role and actions contribute to larger organizational goals. Decisions and actions are guided by their alignment with the organization's purpose and values. Goals are specific, measurable, and tied to the organization's success metrics.

Learning-Oriented Approach: Accountability is seen as a tool for growth and improvement. Mistakes are viewed as learning opportunities rather than causes for punishment. There's an ongoing focus on how processes and performances can be enhanced. Insights and learnings are actively shared across the organization.

Shift from Responsibility-Focused Environment ➡	Shift to Community-Focused Environment
Characteristics: • Task-oriented approach • Emphasis on following instructions • Hierarchical decision-making • Individual role focus • Success measured by task completion	**Characteristics:** • Proactive engagement • Outcome-oriented • Self-driven improvement • Collaborative problem-solving • Emphasis on learning and growth
Advantages: • Clear chain of command • Predictable workflows • Easy to measure individual performance • Clear job descriptions and roles • Efficient in stable, unchanging environments	**Advantages:** • Higher levels of innovation and creativity • Increased employee engagement and satisfaction • More agile and adaptive organization • Stronger alignment between individual actions and organizational goals • Enhanced problem-solving capabilities

Figure 39—Traditional vs. Community Accountability

A New Style of Leadership

Community-enhanced leadership is an approach that fosters intrinsic accountability through shared purpose, transparent communication, and a culture of continuous learning. It operates by aligning individual drive with organizational goals, leveraging peer relationships, and viewing accountability as a pathway to collective growth and success.

Key elements of this leadership style:

- **Vision Alignment:** Leaders clearly communicate the organization's vision and help individuals see how their roles contribute to it.
- **Empowerment:** Leaders provide the autonomy and resources necessary for individuals to take ownership of their responsibilities.
- **Transparency Cultivation:** Leaders create business models and practices that make information, progress, and challenges visible across the organization.
- **Learning Facilitation:** Leaders foster an environment where mistakes are seen as learning opportunities and continuous improvement is the norm.
- **Community Building:** Leaders actively work to create a sense of shared purpose and mutual support within the organization.
- **Outcome Focus:** Leaders shift the focus from mere task completion to achieving meaningful outcomes aligned with organizational goals.
- **Dialogue Promotion:** Leaders encourage open, honest conversations about performance, challenges, and solutions.
- **Trust Development:** Leaders build trust by demonstrating vulnerability, admitting their own mistakes, and showing confidence in their team's capabilities.
- **Business Systemic Thinking:** Leaders help individuals see how their actions impact the entire business model, fostering a sense of interconnectedness and shared accountability.
- **Recognition Reframing:** Leaders celebrate not just successes, but also instances of accountability, problem-solving, and learning from failures.

Accountability, as a critical part of community-enhanced leadership, represents a significant shift from traditional responsibility-focused business models.

⚡⚡⚡⚡

It's the Questions You Ask

Summary: Appendix 3 provides a collection of powerful questions designed to enhance leadership effectiveness and build community. It begins with leadership questions that probe accountability and problem-solving, emphasizing the importance of asking questions rather than providing answers. The appendix then details Block's six categories of transformative questions (Invitation, Possibility, Ownership, Dissent, Commitment, and Gifts), each designed to build different aspects of community engagement. It concludes with additional question sets focused on identifying gifts, exploring potential impact, and implementing changes. Throughout, the appendix emphasizes that leadership effectiveness comes from asking thoughtful, probing questions that encourage accountability and engagement rather than from providing answers or maintaining control.

SAMPLE QUESTIONS

Leadership is demonstrated in the questions you ask about the results as shown on the tools of the business model. Consider these questions to your leadership team:

- What's your accountability for this not being successful?
- How much risk do you plan to take?
- What did you learn from this?

- What part of your accountabilities are you avoiding now?
- What's the most important thing we should be talking about today?
- What is our organization pretending not to know?
- How have we behaved in ways guaranteed to produce results with which we are unhappy?
- What are the conversations out there with our names on them? The ones we've been avoiding for days, weeks, months, years? Who are they with and what are the topics?

These are tough but important types of questions.

When processing issues or fixing problems, think about these questions to your leadership team to help more deeply in solving problems:

- What is your contribution to the very problem you bring up?
- What did you feel when you brought this up?
- Why does that matter to you?
- What are our points of dissent?
- What is the promise you want to make to each other?
- What topic are you hoping I don't bring up?
- Who are your strongest employees? What are you doing to ensure that they're motivated?
- Who are your weakest employees? What is our plan for them?
- If you were hired to compete against us, what would you advise?
- If you were consulting to us, what would you advise?
- What is currently impossible to do that, if it were possible, would change everything?

Processes become a leadership tool, not a bludgeon. Leadership language, and indeed asking the right questions, become the foundational support for ensuring improved performance and scalability. Leaders can ask questions such as:

- Can you help me understand how you could have handled "X" differently?
- The processes are present for good reasons. What could you have done to ensure . . . ?
- By doing it that way (e.g., outside of the accepted process), what did you want to accomplish?
- What was your ideal outcome?
- What results is this situation producing?
- What is at stake for the company if nothing changes?
- How much is it worth to you to resolve this issue?
- What needs to change?

Do not feel compelled to provide all the answers. You don't need to dominate the discussions. You don't need to have the last word. Do not create an environment where everyone looks to you for answers. Learn how to ask great questions (such as those above) and how to listen. The best leaders know that success most often lies in identifying and asking the best questions rather than jumping to conclusions based on personal hunches or faulty assumptions.

Leadership is about the type of questions you ask as relates to accountability.

All these are open-ended-type questions asking the other person to be more accountable. They also avoid the "Why did you . . . ?" question, to which any answer is typically counterproductive to accountability.

Accountability is understanding and following the accepted processes. It is the expectation. Things do change, and if a new situation or a change in the process becomes warranted, change the process; don't let "one-offs" become the norm.

Be the leader your people want you to be; change your mode now from one of answering questions to one of asking questions. Once and for all, work to build a truly accountable community.

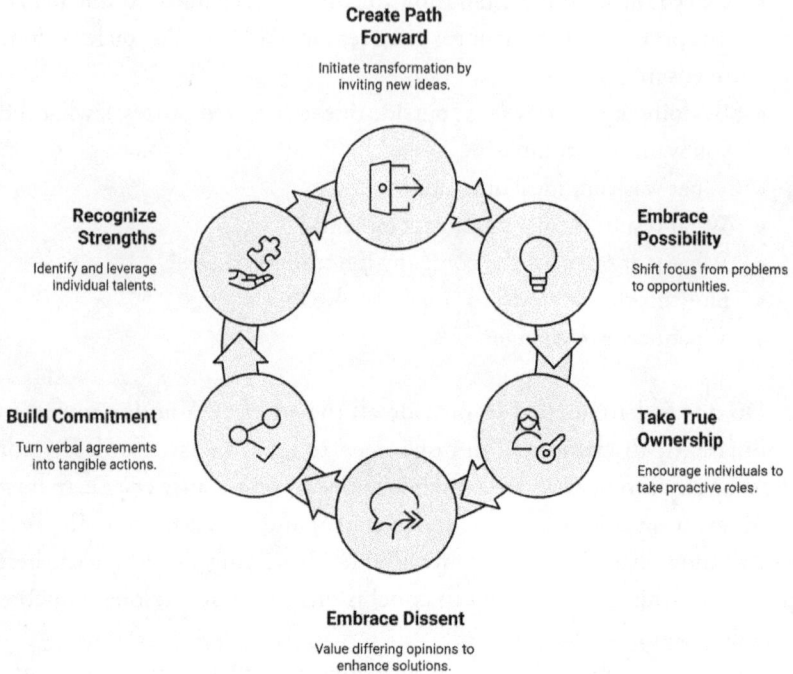

Figure 40—Block's Six Conversations

I. **Invitation:**

Accountability grows out of the act of co-creation. The essence of creating an alternative future comes from employee-to-employee engagement that focuses each step on the well-being of the whole.

- Would an initial meeting be worthwhile if all we did was strengthen our relationships?
- Would a meeting be worthwhile if we learned something of value?
- Suppose in a meeting we simply stated our requests of each other and what we were willing to offer. Would that justify our time together?
- Or, in the gathering, what if we only discussed the gifts we wanted to bring to bear on the concern that brought us together? Would that be an outcome of value?

2. **Jointly Determine Possibility:**
    Focusing on a clear and shared purpose can open our vision to a wide range of possibilities for a different future. This shift in perspective itself can be transformative.

    - What can we create together that will make a difference?
    - What can we create together that you can't create alone?
    - What declaration of possibility can you make that has the power to transform both this community and inspire you?
    - How do we look and feel differently?

3. **Jointly Determine Ownership:**
    It can be easier to focus on what others should change than to accept responsibility for how we contribute to our problems. Focus on how we create a better future.

    - What have I done to contribute to the very thing I complain about or want to change?
    - What's your attraction to your story costing you?

    On a scale of 1–7, in which 1 is the lowest ranking and 7 is the highest, rate the following:

    - How valuable an experience (or project, or community) do you plan for this to be?
    - How much risk are you willing to take?
    - How participative do you plan to be?
    - To what extent are you invested in the well-being of the whole?

4. **Provide Space for Dissent:**
    Block reminds us that as leaders, we have a responsibility to listen and protect space for people's doubt, but we don't necessarily need to respond to each doubt. Some questions for the expression of dissent:

    - What doubts and reservations do you have?
    - What is the "No," or refusal, that you keep postponing?
    - What have you said "Yes" to that you no longer really mean?

- What is a commitment or decision that you have changed your mind about?
- What forgiveness are you withholding?
- What resentment do you hold that no one knows about?

5. **Facilitate Commitment:**
After you have set the context of ownership, explored possibility, and held space for doubt, it comes time for participants to declare their commitment to action. Block writes that honoring our word is the emotional and relational essence of community.

- What promises am I willing to make?
- What measures have meaning to me?
- What price am I willing to pay?
- What is the cost to others for me to keep my commitments or to fail in my commitments?
- What is the promise I am postponing?
- What is the promise or commitment I am unwilling to make?
- What is the promise I'm willing to make that constitutes a risk or major shift for me?

6. **Recognize Gifts:**
Block writes that **community is built by focusing on people's gifts rather than their deficiencies.** In the world of community, deficiencies have no market value; gifts are the point. Citizens in community with each other want to know what you can do, not what you can't do.

- What has someone in your small group done today that has touched you or moved you or been of value to you?
- In what way did a particular person engage you in a way that had meaning?
- What is the gift you currently hold back?
- What is it about you that no one knows about?
- What are you grateful for that has gone unspoken?
- What is the positive feedback you receive that still surprised you?
- What is the gift you have that you do not fully acknowledge?

A FEW OTHER QUESTIONS:

Starting with Gift Questions

- What talents and capacities do we already have?
- What unique perspective do we bring?
- What do we love doing?
- What breaks our hearts about the current reality?
- What contribution are we uniquely positioned to make?

Moving to Impact Questions

- What difference could we make?
- Whom could we serve?
- What could we transform?
- What legacy could we create?
- What future could we enable?

Exploring Implementation Questions

- What would make this possible?
- Who else might contribute?
- What first steps emerge?
- What support would we need?
- How might we begin?

⚡ ⚡ ⚡ ⚡

Leadership

Summary: Appendix 4 provides a detailed comparison of how leadership is conceptualized in Traction and Scaling Up business models. It identifies 12 primary leadership dimensions in Traction (centered around six main areas: Vision, People, Data, Issues, Process, and Traction) and 15 dimensions in Scaling Up (organized around four critical decisions: People, Strategy, Execution, and Cash). While both models share common elements like emphasis on vision, data-driven decision-making, structured meetings, and accountability, they differ significantly in their approach. Traction offers a simpler framework focused on foundational business operations and internal dynamics, while Scaling Up provides a more complex framework designed for managing rapid growth and external challenges. The appendix concludes that the choice between models should depend on an organization's size, growth rate, and specific needs.

HOW DOES LEADERSHIP SHOW UP IN THE TWO BUSINESS MODELS?

Let's take a look at what each of these two business models imply about leadership, remembering that each business model focuses on the tools, not specifically on improving leadership.

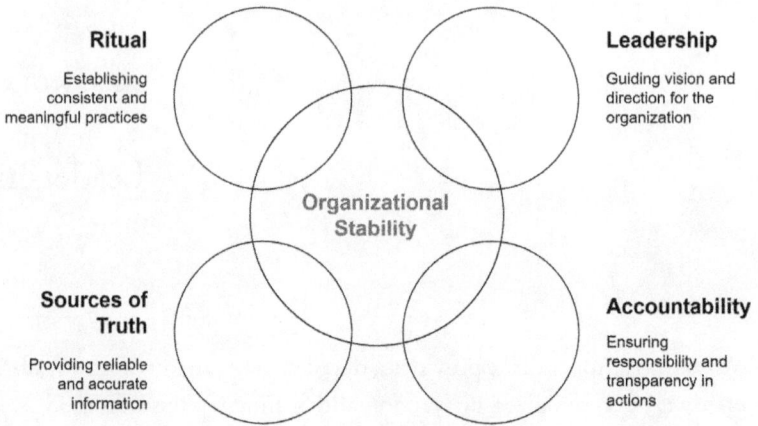

Figure 41—Four Hidden Benefits

PERSPECTIVES ON LEADERSHIP

What are the core perspectives on leadership inherent in Traction as a business model for organizations? The business model is built around six main emphasis areas:

1. Vision
2. People
3. Data
4. Issues
5. Process
6. Traction

While not explicitly called out, within these six areas there seem to be 12 primary leadership dimensions:

1. **Visionary vs. Integrator Roles:** Traction emphasizes the distinction between two key leadership roles. First, the Visionary, typically the entrepreneur or founder, focuses on big-picture thinking and future possibilities. Second, the Integrator, the person who harmonizes the leadership team, manages day-to-day operations and executes the vi-

sion. Effective leadership often requires both roles, typically split between two complementary leaders.

2. **Leadership Team Dynamics:** Traction advocates for a strong, cohesive leadership team. The ideal size is three to seven members who collectively possess the skills to run the entire organization. Each leader should be in the right seat, meaning their role aligns with their strengths and passions.

3. **Accountability:** Leaders are expected to model and enforce accountability throughout the organization. This includes being accountable themselves and asking others for accountability for achieving goals and maintaining commitments.

4. **Clarity and Communication:** Leaders must provide clear direction and effectively communicate the organization's vision, activities, and issues/problems. Open, honest, and regular communication is emphasized, particularly through meeting rituals.

5. **Issue Solving:** Leaders are expected to identify, discuss, and solve issues promptly and effectively. This process is a key tool for leadership in addressing challenges.

6. **Data-Driven Decision-Making:** Traction emphasizes the use of a scorecard, a set of five to 15 key numbers that provide a pulse on the business. Leaders are expected to use this data to make informed decisions and guide the organization.

7. **Maintaining Core Focus:** Leaders are responsible for keeping the organization aligned with its core focus, which includes the company's purpose, cause, or passion, and its niche.

8. **Continuous Improvement:** Traction views leadership as an ongoing process of learning and improvement. Leaders are expected to engage in continuous self-development and to foster a culture of growth within the organization.

9. **Simplicity and Focus:** Traction advocates for simplifying complex business concepts. Leaders are encouraged to maintain focus on what's truly important and avoid getting lost in the details.

10. **Empowerment and Delegation:** Effective leaders in the Traction business model empower their teams by clearly defining roles and responsibilities. They delegate appropriately, trusting their team members to execute within their areas of responsibility.

11. **Quarterly Rocks:** Leaders set and commit to three to seven key priorities (Rocks) each quarter. They are responsible for achieving these Rocks and helping their teams do the same.

12. **Living the Company Values:** Leaders are expected to embody and reinforce the core values of the organization, which stem from the leaders. They play a crucial role in hiring, firing, reviewing, rewarding, and recognizing based on these values.

In this business model, leadership is viewed as a crucial element in creating an organization that can execute the organization's vision. It emphasizes clarity, accountability, and a business systematic approach to running a business. The leadership perspectives in the business model are designed to create a cohesive team that can effectively drive the organization towards its goals while maintaining a healthy and productive company culture.

Scaling Up's perspective on leadership can be summarized around four critical decision areas:

1. **People:** Getting the right people in the right roles
2. **Strategy:** Setting the direction and differentiation of the company
3. **Execution:** Implementing effectively to achieve goals
4. **Cash:** Ensuring sufficient cash to weather storms and fund growth

Within these four critical decision areas there seem to be 15 primary leadership dimensions:

1. **Face Time with Employees:** Leaders should spend significant face time with employees at all levels. The business model recommends a rhythm of daily, weekly, monthly, quarterly, and annual interactions.

2. **Continuous Learning and Teaching:** Leaders are expected to be lifelong learners. They should actively teach what they learn to develop others in the organization.

3. **Setting the Pace:** Leaders set the pace for the entire organization. Their energy and focus directly impact the company's performance.

4. **Clarity of Vision and Purpose:** Leaders must clearly articulate and constantly reinforce the company's vision and purpose. This includes defining core values, purpose, BHAG, and brand promises.

5. **Data-Driven Leadership:** Emphasis on using KPIs and other metrics to guide decisions. Leaders should establish and monitor a "Data Dashboard."

6. **Rhythm of Planning and Execution:** Leaders are advocates for a structured approach to planning and execution which includes daily huddles, weekly meetings, monthly reviews, quarterly planning sessions, and annual strategic planning.

7. **Focus on Priorities:** Leaders should help the organization focus on a few key priorities at a time. Leaders utilize the "One-Page Strategic Plan" to align efforts across the organization.

8. **Building a Strong Executive Team:** Leaders emphasize the importance of a cohesive and high-performing executive team. The business model recommends regular team health checks and development activities.

9. **Developing Future Leaders:** Leaders are responsible for identifying and developing future leaders within the organization, encouraging mentoring, and providing growth opportunities.

10. **Managing Complexity:** As companies scale, leaders must manage increasing complexity and are advocates for business models and processes that allow for scalable growth.

11. **Balancing Short-Term and Long-Term:** Leaders must balance short-term performance with long-term value creation and encourage thinking in terms of both quarterly goals and three- and five-year plans.

12. **Customer-Centric Focus:** Leaders should maintain a strong focus on customer needs and feedback and encourage regular interaction with key customers.

13. **Accountability and Transparency:** Leaders promote a culture of accountability starting from the top and are advocates for transparency in communication and decision-making.

14. **Cash Flow Management:** Leaders must have a keen understanding of cash flow and emphasize the importance of financial acumen in leadership.

15. **Adaptability and Innovation:** Leaders should foster a culture of adaptability and innovation, which encourages experimentation and learning from failures.

The leadership perspectives in Scaling Up are designed to help leaders navigate the challenges of rapid growth while maintaining a strong, purposeful organization. The focus is on creating business models and rhythms that allow for scalable leadership as the company expands.

Similarities Between Models:

These two views (from the business models) of leadership sound convincing but perhaps with different words and methods. When you study the two business models there are some similarities regarding leadership:

- **Emphasis on Vision and Purpose:** Both business models stress the importance of leaders clearly articulating and reinforcing the company's vision, purpose, and core values.
- **Data-Driven Decision-Making:** Traction uses a scorecard, while Scaling Up employs a Data Dashboard. Both emphasize the use of key metrics to guide leadership decisions.
- **Structured Meeting Rituals:** Both business models advocate for regular, structured meetings at various intervals (daily, weekly, quarterly, annually) to maintain alignment and address issues.
- **Focus on Priorities:** Traction uses "Rocks," while Scaling Up uses the "One-Page Strategic Plan." Both aim to help leaders focus on key priorities.
- **Importance of the Right Team:** Both emphasize building a strong leadership team and ensuring the right people are in the right roles.
- **Accountability:** Both business models stress the importance of accountability in leadership and throughout the organization.
- **Continuous Improvement:** Both approaches view leadership as an ongoing process of learning and improvement.

Significant Differences Between the Models:

There should be no surprises here as both business models are designed to improve operations, even though the "how to improve leadership" question remains unaddressed. From the above perspectives of leadership either business model could satisfy your needs. However, there are other significant differences between the two which you may want to consider.

- **Leadership Roles:** Traction emphasizes the distinction between Visionary and Integrator roles. Scaling Up focuses more on a single leader mastering the Four Decisions (People, Strategy, Execution, Cash).
- **Complexity of Framework:** Traction tends to emphasize simplicity and focuses on six key components. Scaling Up offers a more complex framework with multiple tools and concepts.
- **Growth Focus:** Traction is designed for small- to medium-sized businesses, focusing on establishing foundational business models. Scaling Up is specifically tailored for rapid growth and scaling, addressing challenges of larger, fast-growing companies.
- **Financial Emphasis:** Traction includes financial considerations but doesn't emphasize them as a separate leadership focus. Scaling Up puts significant emphasis on cash and financial acumen as a key leadership responsibility.
- **Customer Focus:** Traction's customer focus is implicit in the business model but not explicitly emphasized in leadership roles. Scaling Up explicitly emphasizes customer-centric leadership and regular interaction with key customers.
- **Leadership Development:** Traction focuses more on optimizing current leadership team dynamics. Scaling Up puts more emphasis on developing future leaders and succession planning.
- **External Orientation:** Traction is more internally focused on organizational health and execution. Scaling Up is more externally oriented, emphasizing market dynamics and competitive positioning.
- **Handling Complexity:** Traction aims to simplify complex business concepts for easier execution. Scaling Up acknowledges increasing complexity with growth and provides tools to manage it.
- **Time Horizon:** Traction tends to focus more on shorter-term execution (quarterly Rocks), while Scaling Up emphasizes balancing short-term performance with long-term (three to five year) value creation.
- **Leadership Interaction:** Traction focuses on leadership team dynamics and cascading communication. Scaling Up emphasizes direct leader interaction at all levels, including significant face time with frontline employees.

It appears, then, these two business models also differ in their specific focus and the complexity of their approaches and leadership. Traction offers a simpler, more streamlined business model suitable for establishing basic business operations, while Scaling Up provides a more comprehensive framework designed for managing the complexities of rapid growth. The choice between these business models often depends on the size, growth rate, and specific needs of you, your leadership team, and the organization.

⚡ ⚡ ⚡ ⚡

Accountability

Summary: Appendix 5 examines how accountability is structured in Traction and Scaling Up business models. Traction approaches accountability through ten tools (including Accountability Chart, Rocks, Level 10 Meetings) focused on creating clear organizational structure and measurable goals. Scaling Up similarly offers ten accountability areas (including Function Accountability Chart, Rockefeller Habits Checklist, One-Page Strategic Plan) but with a broader scope. While both models share common elements like visual accountability tools, regular meetings, and focus on metrics, they differ significantly in their approach: Traction emphasizes internal operational accountability with a simpler framework, while Scaling Up provides a more comprehensive framework that includes external relationships and broader business functions. The appendix concludes that effective accountability in either model creates an environment where expectations are clear, progress is visible, and challenges are addressed promptly.

How Does Accountability Show Up in the Two Business Models?

Where the previous appendix took a deeper dive in into the perspectives of leadership inherent in each business model, we will shift to accountability in this one.[66] Each business model talks about accountability, but neither specifically defines it nor addresses how the respective business model can be used.

---

66. See Chapter 16 for an expansion on Accountability.

PERSPECTIVES ON ACCOUNTABILITY

Traction's approach to accountability, again while not specifically defined, revolves around the use of ten tools:

1. **Accountability Chart:** This chart replaces traditional command-and-control organizational charts with a clear structure showing who is accountable for what. It defines key roles and accountabilities within the organization.
2. **Right Person, Right Seat:** The business model emphasizes placing people in roles that match their strengths and the company's needs and uses Get it, Want it, Capacity to do it (GWC™) to assess fit.
3. **Rocks:** These are quarterly priorities that individuals commit to achieving in clear, measurable goals that drive accountability.
4. **Measurables:** Additionally, the business model has KPIs for each role, which provide objective data to assess performance and drive accountability.
5. **Level 10 Meetings:** These are weekly team meetings with a structured format, including a scorecard review and accountability for to-dos and rocks.
6. **Issue Solving:** There is a standard process for addressing problems, which promotes accountability in both problem-solving and decision-making.
7. **Quarterly Conversations:** Regular check-ins to discuss performance, goals, and alignment are recommended quarterly, which reinforces accountability through consistent communication.
8. **Core Values:** Belief in deeply held values is used as a basis for hiring, firing, reviewing, rewarding, and recognizing, which holds individuals accountable to the company's fundamental beliefs.
9. **Scorecard:** These weekly metrics provide a pulse on the business, which further creates accountability for key business results.
10. **To-Do Lists:** Action items are assigned and reviewed weekly ensuring follow-through on commitments.

Accountability is enhanced when leadership creates and maintains a clear and simple organizational structure where:

1. Every individual understands their role and accountabilities (Accountability Chart).
2. People are matched to roles based on their abilities and passion (Right Person, Right Seat).
3. Clear, measurable goals are set and consistently pursued (Rocks and Measurables).
4. Regular, effective communication and problem-solving occur (Level 10 Meetings and IDS).
5. Performance is objectively measured and discussed (Scorecard and Quarterly Conversations).
6. The organization's core values and vision are consistently reinforced and lived.
7. Leaders model accountability and empower others to take ownership of their areas of responsibility.

Effective leaders in this business model create an environment of clarity, focus, and discipline, where accountability is seen as a tool for growth and achievement rather than punishment. They balance setting clear expectations with providing the necessary support and resources for their team to succeed.

Scaling Up's Approach to Accountability is focused in ten areas:

1. **Function Accountability Chart (FACe):** Clearly defines who is accountable for what functions in the organization and assigns KPIs to each function.
2. **Rockefeller Habits Checklist:** A set of ten habits that drive accountability and execution, which includes elements like setting priorities, gathering employee input, and live reporting of data.
3. **One-Page Strategic Plan (OPSP):** Aligns the entire organization around key goals and metrics and creates accountability for strategic objectives at all levels.
4. **Meeting Rhythm:** Daily huddles, weekly meetings, monthly management meetings, quarterly and annual planning sessions, which ensure regular check-ins on goals and accountability.
5. **Critical Numbers:** Key metrics that the organization focuses on quarterly and annually, which creates shared accountability for the most important outcomes.

6. **Cash Acceleration Strategies (CASh):** Focus on financial account-ability and cash flow management, assigning specific responsibilities for improving cash position.
7. **Strengths, Weaknesses, Opportunities, Threats (SWOT):** Regular analysis to keep leaders accountable for addressing key issues and cap-italizing on opportunities.[67]
8. **Process Accountability Chart (PAC):** Defines who is accountable for each of the core processes in the organization, which ensures clear ownership of process improvement.
9. **Key Relationships:** Identifies who is accountable for managing key stakeholder relationships, ensuring important external relationships are nurtured.
10. **Coaching and Feedback:** Emphasizes the importance of regular coaching and feedback sessions, which ask leaders to be accountable for developing their team members.

Accountability then is enhanced when leadership drives sustainable growth by creating a culture of execution in which:

1. Every function and process have clear ownership and measurable out-comes (FACe and PAC),
2. The entire organization is aligned around a coherent strategy and key priorities (OPSP),
3. Regular rhythms of communication and planning maintain focus and drive results (Meeting Rhythm),
4. Financial stewardship and cash flow management are prioritized (CASh),
5. The external environment is continuously monitored and addressed (in the OT part of SWOT),

67. Both business models misrepresent a portion of SWOTs: the word "Opportunity" is not explained according to strategic planning, and it potentially leads teams astray when doing the exercise. In everyday vernacular, an "opportunity" is something you might want to do, such as make an acquisition (i.e., it's an opportunity). Not so in strategic planning, where an "opportunity" is something in the exterior environment that might be conducive for a strategy such as acquisition. An Opportunity in a SWOT analysis is simply some-thing external to the organization (such as a growing economy or other favorable future conditions), not something leadership should, would, or ought to do.

6. Key stakeholder relationships are actively managed, and
7. Team members are developed through consistent coaching and feedback.

Effective leaders in this business model balance strategic thinking with meticulous execution. They create business models that drive accountability across all levels of the organization, while maintaining a focus on the critical factors that enable scalable growth. Leaders are expected to be both visionaries and operators, capable of setting a compelling direction while also ensuring the organization has the discipline and processes to achieve its goals.

In essence, Scaling Up views leadership as the art of creating a growth-oriented organization with the business models, people, and discipline necessary to scale successfully. Leaders are expected to be equally comfortable with high-level strategy and ground-level execution, always maintaining a balance between future vision and current performance.

As with leadership, there are comparisons and contrasts on each business model's approach to accountability.

Similarities between business models:

1. Both use visual tools to clarify accountability (Accountability Chart vs. Functional Accountability Chart).
2. Both emphasize regular meetings to maintain accountability (Level 10 Meetings vs. Meeting Rhythm).
3. Both focus on key metrics and KPIs (Measurables/Scorecard vs. Critical Numbers).
4. Both incorporate quarterly goal setting and review (Rocks vs. One Page Strategic Plan's quarterly goals).
5. Both stress the importance of clear, measurable objectives.

Differences between the two on accountability:

1. **Scope:** Traction focuses more on internal operational accountability, while Scaling Up extends to external relationships and broader business functions.
2. **Complexity:** Traction offers a simpler, more streamlined approach, while Scaling Up provides a more comprehensive framework.

3. **Financial Focus:** Scaling Up places more explicit emphasis on financial accountability (Cash Acceleration Strategies).
4. **Strategic Alignment:** Scaling Up's One Page Strategic Plan provides a more detailed tool for strategic accountability across the organization.
5. **Process Focus:** Scaling Up's Commercial Action Plan provides explicit accountability for core business processes.

Effective accountability, therefore, creates an environment where expectations are clear, progress is visible, challenges are addressed promptly, and success is recognized and reinforced. It serves as a driving force for organizational performance, enabling sustainable growth and fostering a culture of ownership and continuous improvement.

⚡⚡⚡⚡

Ritual

Summary: Appendix 6 compares how rituals are structured in Traction and Scaling Up business models. While Traction embeds six key rituals (including weekly Level 10 meetings, quarterly rocks setting, and annual planning), Scaling Up features seven rituals (including daily huddles, weekly meetings, and quarterly planning). Though both models share common elements like weekly team meetings, quarterly planning, and annual reviews, they differ significantly in their approach. Traction offers more prescriptive, structured rituals suited for small to medium businesses, while Scaling Up provides a more flexible framework designed for larger, complex organizations.

How Does Ritual Show Up in the Two Business Models?

This Appendix explores the third of four main benefits of using either business model: rituals.

First, an examination of each business model.

Traction seems to have rituals embedded in six parts of the business model:

- **Weekly Level 10 Meetings:** The 90-minute structured weekly meeting with a specific agenda
- **Quarterly Rocks Setting:** Establishing three to seven priorities for the next 90 days
- **Quarterly Conversations:** One-on-one meetings between leaders and direct reports

- **Annual Planning Session:** Two-day offsite meeting to review and set direction for the coming year
- **Quarterly Meeting Checks:** Reviewing overall company performance and rocks
- **5-5-5 Communication Structure:** Includes personal sharing, performance review, and feedback each week between leaders and direct reports

Scaling Up also has embedded rituals:

- **Daily Huddle:** Five- to 15-minute stand-up meeting to align the team daily
- **Weekly Meeting:** 60- to 90-minute meeting focused on tactical issues
- **Monthly Management Meeting:** Half-day meeting to address key strategic issues
- **Quarterly Planning Session:** One- to two-day offsite to review progress and set priorities for the next quarter
- **Annual Planning Retreat:** Two- to three-day offsite to set the strategy for the coming year
- **One-on-One Coaching:** Regular meetings between leaders and team members for development and alignment
- **Theme Implementation:** Quarterly or annual themes to focus the entire organization

Similarities of the Models on Rituals:

It is apparent there are similarities in the rituals created by using the business model:

- **Weekly Team Meetings:** Both business models emphasize a structured weekly meeting to address issues and maintain alignment.
- **Quarterly Planning:** Both have a ritual for setting priorities and goals for each quarter.
- **Annual Planning:** Both recommend an annual offsite to set long-term direction.

- **One-on-One Meetings:** Both business models include regular one-on-one meetings between leaders and team members.
- **Data Review:** Both incorporate regular review of key metrics in their meeting structures.

Differences Between the Models on Rituals:

Despite the similarities there are significant differences between the rituals created by implementing either business model:

- **Meeting Frequency:** Scaling Up includes daily huddles and adds a monthly management meeting, neither present in Traction.
- **Meeting Duration:** Traction's Level 10 meeting is specifically 90 minutes long, while Scaling Up's weekly meeting is more flexible, 60 to 90 minutes.
- **Priority Setting:** Traction uses the term "Rocks" for quarterly priorities, while Scaling Up typically refers to these as priorities or goals within the One-Page Strategic Plan.
- **Thematic Approach:** Scaling Up incorporates the concept of organizational themes, which is not a standard part of Traction.
- **Structure of One-on-Ones:** Traction recommends the 5-5-5 structure for weekly check-ins, and Scaling Up is less prescriptive about the structure of one-on-ones.
- **Issue Resolution:** Traction has a specific process built into weekly meetings, while Scaling Up addresses issue resolution but doesn't prescribe a specific method.

Both Traction and Scaling Up emphasize the importance of regular, structured rituals to maintain organizational alignment and drive execution. Traction tends to offer a more prescriptive approach with specific formats for meetings and interactions. Scaling Up provides a more flexible framework that can be adapted to different organizational sizes and complexities.

Scaling Up's rituals seem designed to accommodate larger, more complex organizations with its inclusion of daily huddles and monthly management meetings. Traction's rituals are more focused on establishing fundamental business rhythms, which may be more suitable for small- to medium-sized businesses.

The choice between these business models often depends on the size, growth rate, and complexity of the organization. Some businesses might even find value in combining elements from both approaches, adapting the rituals to fit their specific needs and culture.

⚡⚡⚡⚡

Sources of Truth

Summary: Appendix 7 examines how sources of truth manifest in Traction and Scaling Up business models, though neither explicitly describes their tools as such. Traction employs nine key elements as sources of truth (including Vision/Traction Organizer, Accountability Chart, and Scorecard), focusing on streamlined, fundamental business practices. Scaling Up offers 11 sources of truth (including One-Page Strategic Plan, Function Accountability Chart, and Cash Acceleration Strategies) with greater complexity and detail. While both models share common elements like strategic vision documents and core values, they differ significantly in their approach—Traction emphasizes simplicity for small to medium businesses, while Scaling Up provides more sophisticated tools for managing rapid growth and complexity.

How Do Sources of Truth Show Up in the Two Business Models?

The last of the four main benefits of implementing one of these two business models is about developing and using Sources of Truth.

First, neither business model explicitly describes how their respective tools can be used as sources of truth. However, the tools of each business model serve as evidence of fact, the black-and-white properties of data.

Traction relies on several key elements that serve as sources of truth within the business model. These are the fundamental, authoritative references that guide decision-making, alignment, and execution throughout the organization:

- **Vision/Traction Organizer:** The Vision/Traction Organizer, though only two pages long, is a comprehensive document that captures the organization's core focus, ten-year target, marketing strategy, and three-year picture. It becomes the source of truth for:
  ○ long-term direction,
  ○ core values and purpose, and
  ○ key strategies and goals.

  This form serves as the central reference point for all major decisions and actions, ensuring alignment with the organization's overarching vision and strategy.

- **Accountability Chart:** This chart replaces the traditional organization chart, clearly defining roles, accountabilities, and reporting structures and is an inherent source of truth for:
  ○ organizational structure,
  ○ role clarity, and
  ○ decision-making authority.

  It provides a clear, visual representation of who is responsible for what, eliminating confusion and overlap in responsibilities.

- **Rocks:** Rocks are the top three to seven priorities for the next 90 days. They become the source of truth for:
  ○ short-term priorities, and
  ○ focus and resource allocation.

  Rocks guide day-to-day activities and decision-making, ensuring that efforts are aligned with the most important quarterly objectives.

- **Scorecard:** The Scorecard is a weekly report of five to 15 key numbers that provide a pulse on the business. It becomes a source of truth for:
  ○ current performance,
  ○ trend analysis, and
  ○ early problem detection.

It provides objective, data-driven insights into the health and performance of the business, guiding operational decisions.

- **Level 10 Meeting Agenda:** This is a structured agenda for weekly team meetings, designed to focus on solving real issues. It becomes a source of truth through:
  ○ meeting productivity,
  ○ issue identification and resolution, and
  ○ team communication.

It standardizes the way teams communicate and solve problems, ensuring consistency and efficiency in team interactions.

- **Issues List:** A compiled list of obstacles, problems, and opportunities that need to be addressed. This list is a source of truth for:
  ○ current challenges and opportunities, and
  ○ problem-solving priorities.

It serves as a central repository for all issues that need attention, ensuring that nothing falls through the cracks.

- **Core Values:** A set of three to seven essential beliefs that define the culture of the organization. These values are a source of truth for:
  ○ behavioral expectations,
  ○ hiring and firing decisions, and
  ○ cultural alignment.

Core values guide decision-making, especially in people-related matters, ensuring cultural consistency throughout the organization.

- **Core Focus:** A simple statement that defines the organization's reason for existing and its niche. This focus sets the source of truth for:
  ○ strategic direction, and
  ○ opportunity evaluation.

It serves as a filter for decision-making, helping to evaluate whether potential actions or opportunities align with the organization's fundamental purpose and strengths.

- **Process Documentation:** The documentation of the organization's core processes is a source of truth for:
  ○ operational standards,
  ○ training and onboarding, and
  ○ consistency in execution.

This documentation provides a standardized reference for how key activities should be performed, ensuring consistency and quality across the organization.

These sources of truth embedded in the Traction business model provide a framework of authoritative references that guide decision-making, alignment, and execution throughout the organization. Relying on these source of truth elements upon implementation creates a business model where subjectivity is reduced, clarity is increased, and everyone in the organization can refer to the same set of fundamental truths when making decisions or taking actions.

Scaling Up relies on several key elements that serve as sources of truth within the business model, although these key elements are not described as sources of truth. They are, however, the fundamental, authoritative references that guide decision-making, alignment, and execution throughout the organization as it scales.

- **One-Page Strategic Plan:** A comprehensive document that captures the organization's long-term and short-term goals, strategies, and key initiatives on a single page. It serves as a source of truth for:
  ○ strategic direction,
  ○ alignment of goals across time horizons and organizational levels, and
  ○ key priorities and metrics.

This serves as the central reference point for all strategic decisions and actions, ensuring alignment from the long-term vision down to quarterly priorities.

- **Core Values and Purpose:** Clearly defined set of core values and a purpose statement that guide the organization's culture and decision-making. These serve as a source of truth for:
  - organizational culture,
  - behavioral expectations, and
  - long-term direction.

These serve as a filter for decisions, particularly in hiring, firing, and strategic choices, ensuring cultural consistency as the organization grows.

- **Function Accountability Chart:** A chart that clearly defines the primary functions of the business and who is accountable for each. This serves as a source of truth for:
  - organizational structure,
  - role clarity and accountability, and
  - key performance indicators for each function.

It provides a clear reference for who is responsible for what, reducing confusion and overlap as the organization becomes more complex.

- **Process Accountability Chart:** A document that outlines the core processes of the organization and who is accountable for each. This serves as a source of truth for:
  - operational standards,
  - process ownership, and
  - efficiency and scalability of operations.

It serves as the go-to reference for how key activities should be performed and improved, ensuring consistency and scalability.

- **Rockefeller Habits Checklist:** A set of ten habits derived from John D. Rockefeller's practices, adapted for modern business. These habits from the source of truth for:
  - execution discipline,
  - alignment practices, and
  - leadership behaviors.

The checklist serves as a constant reference for leaders to ensure they're following key practices that drive growth and alignment.

- **Meeting Rhythm:** A structured business model of daily, weekly, monthly, quarterly, and annual meetings, each of which serves as a source of truth for:
  - communication cadence,
  - performance review, and
  - strategic adjustment.

Collectively, they provide a consistent framework for when and how key discussions and decisions should occur at various organizational levels.

- **Cash Acceleration Strategies:** A set of practical tools and metrics focused on improving cash flow. These serve as a source of truth for:
  - financial health,
  - cash flow management, and
  - growth funding.

These strategies serve as the primary reference for financial decision-making and cash management practices.

- **KPIs and Critical Numbers:** A defined set of metrics that provide insight into the organization's performance. These provide a source of truth for:
  - current performance,
  - trend analysis, and
  - focus areas for improvement.

These metrics provide objective, data-driven insights into the health and performance of the business, guiding operational and strategic decisions.

- **BHAG:** A bold, long-term goal that aligns and motivates the entire organization. This provides a source of truth for:
  - long-term vision,

○ ambitious target setting, and
○ organizational motivation.

They serve as a north star for the organization, guiding long-term strategy and decision-making.

- **Brand Promise and Brand Promise Guarantee:** A clear statement of what the company promises to deliver to customers, backed by a specific guarantee. This serves as a source of truth for:
  ○ customer value proposition,
  ○ operational focus, and
  ○ quality standards.

It provides a clear reference point for what the organization stands for in the market and what it commits to delivering to customers.

These Sources of Truth in Scaling Up provide a comprehensive framework of authoritative references that guide decision-making, alignment, and execution as an organization grows. By relying on these elements, Scaling Up creates a business model where complexity is managed, clarity is maintained, and everyone in the organization can refer to the same set of fundamental truths when making decisions or taking actions, even as the organization scales rapidly.

Similarities of the Models on Sources of Truth:

As with the previous three main benefits of the business models, there are similarities in the two:

- **Strategic Vision Document:** Traction's Vision/Traction Organizer and Scaling Up's One-Page Strategic Plan both serve as comprehensive references for strategic direction and goals.
- **Core Values and Purpose:** Both business models emphasize these as fundamental guides for organizational culture and decision-making.
- **Organizational Structure Clarity:** Traction's Accountability Chart and Scaling Up's Function Accountability Chart (FACe) both provide clear references for roles and responsibilities.

- **Key Performance Metrics:** Traction's Scorecard and Scaling Up's Key Performance Indicators and Critical Numbers all emphasize data-driven performance tracking.
- **Meeting Structure:** Traction's Level 10 Meeting Agenda and Scaling Up's Meeting Rhythm both provide models for regular, structured communication.
- **Short-Term Priorities:** Traction's Rocks and Scaling Up's Priorities both focus on key short-term (often quarterly) objectives.
- **Process Documentation:** Traction's Process Documentation and Scaling Up's Process Accountability Chart both emphasize standardizing core processes.

As before, the two business models also have their differences. It is notable to point out:

- **Complexity and Detail:** Traction tends to offer simpler, more streamlined tools, while Scaling Up provides more detailed and complex models, suitable for larger or rapidly growing organizations.
- **Financial Focus:** Traction includes financial considerations within its overall framework. In comparison, Scaling Up has a specific tool: Cash Acceleration Strategies (CASh) which is dedicated to financial management.
- **Long-Term Vision:** Traction includes a 10-year target in their V/TO, while Scaling Up emphasizes the Big Hairy Audacious Goal (BHAG) as a separate, central concept.
- **Issue Management:** Traction has a specific Issues List as a Source of Truth, while Scaling Up addresses issues within its meeting rhythm but doesn't highlight them as a separate Source of Truth.
- **Market Positioning:** Scaling Up includes Brand Promise and Brand Promise Guarantee as specific Sources of Truth, while Traction incorporates market positioning within the Vison/Traction Organizer but doesn't highlight it as a separate element.
- **Execution Framework:** Scaling Up has the Rockefeller Habits Checklist as a specific Source of Truth for execution practices, while Traction embeds execution practices within its overall business model, without a separate checklist.

- **Growth Focus:** Scaling Up's tools are more explicitly designed for managing rapid growth and increasing complexity, and Traction's tools are more focused on establishing fundamental business practices.

Differences of the Models on Sources of Truth:

Finally, there are several elements that are unique to each business model:

Traction:

- **Core Focus:** A simple statement of purpose and niche, more concise than Scaling Up's approach, and
- The **Traction component** with its specific emphasis on discipline and accountability.

Scaling Up:

- **BHAG:** Emphasized as a central, long-term visionary goal.
- **Cash Acceleration Strategies:** Specific focus on cash flow management.
- **Function and Process Accountability Charts:** Separates functional and process responsibilities.

Both Traction and Scaling Up provide comprehensive sets of sources of truth to guide organizational decision-making and alignment. Traction offers a more streamlined, simplistic approach suitable for small- to medium-sized businesses for focusing on establishing strong foundational practices. Scaling Up provides a more detailed and complex set of tools designed to manage the challenges of rapid growth and increasing organizational complexity.

The choice between these business models is up to you and often depends on the size, growth rate, and complexity of your organization. Some businesses might even find value in combining elements from both approaches as they grow and evolve.

⚡⚡⚡⚡

Strategies to Disentangle Oneself

Summary: Appendix 8 provides nine practical strategies to help leaders transition from traditional to community-enhanced leadership styles. These strategies include starting with small initiatives and celebrating wins, investing in personal leadership development, creating opportunities to showcase employee capabilities, reframing perspectives on time and results, practicing vulnerability, implementing structured collaboration models, building personal connections throughout the organization, engaging with peer CEOs who have successfully made similar transitions, and gradually delegating authority. Each strategy is designed to address specific fears and challenges leaders face when moving away from command-and-control approaches, helping them build confidence and comfort with more collaborative leadership methods.

As you evolve to a more community-enhanced leadership style, you may find yourself wishing to leave some old patterns/habits of behavior behind. Sometimes this is not an easy task, because, at a minimum, it requires you to acknowledge that what you are currently doing may not be the best answer.

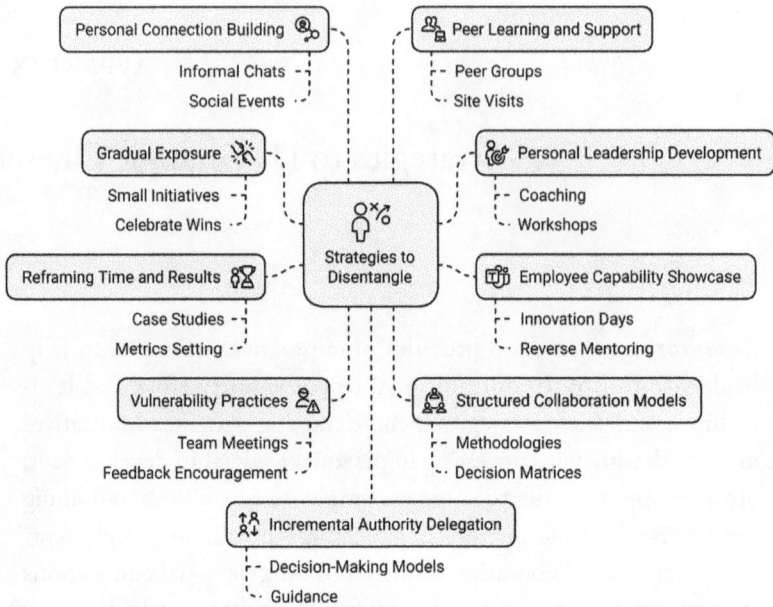

Figure 42—Strategies to Disentangle Oneself

Some suggestions to help you break free and untangle yourself from your own past:

- **Gradual Exposure and Celebration of Small Wins:** Start with small, low-risk initiatives using community-based approaches, such as beginning with a single project, setting clear, achievable goals for yourself in this initial effort, and celebrating and publicizing successes, no matter how small. This strategy addresses the fear of losing control or fear of chaos by building your confidence in the approach without feeling overwhelmed.

- **Personal Leadership Development:** Invest in personal growth and leadership coaching such as working with a coach who is experienced in collaborative leadership styles, attending workshops or retreats focused on emotional intelligence and collaborative/community-enhanced leadership, and practicing self-reflection and journaling about leadership experiences. This strategy addresses insecurity about leadership abilities, fear of vulnerability by enhancing self-awareness and confidence in diverse leadership styles.

- **Employee Capability Showcase:** Create opportunities to witness and acknowledge employee capabilities; for example, organizing "innovation days" or hackathons where employees can showcase ideas; implement a reverse mentoring program in which junior staff members mentor executives; or regularly rotate meeting leadership among team members. This strategy works to eliminate distrust in employees' capabilities by building trust in the team's abilities and opens eyes to hidden talents.

- **Reframing Time and Results:** Shift perspective on the relationship between time, process, and outcomes by reviewing case studies of successful community-led initiatives and their long-term benefits, setting both short-term and long-term metrics for initiatives, or practicing patience and celebrating progress, not just end results. This strategy addresses the perceived need for quick results and develops a more nuanced understanding of success and timelines.

- **Vulnerability Practices:** Gradually introduce practices that encourage openness and vulnerability, such as starting team meetings by sharing a personal challenge or learning, publicly acknowledging mistakes and what was learned from them, and encouraging and rewarding honest feedback from all levels. This strategy addresses the fear of vulnerability and creates a culture of trust and authenticity.

- **Structured Collaboration Models:** Implement structured models (e.g., the community-enhanced leadership business model) for collaborative decision-making and problem-solving. For example, adopting different methodologies (like Design Thinking or Agile) for specific projects, using tools like decision matrices that incorporate input from various levels, or setting clear parameters for collaborative processes to maintain focus. This strategy addresses the fear of chaos or losing focus while providing a sense of order and direction within collaborative approaches.

- **Personal Connection Building:** Focus on building personal connections throughout the organization, such as regularly scheduling informal chats with employees at all levels, participating in company social events and team-building activities, and sharing appropriate personal stories and encouraging others to do the same. This strategy addresses the fear of losing authority, insecurity about leadership abilities and builds trust and rapport, making the transition to a community-based approach feel more natural.

- **Peer Learning and Support:** Engage with peer business owners/ CEOs who have successfully implemented community-based approaches; examples include joining business owner/CEO peer groups or forums focused on modern leadership styles, arranging site visits to organizations successfully using community-based leadership, or inviting guest speakers to share their community leadership journeys. This strategy addresses attachment to traditional power structures and insecurity about new approaches and provides real-world examples and peer support for the transition.

- **Incremental Authority Delegation:** Gradually delegate decision-making authority to build comfort with shared leadership by identifying low-risk decisions that can be delegated to teams, providing clear models for decision-making processes, and offering support and guidance, but resist the urge to overrule decisions. This strategy addresses the fear of losing control, distrust in employees' capabilities while building trust in the team's abilities and comfort with shared leadership.

$$\not{f} \not{f} \not{f} \not{f}$$

Transformational Capabilities
Development Checklist

Summary: Appendix 9 provides a comprehensive self-assessment checklist for leaders and organizations to evaluate their capabilities across six key development areas: Facilitation, Question-Asking, Listening, Pattern Recognition, Support Systems, and Integration. Each area is broken down into foundation, intermediate, and advanced levels (or specific components for Support Systems and Integration), allowing leaders to honestly assess their current capabilities and identify areas for growth. The checklist is designed to be used as a developmental guide rather than a performance evaluation, emphasizing steady improvement over perfect scores and encouraging regular review and adaptation to specific organizational contexts.

NOTES FOR USING THIS CHECKLIST:

- ☐ Use as a developmental guide, not performance evaluation.
- ☐ Review regularly to track progress.
- ☐ Focus on steady improvement rather than perfect scores.
- ☐ Adapt to specific organizational context.
- ☐ Update based on emerging needs and learning.

Check off all that apply in each of the six categories below. Be honest and see where your organizational capabilities lie. Note: you also want to do this with your leadership team, individually or collectively.

APPENDIX 9

FACILITATION DEVELOPMENT

Foundation Level

- ☐ Can establish clear context for group conversations
- ☐ Manages basic time boundaries effectively
- ☐ Ensures all participants have opportunity to contribute
- ☐ Captures key discussion points accurately
- ☐ Maintains basic group focus on topic

Intermediate Level

- ☐ Reads and responds to group energy shifts
- ☐ Navigates basic conflict situations
- ☐ Balances participation across different voices
- ☐ Supports natural emergence of ideas
- ☐ Guides groups toward clear decisions

Advanced Level

- ☐ Holds creative tension in complex situations
- ☐ Works effectively with emergent dynamics
- ☐ Enables access to collective wisdom
- ☐ Supports transformative conversations
- ☐ Builds group's self-facilitation capacity

QUESTION-ASKING DEVELOPMENT

Foundation Level

- ☐ Shifts from statements to questions regularly
- ☐ Asks basic clarifying questions effectively
- ☐ Explores different perspectives through questions
- ☐ Checks assumptions through inquiry
- ☐ Identifies needs through questioning

Intermediate Level

- ☐ Creates questions that open new possibilities
- ☐ Challenges assumptions constructively
- ☐ Reveals patterns through questioning
- ☐ Explores implications effectively
- ☐ Discovers deeper meaning through inquiry

Advanced Level

- ☐ Enables breakthrough thinking with questions
- ☐ Accesses collective wisdom through inquiry
- ☐ Reveals unexpected possibilities
- ☐ Creates paradigm shifts through questions
- ☐ Enables transformation through powerful questions

LISTENING DEVELOPMENT

Foundation Level

- ☐ Maintains physical presence in conversations
- ☐ Focuses mental attention effectively
- ☐ Demonstrates basic emotional awareness
- ☐ Notices energy in interactions
- ☐ Recognizes basic patterns in dialogue

Intermediate Level

- ☐ Creates safe space for others' expression
- ☐ Senses underlying currents in conversations
- ☐ Works comfortably with silence
- ☐ Reads non-verbal communications
- ☐ Understands contextual influences

Advanced Level

☐ Accesses collective field in groups
☐ Senses emerging possibilities
☐ Understands systemic patterns
☐ Enables transformative dialogue
☐ Builds collective listening capacity

PATTERN RECOGNITION DEVELOPMENT

Foundation Level

☐ Notices recurring themes in conversations
☐ Tracks basic energy patterns
☐ Observes simple relationship dynamics
☐ Monitors decision-making patterns
☐ Recognizes emerging trends

Intermediate Level

☐ Understands organizational dynamics
☐ Recognizes cultural patterns
☐ Maps relationship networks
☐ Identifies power structures
☐ Tracks change processes

Advanced Level

☐ Anticipates future trends
☐ Identifies emerging possibilities
☐ Recognizes strategic implications
☐ Spots innovation opportunities
☐ Senses transformation potential

SUPPORT SYSTEM DEVELOPMENT

Learning Infrastructure

- ☐ Establishes daily reflection practices
- ☐ Holds regular weekly learning exchanges
- ☐ Holds monthly capability review process
- ☐ Holds quarterly development assessment
- ☐ Holds annual capability planning

Knowledge Management

- ☐ Has system in place for capturing learning
- ☐ Has process in place for sharing practices
- ☐ Has method in place for documenting insights
- ☐ Has structure in place for wisdom harvest
- ☐ Has approach in place for scaling learning

Development Support

- ☐ Has mentoring relationships established
- ☐ Has active practice communities
- ☐ Has feedback systems functioning
- ☐ Has regular learning celebrations
- ☐ Has clear growth pathways

INTEGRATION ASSESSMENT

Daily Integration

- ☐ Morning capability focus established
- ☐ Practice opportunities identified
- ☐ Reflection moments scheduled
- ☐ Learning captured regularly
- ☐ Evening review process in place

Weekly Development

- ☐ Skill practice sessions scheduled
- ☐ Learning exchanges happening
- ☐ Feedback processes active
- ☐ Pattern recognition practiced
- ☐ Celebration moments included

Monthly Deepening

- ☐ Capability assessment process active
- ☐ Learning integration happening
- ☐ Practice adjustments made
- ☐ Support systems aligned
- ☐ Growth planning active

⚡⚡⚡⚡

Acknowledgements

Living a life full of enrichment and satisfaction is due to many, many influencers, and acknowledging their impact is a gift.

Where to start is a bit problematic, though.

First, and foremost, to my family. My wife, Louise, is a constant source of encouragement and glee. She not only supports my efforts but also serves as both a counterpoint and an anchor to my chasing of shiny objects. She is simply the right person at the right time for me, and I give thanks daily for her presence.

My two children, Gina and Drew, and their respective spouses, are examples of adults who have each matured and become successful, despite my efforts or examples to the contrary. I am proud of who they each have become and what they've achieved. I couldn't have written a better script for each. Thanks to each of you.

Early in my career, I was hired into consulting by Nathaniel Hill, who owned a small boutique consulting firm in Raleigh, NC. His mentorship was both incredible and excruciating at the same time. His "lessons" in consulting and comportment were foundational to my successes over the past 51 years, and I use them even today, primarily his emphasis on ethics and professionalism.

While a member of the National Board of Directors of the Institute of Management Consultants USA, I was introduced to Peter Block and his book *Community: The Structure of Belonging* at an IMC USA annual conference in 2016. His powerful message about building communities and his piercing questions continue to resonate today with me, especially as foundational to the principles of true leadership.

Further, I found EOS when with Vistage International as a business coach in Charlotte, NC. As a coach to small- to mid-sized business owners, Traction/

EOS became that set of foundational tools that helped my clients succeed. As important, the community of EOS Implementers who met quarterly was as much about my professional development as it was about community.

For over 51 years, I have served as a management consultant to innumerable closely held businesses, and each one provided learning lessons and were instrumental, directly or indirectly, in helping me write *Supercharge: A New Playbook for Leadership*. I acknowledge and thank each.

There are thousands of others who have had an influence on me, and while I can't acknowledge each by name, you know who you are, from friends, to peers, to clients, to past workmates, to . . . and the list goes on. Thanks.

⚡⚡⚡⚡

About the Author

David Norman,
CMC, FIMC, CMC-AF
President, David Norman & Associates
Chair, The Consultants Peer Group and High
Country Peer Group.

David Norman holds two certifications: the **Certified Management Consultant**® (CMC®), from the Institute of Management Consultants, the only accrediting body requiring client references, evidence of successful engagements, and completion of a sitting examination on ethics; and the **Certified Business Manager** (CBM), from the Association of Professionals in Business Management, the only masters-level certification and the most integrated certification available for business professionals.

Overall, Norman has over 51 years' experience consulting concurrent with 15 years' experience as executive coach with the owners/executives of a wide variety of, mostly, closely held clients. In addition, Norman has helped management through development of long-range plans and strategic plans and assisted in resolving succession issues. He has served as chair of three nonprofits and as interim executive director at three nonprofits undergoing change. He has assisted troubled organizations with improving operations, strengthening management, and increasing profitability.

Norman founded his own consulting firm, David Norman & Associates, in 1995 to offer results-oriented services to small and mid-sized companies, nonprofit organizations, and governmental agencies. The firm specializes in financial, operational, and general management consulting services tailored to the client's specific needs. Norman has extensive experience in EOS, Entrepreneurial Operating Business model, as a former Certified EOS Implementer.

Norman has been recognized for his consulting; first, internationally in 2017 with the CMC-AF (Academic Fellow by ICMCI); second, in 2018 as a Fellow of IMC USA (FIMC); and third, as only the 21st recipient of IMC USA's Lifetime Achievement Award, in 2021.

Norman served on the Institute of Management Consulting USA (IMC USA), Carolinas Chapter Board, the National Board of Directors, served as CEO and Chair of the National Board of Directors, and currently is Acting Secretary of the Board. He is also chair of the Board of IMC USA Foundation, a nonprofit organization promoting ethics education. Norman also served as founding Chair of the Board of Lost Province Center for Cultural Arts in Ashe County, NC. He and his wife, Louise, have a lavender farm in the county, near Lansing, NC.

After graduating from Furman University, Norman earned an MBA from the University of North Carolina at Chapel Hill. Norman has had over 25 years' experience as an adjunct professor at McColl School at Queens University and at Pfeiffer University. He taught investments, strategic management, corporate finance, organizational behavior, principles of management, and principles of marketing. Norman has published a wide variety of blogs on consulting, leadership, and EOS; reports on technology and productivity; articles for magazines and newsletters on sales compensation, costing, creative problem solving, and increasing profitability; and three books on costing, pricing, and cost control.

⚡⚡⚡⚡

How Others Leveraged This Process

"Our EBITDA will improve by 200% this year by focusing on solving real problems. Enough said!"

"By allowing others around me to help me do what I do best. It helps me be a better visionary, leader, and person."

"The value is on keeping the company focused, in lieu of the alternative where employees get bogged down with the day to day and lose sight of the future goals and path to make those goals happen."

"I just wanted to take a moment to thank you for the excellent leadership guidance you provided last Friday. We have a great group and the skills you are providing us with have enhanced how we look and react to opportunities. It shows us how to really drill down to the meat. The result is that we tackled the top items and focused on them rather than trying to get through the whole Issue list and trying to 'resolve' them just on the top level."

"Our communication has improved, our meetings have become shorter and more productive, and we are not wasting as much time as we used to talking about the same ole issues. We are now able to more effectively identify what

---

68. As has been my practice for over 51 years of management consulting and coaching, to ensure confidentiality I do not share the names of clients and/or their personnel. No ego brag page on my website.

our current issues are, determine what the real root cause is and solve the issue once and for all.

"Providing a clear and confident path towards real results among a leadership team with big egos."

"I have learned that before [David's involvement] I wasn't very interested in letting others have a voice. Now it is so important that the trust is there, and everyone feels that they can speak their mind."

"It was educational and challenging. It takes a while for the process to fall into place and you begin to understand how it can apply to your situation. Finding the right ways to have the process work for you is part of the challenge and changing the mindset of some people who are reluctant to change. David did a great job of leading us through that and helping us all find value where we were headed. Finding Traction is not easy sometimes but always worth the effort."

"Mostly involve people and processes. Getting the right people in the right seats. Understanding that setting expectations and having minimal step by step instructions grows the team and creates a positive culture. We are better delegators. We are dealing with real issues and not just dumping info during meetings.

"We know how to actually run an effective meeting, and I think most importantly the true definition of accountability."

"Don't ask a 'why' question. Lean into conflict. Set and reset expectations. Hold yourself and others accountable. Ask questions, emotional questions that get to the heart of the issue. Leadership is about helping others. Embrace change and learn from mistakes. Set big hairy goals and don't back off reaching them and delegate properly with clear expectations. People will fire themselves if they don't fit your culture. Your Why."

"How long it took me to get to a good place but then, afterwards, how quickly the transition was."

"David has the ability to push us farther. He may not know where or what the answer/issue is, but he knows when we have to go deeper or push our limits. He does not let us settle or take the easy answer."

"David is quite capable of sorting through a company's people, problems, and 'stuff' to arrive at the deeper issue. He has a great way of keeping everyone on the same page, even owners."

"Integration [of the business model], through David's leadership, equips the leadership of a company to make real change on a weekly basis while enabling the entire leadership team to promote the vision of the company."

"David is excellent and makes us focus on real issues, rather than glossing over problems in our organization. He helps us focus on the real problem, rather than symptoms.

"David doesn't tell you what you want to hear, but he does tell you what you need to hear and he does it in a way that is not off-putting. In other words, he knows how to step on your shoes without messing up the shine."

"At the end of our lives, I am convinced we will look back at a few defining moments and see the impact that they had. Your guidance and ability to bring to the surface the courageous conversation that needed to happen will be felt for years to come I feel. You really pulled back the curtain and allowed us to be 'exposed.' It's about the organization not the individual, but when emotions and personal agendas get involved, it is hard to separate the two. You made a difference in our future going forward. Your wisdom and credibility were evident in the way you allowed the group to be open and honest."

Net Promoter Score: 9.22 (out of 10)

⚡⚡⚡⚡⚡

Table of Figures

Index

⚡ ⚡ ⚡ ⚡ ⚡

Bibliography

Banks, Simon (@simonbanksvisualfunk). "You are not a leader until you have produced a leader who can produce another leader." LinkedIn. August 16, 2017. https://www.linkedin.com/pulse/you-leader-until-have -produced-who-can-produce-another-simon-banks/.

Beck, Randall J. and Jim Harter. "Why Great Managers Are So Rare." Gallup. Last modified July 21, 2023. https://www.gallup.com/workplace /231593/why-great-managers-rare.aspx.

Block, Peter. *Community: The Structure of Belonging.* Barrett-Joehler Publishers. 2008.

Block, Peter. Workshop on Leadership. Institute of Management Consultants Annual Conference. 2016.

Blount, Sally and Paul Leinwand. "Why Are We Here?" *Harvard Business Review.* November-December 2019. https://hbr.org/2019/11/why-are -we-here.

Carucci, Ron. "How to Actually encourage Employee Accountability." *Harvard Business Review.* November 23, 2020. https://hbr.org/2020/11 /how-to-actually-encourage-employee-accountability.

Cohen, Chantel. "The Entrepreneur's Roadmap to Overcoming Impostor Syndrome." *Inc.* March 11, 2024. https://www.inc.com/entrepreneurs -organization/the-entrepreneurs-roadmap-to-overcoming-imposter -syndrome.html.

Collins, Jim and Jerry Porras. *Built to Last: Successful Habits of Visionary Companies.* Harper Business. 1994.

Covey, Stephen R. *The Seven Habits of Highly Effective People.* Simon & Schuster. 1989.

Fishner, Kevin. "Focus on Your First 10 Systems, Not Just Your First 10 Hires:

This Chief of Staff Shares His Playbook." First Round Review. Last modified February 29, 2024. https://review.firstround.com/focus-on -your-first-10-systems-not-just-your-first-10-hires-this-chief-of-staff-s hares-his-playbook/?action=subscribe&success=true#why-your-first -10-systems-are-crucial.

Gino, Francesca and Michael I. Norton. "Why rituals Work. *Scientific American.* May 14, 2013. https://www.scientificamerican.com/article/why -rituals-work/.

Greiner, Larry E. "Evolution and revolution as Organizations Grow." *Harvard Business Review.* July-August 1972; last modified May-June 1998. https://hbr.org/1998/05/evolution-and-revolution-as-organizations -grow#:~:text=This%20article%20originally%20appeared%20in,%2C %E2%80%9D%20to%20update%20his%20observations.

Hall, Randy. "Self-Leadership—The Toughest Kind." 4thGearConsulting. com. June 26, 2009. https://4thgearconsulting.com/coaching/self -leadership-the-toughest-kind/.

Harter, Jim. "Thriving Employees Create a Thriving Business." Gallup Workplace. Last modified April 14, 2021. https://www.gallup.com/work place/313067/employees-aren-thriving-business-struggling.aspx.

McLeod, Melvin. "There's No Place to Go but Up: bell hooks and Maya Angelou in conversation." Lion's Road. January 1, 1998. https://www.lions roar.com/theres-no-place-to-go-but-up/.

Mihalicz, Dwight. "Building High-Performance Cultures with the Effective Point of Accountability." Effective Managers. October 8, 2024. https:// effectivemanagers.com/dwight-mihalicz/building-high-performance -cultures-with-the-effective-point-of-accountability/.

Odate, Toshio. *Japanese Woodworking Tools: Their Tradition, Spirit and Use.* Taunton Press. 1984.

Overfield, Darren and Rob Kaiser. "One Out of Every Two Managers Is Terrible at Accountability." *Harvard Business Review.* November 9, 2012. https://hbr.org/2012/11/one-out-of-every-two-managers-is-terrible-at -accountability.

Rauch, Allison. "Butterfly effect." Britannica. December 21, 2024. https:// www.britannica.com/science/butterfly-effect

Samuel, Mark. "8 Behaviors that Help Develop Personal Accountability." B State. March 3, 2021. https://bstate.com/2021/03/03/behaviors-that -help-develop-personal-accountability/.

Senge, Peter M. *The Fifth Discipline: The Art and Practice of the Learning Organization.* Doubleday/Currency. 1990.

Spencer, E. A. and K. Mahtani. "Hawthorne Effect." Sackett Catalogue of Bias Collaboration. 2017. https://catalogofbias.org/biases/hawthorne-effect/.

Tulgan, Bruce. "Seven Leadership Myths That Are Holding Managers Back." *Forbes.* January 26, 2024. https://www.forbes.com/sites/brucetulgan /2024/01/24/seven-leadership-myths-that-are-holding-managers -back/.

U.S. Small Business Administration Office of Advocacy. "2024 Small Business Profile." 2024. https://advocacy.sba.gov/wp-content/uploads/2024 /11/United_States.pdf.

Zhou, Luisa. "Small Business Statistics: The Ultimate List in 2025." *Luisa Zhou* (blog). January 23, 2025. https://luisazhou.com/blog/small -business-statistics/.

THE B CORP MOVEMENT

Dear Reader,

Thank you for reading this book and joining the Publish Your Purpose community! You are joining a special group of people who aim to make the world a better place.

WHAT'S PUBLISH YOUR PURPOSE ABOUT?

Our mission is to elevate the voices often excluded from traditional publishing. We intentionally seek out authors and storytellers with diverse backgrounds, life experiences, and unique perspectives to publish books that will make an impact in the world.

Certified

B

®

Corporation

Beyond our books, we are focused on tangible, action-based change. As a woman- and LGBTQ+-owned company, we are committed to reducing inequality, lowering levels of poverty, creating a healthier environment, building stronger communities, and creating high-quality jobs with dignity and purpose.

As a Certified B Corporation, we use business as a force for good. We join a community of mission-driven companies building a more equitable, inclusive, and sustainable global economy. B Corporations must meet high standards of transparency, social and environmental performance, and accountability as determined by the nonprofit B Lab. The certification process is rigorous and ongoing (with a recertification requirement every three years).

HOW DO WE DO THIS?

We intentionally partner with socially and economically disadvantaged businesses that meet our sustainability goals. We embrace and encourage our authors and employee's differences in race, age, color, disability, ethnicity, family or marital status, gender identity or expression, language, national origin, physical and mental ability, political affiliation, religion, sexual orientation, socio-economic status, veteran status, and other characteristics that make them unique.

Community is at the heart of everything we do—from our writing and publishing programs to contributing to social enterprise nonprofits like reSET (www.resetco.org) and our work in founding B Local Connecticut.

We are endlessly grateful to our authors, readers, and local community for being the driving force behind the equitable and sustainable world we are building together.

To connect with us online or publish with us, visit us at www.publishyourpurpose.com.

Elevating Your Voice,

Jenn T Grace

Jenn T. Grace
Founder, Publish Your Purpose

www.ingramcontent.com/pod-product-compliance
Lightning Source LLC
Chambersburg PA
CBHW021551210326
41599CB00010B/393